Successful Use of Expert Witnesses
in Civil Disputes

SUCCESSFUL USE
of
EXPERT WITNESSES
in Civil Disputes

Suzanne Burn
B.A. (Hons.), M.Phil., LL.B., LL.M., District Judge

Written in association with **Bond Solon Training**

Shaw & Sons

Shaw's
Since 1750

Published by
Shaw & Sons Limited
Shaway House
21 Bourne Park
Bourne Road
Crayford
Kent DA1 4BZ

www.shaws.co.uk

© Shaw & Sons Limited 2005

Published September 2005

ISBN 0 7219 1450 0

A CIP catalogue record for this book is available from the
British Library

Printed in Great Britain by
Bell & Bain Limited, Glasgow

CONTENTS

Contents

Contents

Contents

Contents

FOREWORD

The expert witness occupies a central position in our system of civil justice. Without expert evidence, judges would be quite incapable of resolving many of the cases which they have to try. Even the most straightforward personal injury claim often involves an issue of a sufficiently technical nature to require the assistance of an expert witness. As litigation becomes more complex, so the need for experts skilled in many diverse disciplines becomes ever more pressing.

The publication of this book could not be more timely. It is now more than six years since the Woolf Civil Justice Reforms were introduced, and a good time to take stock. Lord Woolf made a number of important changes in relation to expert evidence. These are all discussed in considerable detail by Suzanne Burn primarily, but not exclusively, from the point of view of the instructing lawyer. This is an intensely practical book which provides invaluable guidance on such topics as the role of the expert, instructing the expert, experts' reports, experts' meetings, the vexed and difficult issue of the single joint expert and experts at trial.

Ms Burn tackles some of the problem areas and is not afraid to express her opinion. This book is no mere catalogue of uncontroversial facts. And her advice often shows real insight. All lawyers who engage in civil litigation should add the book to their libraries. I commend it to practitioners.

Rt. Hon. Lord Justice Dyson
Deputy Head of Civil Justice
20th July 2005

ACKNOWLEDGEMENTS

The idea for this book came from Bond Solon, the witness training company. In 1997 Catherine Bond, Mark Solon and Penny Harper of Bond Solon wrote the first edition of *The Expert Witness in Court**, a practical guide for experts. I met Catherine and Mark in the 1990s when I was the Secretary to the Civil Litigation Committee of the Law Society: their enthusiasm for the role of expert witnesses in the civil justice system encouraged me to develop a particular interest in the subject, which I have continued to this day. In 1999 I updated *The Expert Witness in Court** for a second edition following the implementation of the Civil Procedure Rules. I also began to write and teach a number of courses for Bond Solon, and to speak at their conferences for expert witnesses, initially on how the new rules would change their work and later to keep experts up to date with practice and procedure in the civil courts. Bond Solon also run training courses for lawyers and in 2000/1 Mark Solon and I wrote and delivered a number of courses entitled 'The Successful Use of Expert Witnesses'. Mark suggested a companion book for lawyers to *The Expert Witness in Court**; hence the idea for this book was born.

I would also like to thank:

- Lord Woolf and the then Lord Chancellor's Department team working on the civil justice reforms between 1994 and 1999, and the Law Society Civil Litigation Committee members during that time, particularly chairmen Phillip Sycamore (now HH Judge Sycamore) and Michael Napier, for providing me with the opportunity to become closely involved with the reforms and with the development of the CPR, and who all helped to frame my views.

- The several other organisations and individuals who have encouraged and supported my work on the CPR, and on expert evidence in the last five years, especially the Association of Personal Injury Lawyers (particularly Nigel Tomkins with whom I ran a number of courses for experts and had lots of fun), the Expert Witness Institute (especially Brian Thomson and Sir Louis Blom Cooper) for involving me in several of their seminars and conferences for expert witnesses, the Inns of Court School of Law (especially Penny Cooper) also for providing me with opportunities to write and teach on expert evidence, and the members and staff servicing the Civil Justice Council, of which I have been a member since 2001, for involving me in several 'awaydays' and events about expert evidence.

- The many solicitors and expert witnesses with whom I have exchanged views (often lively ones) on expert evidence at training events, seminars and conferences over the years.

- Crispin Williams and the team at Shaws for their patience with my delay in getting started on the book and for their speedy editing once it was produced.

- Lord Justice Dyson for contributing an incisive and complimentary foreword at a very busy time in the legal year.

Finally, this book would never have been written without the forbearance of my husband and partner David Burn, himself an occasional expert witness, who uncomplainingly looked after our domestic life whenever I disappeared to the computer to work on another chapter, and who has unfailingly supported me in all my varied work ventures over the last 33 years.

Suzanne Burn

* *The Expert Witness in Court: A Practical Guide, Second Edition*, is available from Shaw & Sons Ltd, 21 Bourne Park, Bourne Road, Crayford, Kent DA1 4BZ at £25.00, post free.

THE AUTHOR

Suzanne Burn, B.A. (Hons.)., M.Phil., LL.B., LL.M. is a District Judge. Her early career was in the public sector – in central and local government and as a senior officer of the Local Government Ombudsman. She became a solicitor in 1989 and specialised in civil litigation, particularly serious personal injury claims. From 1994 to 1999 Suzanne was Secretary to the Law Society's Civil Litigation Committee, leading the Society's work on the Woolf civil justice reforms and on the Civil Procedure Rules and acquiring an LL.M. in advanced litigation.

From 1999-2005 she had a 'portfolio' of roles, including lecturing and training lawyers and expert witnesses on civil litigation for the College of Law, Inns of Court School of Law, Central Law Training, the Association of Personal Injury Lawyers and Bond Solon, sitting as a Deputy District Judge, and acting as a legal assessor to the General Medical Council and as a non-executive Director of the London Ambulance Service NHS Trust. From 2003 to 2005 Suzanne chaired the Clinical Disputes Forum and she has been a member of the Civil Justice Council since 2001.

Suzanne was appointed a District Judge in January 2005 and sits in the London county courts. She writes widely on civil litigation, including for Sweet and Maxwell's *Civil Procedure* (the White Book) and *Litigation Practice*, for Tottel's *Accountancy Litigation Support*, and for the *Legal Action* journal. She was consultant editor of the first edition of the Law Society's *Civil Litigation Handbook* and is general editor of the forthcoming second edition. Suzanne is also a co-author, with Catherine Bond and Mark Solon, of the second edition of Shaw & Son's *The Expert Witness in Court*, and of GMM's *Healthcare Professionals as Witnesses to the Court*.

BOND SOLON TRAINING

Bond Solon is the UK's leading legal training consultancy for non-lawyers. They are the market leaders in providing innovative, relevant and experiential courses that are designed to improve performance in the work place. They have won several awards including, in 2004, a Highly Commended National Training Award.

Since Bond Solon began in 1992, nearly a half million people have attended their programmes. They have a sister company in Ireland, La Touche Bond Solon, and in 2001 Bond Solon joined forces with Central Law Training, the largest provider of post-qualification legal education for lawyers in the UK. Bond Solon and Central Law Training are part of the Wilmington group.

Bond Solon have led the way in training for expert witnesses and have the only university certified programme for experts in the UK. They have designed a practical and intense programme with Cardiff University that has improved standards considerably. Since 1993, they have held the largest annual expert witness conference every autumn. Bond Solon regularly conduct surveys of experts and provide media comment on expert issues.

Tel: 020 7253 7053
www.bondsolon.com

TABLE OF CASES

INTRODUCTION

Expert advice and evidence can be crucial to the outcome of many civil disputes. Solicitors and their clients invariably benefit from early specialist advice in disputes about technical or scientific matters, and in potential professional negligence claims. The right expert advice at the right time can prevent weak claims from being pursued, and can help to isolate the key issues in claims with a good prospect of success. Judges are greatly assisted by explanations by experts of the facts and issues in many technical cases; they frequently rely upon medical and valuation reports to assess the quantum of claims as varied as personal injury and those arising from building projects, and are dependent upon quality opinion evidence, often from more than one source, to help them to decide professional negligence claims. Conversely, unnecessary or inappropriate evidence from experts can add considerable expense but little value, and poor reports or oral evidence from experts with insufficient expertise, or who fail to understand their role, can lose a case. Selecting and instructing the right expert is an important part of a litigation solicitor's function, as is subjecting the expert's advice and report to careful, and maybe rigorous, scrutiny as early as possible in the dispute.

Undoubtedly there was a period, in the 1970s and 80s, when some parties too often tried to use expert evidence to bolster their cases. This in turn encouraged some experts to provide their services to the litigation industry who were prepared to be, or even thought it was their job to be, partisan. The damage was not always readily apparent until a case came to court, as pre-trial disclosure of expert reports was not the norm until the 1980s.

It is not surprising therefore that successive civil justice reviews have sought to grapple with the problems posed by expert evidence. Lord Woolf, in his *Access to Justice* reports of the late 1990s, focused considerable attention on expert evidence that he saw as too often contributing to the delay, complexity and cost of many disputes. The Civil Procedure Rules, which emerged from Lord Woolf's review, certainly give the judges much greater power to control expert evidence, and emphasise that the expert's duty is to the court, not to the party that instructs them.

1

However, the CPR have not solved all of the problems: six years after their implementation, the Appellate Courts are still frequently required to decide upon difficult 'procedural' issues in relation to expert evidence, and trial judges too often find it necessary to comment unfavourably on an expert's report or oral evidence.

Post-CPR, a number of useful texts have been written to guide expert witnesses through the civil justice system. However, the aim of this book is to provide guidance to *lawyers* on how to make the best use of expert evidence for the benefit of the clients, and how to work co-operatively and successfully with expert witnesses.

The book concentrates solely on civil cases, but with occasional reference to useful sources of guidance in the family and criminal jurisdictions. It does not attempt to cover the particular issues in relation to expert evidence in specific types of dispute or litigation – practitioners should refer to the standard textbooks in those fields for these. The book is likely to be of most value to recently qualified solicitors or general practitioners who only occasionally need to rely upon expert evidence. More experienced and specialist litigators should also appreciate the summaries and analysis of the not inconsiderable post-CPR case law on expert evidence issues, and more experienced expert witnesses should also find material of interest. The law is stated as at May 2005.

Chapters 1-3 cover when expert evidence is likely to be permitted by the courts, explain the CPR changes in relation to expert evidence, summarise judicial guidance on the meaning of experts' independence and duty to the court and consider the different roles experts fulfil in civil disputes.

Chapters 4-6 give practical advice on the selection and instruction of experts and on the thorny topic of experts' fees – agreeing fees with an expert, payment arrangements and court control of fees.

Chapter 7 looks at expert advice and reports pre-action, particularly in relation to the pre-action protocols.

Chapter 8 covers experts' reports – the CPR requirements, style and presentation, checking and disclosing reports, and the difficult question of privilege.

2

Chapter 9 focuses on single joint experts, a species created by the CPR – when might the court order evidence to be given by an SJE, and the nuances of selecting and working with SJEs that may be different from working with party-instructed experts.

Chapters 10-11 cover the varied tasks that experts might carry out in addition to writing reports, changing or adding experts late in the day, experts who change their minds, and dealing with questions on experts' reports and discussions between experts.

Chapter 12 has two functions: first, to give some guidance on the practical issues in relation to experts giving oral evidence at court; secondly, to analyse, from recently decided cases, how judges handle expert evidence at trial.

Chapter 13 deals with the downside of expert evidence – what can go wrong and what, if anything, can be done when it does.

Chapter 14 turns the coin over briefly and looks at how experts view their relationship with lawyers in civil disputes from recent surveys.

Chapter 15 looks back at what the CPR tried to achieve in relation to expert evidence and evaluates the experience to date.

Chapter 1
WHAT IS EXPERT EVIDENCE AND WHEN IS IT NECESSARY?

Deciding whether and when to instruct which experts in a civil dispute is a difficult task. The solicitor and the client might decide that they need technical help in investigating the facts and issues, or specialist advice to understand the strengths and weaknesses of the client's case. There are no restrictions on seeking advice early in a dispute (apart from financing it), but the court might take a very different view of the need for expert evidence to resolve the dispute after proceedings are issued. Decisions taken at the outset on the type of expert, their seniority and experience, and on whether the expert's investigations and advice might be shared with the other party, can significantly influence the outcome and costs of a dispute.

Solicitors need to have an understanding of the position of expert evidence in the English legal system, what the judges consider to be the functions of expert witnesses, and when permission is likely to be given for reliance upon expert evidence. Lord Woolf, in his *Access to Justice* review in the mid-1990s, was determined to reform what he perceived as a misuse of expert evidence. The implementation of the Civil Procedure Rules (CPR) in April 1999 focused the attention of lawyers and expert witnesses on a more controlled role for experts in civil disputes and upon experts' duties to the court.

This chapter looks at the role of expert evidence in English law in civil cases, why judges began to be concerned about inappropriate use of expert evidence, the skills and qualities required of experts, when the court will give permission for expert evidence, how the conduct of experts is governed outside the court process and whether an official accreditation scheme for expert witnesses might assist.

THE ROLE OF AN EXPERT IN CIVIL DISPUTES

What is an expert?

The Concise Oxford Dictionary defines an **expert** as "a person with a high degree of skill or knowledge in a certain subject".

CPR 35.2 simply defines an **expert** as a person "who has been instructed to give or prepare evidence for the purposes of court proceedings". It could be said that this is not very helpful, but the Part 35 Practice Direction does expand upon the role and responsibilities of experts – see Appendix A.

The definition in the Australian Federal Court Rules is somewhat fuller:

"An expert witness means a person who is called, or is to be called, by a party to give opinion evidence, based upon the person's specialised knowledge or based upon the person's training, study or experience."

The function of an expert

Parties and their lawyers often need assistance to investigate the technical aspects of a problem or dispute, and advice on how to resolve these, sometimes including whether to pursue or to defend a claim.

Judges also often need assistance to understand technical matters and benefit from specialist interpretation of the essential facts and matters in issue in the case. An expert may be needed to give clear, independent technical assistance or opinion evidence on a subject within his or her field. This field is defined by reference to the expert's experience and qualifications. An expert should not give opinion evidence outside his or her field of expertise and should not accept the role at all in cases outside their expertise.

Expert witness evidence for court proceedings is often very important. It must be based on a sound foundation of facts that have been properly and rigorously investigated. Acquiring these facts may involve such activities as examining a patient, inspecting a building and conducting tests. Experts should always explain why they reached their expert opinion given a certain set of facts.

An expert's role is thus primarily as an educator. First, their role involves assisting the party and their lawyers in the preparation of the case, which may include providing some written advice. Secondly, if the case goes to court, they must prepare a report for the court and, occasionally, they might give oral evidence at trial to assist the judge to reach a fair decision.

The distinction between a witness of fact and an expert witness

The distinction between an expert witness and a witness of fact is that an expert is allowed to give opinion evidence on matters at issue within his expertise, based upon his knowledge skills and experience. A witness of fact describes what they saw or did, and may be permitted to interpret that according to their experience. Witnesses of fact should not give opinion evidence.

Some blurring of this distinction may occur when:

- An expert gives evidence based on his investigations, e.g. a forensic pathologist who carries out an autopsy or a clinician who medically examines an accident victim – the expert's evidence is then partly factual.

- A witness of fact is also a specialist or professional – when their interpretation of the events in which they were involved inevitably is based upon their professional experience.

The distinction matters in relation to:

1. Whether the party needs permission to rely on the evidence – only necessary for expert evidence (see later in this chapter).

2. Whether the witness can charge fees that may be recovered (see *Admiral Management Services v Para-Protect Europe Ltd* [2002] EWHC 233 Ch, discussed in Chapter 2).

3. The equality of arms between the respective parties' evidence (see *ES v Chesterfield Royal Hospital NHS Trust* [2003] EWCA Civ 1284, when a claimant in a clinical negligence claim was allowed to instruct a second expert, because the defendant had two witnesses of fact and one expert from the same discipline – discussed in more detail in Chapter 10).

4. The weight which the trial judge attaches to the evidence (see Chapter 12).

In *DN v Greenwich London Borough* [2004] EWCA Civ 1659, a negligence claim arising from the failure of an educational psychologist to identify the child claimant's complex needs, the local authority, unusually, did not seek to rely upon independent expert evidence on liability. The authority appealed against the trial judge's decision that there had been negligence, on the ground that he had failed to assess properly the evidence of the psychologist in question and had held, wrongly, that he could not give expert evidence because he was a witness of fact. The Court of Appeal held that the psychologist's evidence (as to why he considered that his conduct did not fall below the standard of care reasonably to be expected of him) was admissible, the fact that it might lack the objectivity of an independent expert went to cogency and not admissibility (see below). Nonetheless, they dismissed the appeal because they concluded that the judge had, in fact, adequately considered the psychologist's evidence.

Experts are not advocates

Lawyers represent their client's case in court. They are paid to do their best for their clients but have a professional duty to assist the court. They have discretion in deciding which evidence to use and how to present it, subject to the court's control, and will marshal it in a way that is most favourable to their client's case. Lawyers must not knowingly present false evidence and have a duty not to mislead the court, but their main duty is to their client. Lawyers do not give evidence; they are not witnesses. Their role is to argue and seek to persuade the judge to decide in favour of their client. Lawyers will often argue matters of law.

By contrast, the role of the expert witness is to give an opinion on technical matters on behalf of whoever instructs him, but in an impartial, objective and independent way. Experts must not be selective in the facts and evidence that are relevant and cannot rely only on evidence favourable to the client's case. An expert's main duty is to the court and, in proceedings, their duty to the client becomes secondary. An expert is not an advocate, and should not adopt that role. Those that do may be criticised by the trial judge, or worse (see Chapters 2 and 13). Experts should not be concerned directly with matters of law.

Some judicial comments pre-CPR on the functions of an expert

The pre-CPR adversarial system and rules did not sufficiently discourage parties from using expert evidence in a partisan way to 'bolster' their case. This led to some misuse of expert evidence, as well as misunderstanding by many experts as to their proper role.

The following quotations (from leading decisions prior to the implementation of the CPR), explain why judges increasingly took a somewhat jaundiced view of the value of some expert evidence in civil litigation.

1. "Although the evidence is given on oath, in point of fact the person knows that he cannot be indicted for perjury because it is only evidence as to a matter of opinion... A dishonest man, knowing he could not be punished, might be inclined to indulge in extravagant assertions on an occasion that required it. An expert is not like an ordinary witness, who hopes to get his expenses, but he is employed and paid in a sense of gain, being employed by the person who calls him. Now it is natural that his mind, however honest he may be, should be biased on favour of the person employing him." Sir George Jessel in *Lord Abinger v Ashton* [1873] 17 LREq 358.

2. "It is necessary that expert evidence presented to the court should be, and should be seen to be, the independent product of the expert uninfluenced as to form or content by the exigencies of litigation. To the extent that it is not, the evidence is likely to be not only incorrect but self-defeating." Lord Wilberforce in *Whitehouse v Jordan* [1981] 1 WLR 246.

3. "During the preparation of this judgment, I re-read (the expert's) report on the understanding that it was drafted as a partisan tract with the objective of selling the defendant's case to the court and virtually ignoring everything which could harm that objective. I did not find it of significant assistance in deciding the issues ... An expert should not consider that it is his job to stand shoulder to shoulder through thick and thin with the side who is paying his bill." Laddie J in *Cala Homes v Alfred McAlpine* [1995] FSR 518.

4. "I consider that a misunderstanding on the part of certain of the expert witnesses in the present case as to their duties and

responsibilities contributed to the length of the trial." Cresswell J in the *Ikarian Reefer* case (see below for Cresswell's detailed guidance on expert evidence).

5. It is not the function of an expert to present evidence "in the light that seems most helpful to the immediate cause". Thorpe J in *Vernon v Bosley No 2* [1997] 3 WLR 683.

The Ikarian Reefer guidance

In 1993, Mr Justice Cresswell (as he then was) summarised an expert's duties and responsibilities in a shipping case, *National Justice Compania Naviera SA v Prudential Assurance Company Ltd (Ikarian Reefer)* [1993] 2 Lloyd's Rep 68. His guidance is quoted in full because it now forms the basis of paragraph 1 of the CPR Part 35 Practice Direction:

"1.1 It is the duty of an expert to help the court on matters within his own expertise: rule 35.3(1). This duty is paramount and overrides any obligation to the person from whom the expert has received instructions or by whom he is paid: rule 35.3(2).

1.2 Expert evidence should be the independent product of the expert uninfluenced by the pressures of litigation.

1.3 An expert should assist the court by providing objective, unbiased opinion on matters within his expertise, and should not assume the role of an advocate.

1.4 An expert should consider all material facts, including those which might detract from his opinion.

1.5 An expert should make it clear:

a) when a question or issue falls outside his expertise; and

b) when he is not able to reach a definite opinion, for example because he has insufficient information.

1.6. If, after producing a report, an expert changes his view on any material matter, such change of view should be communicated to all the parties without delay, and when appropriate to the court."

THE SKILLS AND QUALITIES REQUIRED OF AN EXPERT

Skills

The particular skills required of an expert in the post-CPR climate are:

● Current, or at least recent, practical expertise in the particular subject or discipline in question. An expert must speak from expertise based on experience, and keep up to date in his subject.

● Impartiality and objectivity – possessing an independent mind. Parties, and particularly the court, want the expert's honest opinion, not a one-sided picture.

● An analytical mind and an interest in investigation and research.

● Good written communication skills for preparing concise, relevant and jargon-free reports – experts need to be able to explain and give opinions upon technical issues to a 'lay' readership, which may include the judge.

● Sufficient confidence, and good oral communication skills, to be able to cope well in discussions with other experts, at conferences with the client, solicitor and advocate and in giving oral evidence at court.

● A robust but polite personality, and coolness under pressure, to cope with other strong-minded experts, 'controlling' solicitors, tough advocates in cross-examination, and probing questions from judges.

● Basic knowledge of litigation procedure and the law in the area of the dispute.

Other qualities

Experts also need to display the following qualities:

● Efficiency – only accepting work that can be carried out on time, to be able to produce advice and reports to tight timetables, and to plan court appearances.

● Thoroughness, including a real attention to detail.

● Integrity, including not accepting work that could lead to a conflict of interest between clients, keeping client details and information confidential, quoting research findings accurately and honestly, and an ability to change his/her mind in the face of new or better evidence.

- An awareness of cost-effectiveness, 'proportionality' under the CPR (see below).

- A degree of modesty – experts need to know when to decline work outside their qualifications or experience, and to admit the limits of their expertise. (In *Anglo Group plc v Winther Browne & Co Ltd* [2000] 1 WLR 820, the courts said expert witnesses should make it clear when any question or issue in the case falls outside their expertise or when their conclusions are based on inadequate evidence.)

- Commitment to the case and to the interests of justice – accepting that their task is not completed when their report has been written.

Qualifications

Qualifications, academic or professional, are not an essential criterion for acting as an expert witness – but relevant experience and expertise is. The latter can be demonstrated, but only to a degree, by qualifications. Too many experts make the mistake of over-emphasising their qualifications in their reports rather than their expertise (see also Chapter 8).

THE ADVANTAGES AND DISADVANTAGES OF EARLY EXPERT EVIDENCE

(See also Chapter 7)

The advantages

Cases may be won on the strength of experts' evidence, particularly a timely, relevant and well-argued written report.

Clients and solicitors may need expert advice early in a dispute to help in assessing:

a) the strength of the case;

b) the risks if it proceeds;

c) whether to take the case on, especially on a conditional fee basis;

d) how to advise the funder;

e) how to advise the client.

There is certainly an argument that the earlier a liability expert is asked to advise the better, because:

a) a solicitor can avoid a disaster caused by accepting instructions in a weak case;

b) it can save time and money as an expert may quickly grasp the heart of the problem;

c) an expert can advise upon necessary investigations and fact finding; and

d) early advice is privileged (see Chapter 5).

The disadvantages

The CPR provides that a party may only rely on expert evidence once the court has given permission. The court may decide it does not need expert evidence at all or only needs it from a single joint expert.

Hence, there is a real risk that a client may not recover the cost of an expert instructed to advise pre-proceedings – the solicitor needs to warn the client of this. On the other hand, if the solicitor waits to instruct an expert until the court gives permission (usually at directions stage), the client may lose the benefit of the expert's more general advice and guidance on the strengths and weaknesses of the case, the court may restrict the scope of the advice/report and from whom it can be obtained, and the evidence will have to be obtained quickly to suit the court timetable.

Also note that:

- Experts can add significantly to the costs of litigation – a minimum of about £300, excluding costs of the time taken to instruct them and to advise the client on the report.

- As the expert's main duty is to the court, not to the solicitor or the client, a party cannot control the expert, either in terms of the issues he chooses to cover in his report, or his findings and opinions.

13

- A poor expert, or one who does not understand his role or know the CPR, can weaken the client's case, or even cause it to be struck out or lost at trial.

WHEN WILL THE COURT GIVE PERMISSION FOR EXPERT EVIDENCE?

Because only expert witnesses are permitted to offer opinions to the court on the meaning and implication of other evidence that may influence the outcome of the case, the courts are concerned to ensure that opinions are offered by reputable people, following recognised disciplines of knowledge.

The civil courts, under the CPR (rules 32.1, 35.1 and 35.4), now have complete control over evidence, including expert evidence (see Chapter 2). Moreover, the Pre-action Practice Direction states that if parties need an expert pre-action they should if possible engage an agreed expert, and should be aware that if proceedings are issued the court may not allow the use of the expert's report or the recovery of the costs (paragraphs 4.9-10). (See Chapter 7 for a longer discussion of expert evidence pre-action.)

While the courts had the power, under the previous Supreme Court and County Court rules, to refuse to entertain expert evidence, this was used sparingly. In practice, before the implementation of the CPR, the decision as to when to instruct which experts, and when to disclose their reports, was left very much to the parties and their lawyers.

This is no longer the case for the following reasons:

1. The CPR emphasise the role of the expert as adviser to the court, and that experts should be independent from the party who instructs them (CPR 35.3). (See Chapter 2 for a fuller discussion of the expert's duty to the court.)

2. The courts have greater control, through judicial case management, over evidence in general (and expert evidence in particular), and over the costs of litigation. This means that at an early stage in every litigated case, a judge takes a view on whether expert evidence is necessary at all, whether that evidence should be given

14

by a single joint expert instructed by both parties or by one expert for each party, and whether there should be some control over the expert's fees. (This is discussed in more detail in Chapters 2 and 6.)

3. The CPR are more prescriptive than the previous High Court and County Court Rules on the form and content of expert reports, and on other aspects of the procedure in relation to expert evidence, particularly the new provisions for raising questions on experts' reports, and for experts' discussions. (See Chapters 8 and 11.)

Admissibility of expert evidence

A case management judge has to decide first whether expert evidence is admissible under section 3 of the Civil Evidence Act 1972. This provides that:

a) the opinion of a witness on any relevant matter on which he is qualified to give expert evidence shall be admissible, and

b) that a statement of opinion by such a witness on any matter, on which he is not qualified to give expert evidence, is also admissible if made as a way of conveying relevant facts personally perceived by him. (This second limb of section 3 of the Civil Evidence Act means that, for example, an orthopaedic surgeon could say the claimant was upset and seemed depressed even though he has no expertise in psychology or psychiatry.)

The case management judge, usually at allocation and directions stage (see below), considers whether the proposed expert evidence meets the following tests:

1. **The common knowledge test.**

   i.e. whether the court needs help from a third party to understand an issue or whether the judge can decide the issue based on knowledge or common sense. See, for instance, *Thermos Ltd v Aladdin Sales* [2000] FSR 402, an infringement of a patent case, concerning the design of a vacuum flask. Jacob J (as he then was) concluded that expert evidence, although traditional in patent cases, was of little use when the design was for a consumer article bought by ordinary members of the public and the issue was "consumer eye appeal".

2. **The basis of knowledge test.**

   i.e. whether the knowledge and expertise in question is sufficiently recognised as credible by others capable of evaluating it. See, for instance, *Barings plc (in liquidation) v Coopers & Lybrand (No 2)* (*The Times*, 7th March 2001 Ch D), in which the judge permitted expert evidence on practice and procedure in investment banking because there "exists recognised expertise governed by recognised standards and rules of conduct capable of influencing the court's decision on any of the issues which it has to decide".

   However, the judge also said that the court has a discretion to exclude such evidence if it would not help the determination of the issues, and that the "modern view is to regulate such matters by way of weight, rather than admissibility".

   See also *Pride Valley Foods Ltd v Hall and Partners* [2000] EWHC Technology 106, in an action arising out of a fire that destroyed the claimant's factory, evidence from fire experts was held to be admissible and relevant, but the judge disregarded the evidence from project managers because there was no such recognisable profession (and because one of the reports dealt with questions which were for the court, not for the expert).

3. **The expertise test.**

   i.e. whether the proposed witness has sufficient knowledge and experience to be an expert who can help the court (see for instance *R v Luttrell* [2004] EWCA Crim 1344, in which the Court of Appeal concluded that lip-reading evidence from CCTV recordings of a conversation between the co-accused was capable of being relevant and reliable as the condition that study, from experience, to give the opinion of a witness authority, was satisfied. The Court of Appeal also noted that:

   "Although at one time, a more conservative approach had been adopted, the policy of the English courts has been to be flexible in admitting expert evidence and to enjoy the advantages to be gained from new techniques and new advances in science.")

4. **The ultimate issue test.**

   i.e. whether the expert's contribution might have the effect of supplanting the function of the judge in deciding the case. Judges do not usually want experts to give opinions directly on the matters that the judge has to decide e.g. the disputed facts, or whether a defendant has been negligent. (See, for instance, *Secretary of State for Trade and Industry v Baker* (No 5) [2000] 1 BCL, when the judge held that the standard of competence to be shown by a director of a company in directors' disqualification proceedings was a question of law which did not require expert evidence.)

In practice, case management judges rarely itemise these tests, and in civil cases will often give the party requesting reliance upon the expert evidence the benefit of the doubt with regard to admissibility, leaving the trial judge to decide upon the relevance and weight of the evidence (see Chapter 12).

In recent years, the US courts have adopted a more rigorous basis of knowledge test, especially for scientific evidence. This practice, and the Federal Court procedures to apply it, derived from *Daubert v Merrell Dow Pharmaceuticals* 509 US 579 (1993), a case concerning whether a particular drug could cause birth defects. The US Supreme Court held that knowledge requires:

"... more than subjective belief or unsupported speculation. The term applies to any body of known facts or to any body of ideas inferred from such facts or accepted as facts on good grounds.... Proposed testimony must be supported by appropriate validation on good grounds based on what is known."

The US court in Daubert also said that proposed expert testimony could be tested against the following criteria to check that it amounts to "knowledge":

a) whether a theory or technique at issue has been tested;

b) whether it has been subject to peer review or has been published;

c) whether there is a known error rate in the particular technique; and

d) whether the evidence has gained widespread acceptance in the scientific community.

The decision and the procedures (depositions – see Chapter 12) are not without their critics but, in the criminal courts in this jurisdiction at least, questions are beginning to be asked about screening processes for 'kite-flying' expert evidence (see also Chapter 12).

THE COURT'S DUTY TO RESTRICT EXPERT EVIDENCE – COGENCY, RELEVANCE AND PROPORTIONALITY

The court also now has a duty to restrict expert evidence (CPR 35.1) to that which is "reasonably required" to decide the case, i.e. the evidence that the trial judge is likely to find helpful, not the evidence upon which the parties wish to rely.

In *Grobbelaar v Sun Newspapers* (*The Times*, 12th August 1999), the Court of Appeal made it quite clear that the court has jurisdiction to exclude relevant admissible evidence if it will not be helpful to the court.

The court can now decide:

a) the issues on which it requires evidence;

b) the nature of the evidence which it requires to decide those issues; and

c) the way in which the evidence is to be placed before the court.

The modern approach encourages judges to scrutinise parties' requests for expert evidence carefully at directions stage and to consider questions of admissibility and cogency again, immediately before or at trial.

In recent years, the courts have decided that expert evidence will not be required:

1. **When the judge can decide the disputed issues based on factual evidence.**

   Liddell v Middleton [1996] PIQR (p36) was a personal injury claim by a pedestrian, arising from an road traffic accident, in which the Court of Appeal concluded that the evidence of an accident reconstruction expert (for each party) had been wrongly admitted. There were four lay witnesses. The Court of Appeal said the expert evidence was unnecessary because it did not involve technical matters, such as the length of skid marks that required expert interpretation, but was "simply the evaluation of eyewitness accounts". Stuart Smith LJ said:

18

"We do not have trial by expert in this country: we have trial by judge. In my judgement, the expert witnesses contributed nothing to the trial in this case except expense."

Hawkes v London Borough of Southwark [1998] CA (unrep) was a personal injury claim in which an employee was injured when carrying a door upstairs – the judge decided that the risks in this activity were so self-evident that opinion evidence from an expert would not, therefore, assist.

Coker v Barkland Cleaning Co, 6th December 1999 (unrep, except in *Expert Evidence under the CPR,* Sweet and Maxwell, 2001), was a personal injury case in which the claimant was hit from behind by a cleaning machine. The Court of Appeal was very critical of both parties for instructing an engineer expert because, given the circumstances of the accident, and the presence of an eyewitness, expert evidence was unnecessary.

2. **Where the issue is construction of a contract.**

In *LHS Holdings v Laporte plc* [2001] EWCA Civ 278, the issue to be decided was the construction of an agreement for the sale of shares – the court decided that opinion evidence from accountant experts would not assist.

In *Clarke v Marlborough Fine Art (London) Ltd and Another (No 3)* [2002] EWHC 11 Ch, the dispute concerned an agreement between the artist Francis Bacon (now deceased) and an art gallery, about a supply of paintings. The court gave permission for expert evidence in relation to the valuation of, and market for, Bacon's work. However, the claimant was refused permission to obtain a report from a lawyer specialising in art law on how the terms of the agreement compared to those that would have been available on the open market. The judge said that the lawyer's experience concerned the present art market, not that of 40 years ago contemporaneous to the agreement, his assessment would be bound to be subjective, and his report would add no relevant factual information – the issue was not an appropriate one for expert evidence.

Tain Investments Ltd v Loxleys [2004] EWHC 2708 Ch was a professional negligence claim against solicitors arising from a property transaction. The claimant, at first instance and on appeal, was refused permission to adduce expert evidence from a solicitor on an "unusual clause" in a contract; expert evidence would only be appropriate when the transaction in question was likely to be entirely outside the sphere of knowledge of the judge.

3. **Where the costs of the expert evidence will be disproportionate to the amount at issue.**

   This will be particularly significant in claims allocated to the small claims and fast tracks (see also Chapter 2).

   Bandegani v Norwich Union Fire Insurance Society Ltd (Lawtel, 20th May 1999) was a small claim in which the issue to be decided was the pre-accident value of a second-hand car, for which the claimant had paid £1,500. The defendant produced an expert report on the day of the hearing that the judge disregarded. The Court of Appeal said expert evidence in such a case was disproportionate, and that published guides on the prices of second-hand cars would give "better evidential value for money".

   Mann v Chetty and Patel [2000] WL 1544723 was a professional negligence action against solicitors, arising from ancillary relief proceedings, in which the claimant was seeking permission for expert evidence on a number of valuation and handwriting matters, that together would cost about £2,000. The Court of Appeal allowed very limited evidence only by single joint experts on two valuation matters, concluding that more extensive evidence would be disproportionate.

4. **When a party is seeking to introduce marginally relevant expert evidence to bolster their case.**

   Gumpo v Church of Scientology Religious Education College Inc, 26th July 1999 (unrep), in which a dismissed employee wanted to rely upon psychiatric evidence, which the court considered to be superfluous.

5. **Where pure opinion evidence is likely to be very subjective and speculative.**

   Slimani v SOS for the Home Department (Immigration Tribunal case 01/TH/00092), where the issue was the political situation in the country of origin of an asylum seeker. The Tribunal said that it was difficult to obtain objective up-to-date evidence of real value when opinions in this area were so subjective, and that letters or statements from "experts" who could not quote their sources were of little evidential value.

6. **Where the expert is not sufficiently independent.**

This is discussed in Chapter 2.

TYPES OF CASES WHERE EXPERT EVIDENCE WILL BE PERMITTED

The types of cases where expert evidence will usually be permitted, subject to relevance and proportionality, include:

- **Professional negligence claims** (including clinical negligence), on what was the state of knowledge, standards and reasonably competent professional practice at the time in question. The exceptions are claims against solicitors and barristers, where the courts usually consider they have the necessary expertise (see *Midland Bank v Hett, Stubbs & Kemp* [1979] Ch 384), and when the alleged failure by the professional is a matter of 'common sense' (see *Michael Hyde & Associates Ltd v Williams (JD) & Co Ltd* [2001] *PNLR 8* and *Royal Brompton NHS Trust v Hammond (No 7)* [2001] CILL 1714).

- **Personal injury claims** – a medical report on the claimant's condition and prognosis will usually be required except for very minor injuries (see also CPR Part 16).

- **Claims concerning defective products**, especially technical or medical products.

- **Building and property disrepair disputes**, e.g. regarding the condition and costs of repair of an allegedly defective building.

- **Intellectual property claims**, e.g. *IPC Media Ltd v Highbury Leisure Publishing Ltd* [2004] EWHC 1967 Ch, a copyright dispute, in which the parties were given permission only two months before trial to adduce expert evidence on the similarities between the design features of the two magazines. (However, also see *Thermos v Aladdin* above, where design issues may be common sense.)

- **IT disputes,** e.g. *Peregrine Systems Ltd v Stena Ltd* [2004] EWHC 275 (TCC), a dispute arising from a contract to supply an IT system, in which the judge said it was unhelpful that no expert evidence was called.

- **Issues of foreign law** – section 4(1) of the Civil Evidence Act 1972 provides that a person is competent to testify about foreign law if he "is suitably qualified to do so on account of his knowledge and experience". (See CPR 33.7 for the procedure for adducing evidence of a finding on a question of foreign law.)

- **Shipping cases** (see also in relation to Assessors, discussed in Chapter 3).

- **Valuation issues,** e.g. property or shares.

THE DIFFICULT DECISION FOR THE PARTIES

In practice, it can be very difficult for the parties and their lawyers to anticipate in advance of proceedings when the court will decide that expert evidence is or is not required. A party may quite reasonably conclude that he needs advice from an expert early in a dispute as to whether he has grounds for a claim or defence, especially if the case concerns technical issues. However, if the court later decides that evidence from an expert witness is not necessary to assist the trial judge in deciding the issues which remain in dispute at that stage, the costs incurred by the party in obtaining the expert advice may not be recoverable from the other party (see *Coker v Barkland Cleaning Co.*, the facts of which are set out above; the claimant succeeded but did not recover the unnecessary expert's fees). Solicitors need to warn clients that the costs of obtaining early expert advice may not be recovered.

SEEKING THE COURT'S PERMISSION TO RELY UPON EXPERT EVIDENCE

Under CPR 35.4, no party may call an expert or put in evidence an expert's report without the court's express permission. If permission is granted, it is in relation only to the field of expertise identified, and possibly only for a specific named expert.

Parties have to propose the expert evidence they consider is necessary on the Allocation Questionnaire (court form N150) that they both complete soon after a defence is filed. The experts' section in the questionnaire merits careful completion as it is the parties' opportunity to 'make their bids' for the expert evidence they think they require. The parties are required to co-operate in filling in the questionnaires and should copy the completed ones to each other. The specific questions to be answered on expert evidence are:

1. Do you wish to use expert evidence at trial? If yes, list the experts you propose by name and field of expertise and whether they are single joint experts.

2. Have you already copied any expert reports to the other party?

3. Do you consider the case suitable for a single joint expert in any field?

4. Do you want the expert to give oral evidence at trial? If yes, give reasons.

If a party wants to rely on expert evidence in a low value claim, or evidence from an unusual type of expert, or considers that a single joint expert is not appropriate in a low value claim or on a technical issue, now is the time to make out the case. If the boxes on the form do not provide sufficient space, the argument should be made in a letter or attachment. In the author's experience, Allocation Questionnaires are frequently poorly completed, with little justification provided for the expert evidence requested, e.g. often no explanation is offered why the defendant in a fast track personal injury claim is requesting their own condition and prognosis report.

A case management judge looks at the completed questionnaires and statements of case, and either gives directions 'on paper' or invites the parties, through their lawyers, to a case management conference where the decisions on expert evidence (and other matters) will be taken. At that stage, permission will only be given, at best, for a written report from the experts, especially in an action allocated to the fast track. Typical directions on expert evidence in fast and multi-track cases are in Appendix 4. Perhaps judges could take a more rigorous approach at this stage and, when scientific or theory evidence is proposed, subject it to the Daubert criteria applied in the USA (see above)?

A case has to be made later – when the second questionnaire, the Pre-Trial Checklist (Form N170), is completed, about 10 weeks before trial – for the expert(s) to give oral evidence at trial. This will only be permitted if there are expert opinion issues that remain in dispute, or the expert report(s) concern complex or very technical matters which may need to be explained in more detail to the judge. Permission for oral evidence will rarely be granted in a fast track case when the trial will last less than one day (see Chapter 12 for a fuller discussion of the Pre-Trial Checklist).

CHALLENGING THE ADMISSIBILITY, RELEVANCE OR PROPORTIONALITY OF OTHER PARTIES' PROPOSED EXPERT EVIDENCE

This should be done as early as possible and not left until close to, or at, trial. In *Liverpool Roman Catholic Archdiocesan Trustees Inc v Goldberg* (*The Times*, 9th March 2001 (see also Chapter 2)), Neuberger J gave detailed advice on what he considered to be the proper approach when considering an application to exclude expert evidence. He suggested the following:

- Inadmissibility points should be raised as soon as possible.

- If the objection is raised early, the case management judge should normally deal with it rather than leave it to the trial judge.

- If the objection is made late, particularly when it is made very close to trial, the court should be slower to decide it (this is what happened in this case).

- If there is doubt as to whether expert evidence is admissible, the issues should be determined in favour of admissibility.

- Where it is clear that the evidence is likely to be very expensive and very time-consuming, the court should grasp the nettle and exclude it.

CONDUCT OF EXPERT WITNESSES AND THEIR ACCREDITATION

Conduct of expert witnesses

It is difficult for solicitors, when instructing an expert witness for the first time, to check whether that expert understands that his duty is to the court (the expert's duty to the court is discussed in Chapter 2) and whether he is likely to perform his role competently.

However, some professional bodies, whose members act as expert witnesses, have voluntary registration schemes and codes of conduct for their members in that role (e.g. the Royal Institute of Chartered Surveyors and the Institute of Chartered Accountants. The General Medical Council is working on guidance for doctors who give expert witness evidence.) The expert witness organisations, the Academy of Experts and the Expert Witness Institute also have codes that variously provide that an expert:

a) will only accept instructions in matters where s/he has the relevant expertise;

b) will keep their knowledge up-to-date;

c) will maintain client confidentiality except where there is a legal or overriding professional duty to disclose;

d) will not accept instructions where there is a conflict of interest;

e) should not work on a contingency fee basis;

f) shall maintain appropriate professional indemnity cover.

Unacceptable conduct under the codes would be likely to include breaches of the above and the following bad practices:

a) ignoring 'inconvenient' factual evidence or research;

b) providing a report or oral evidence which is incorrect through lack of knowledge or attention to detail; and

c) knowingly giving false testimony in a report or oral evidence.

It is, therefore, good practice for solicitors to check a proposed expert's membership of professional and expert organisations prior to instructing them. Problems caused by experts who act unprofessionally, as well as possible remedies, are discussed in detail in Chapter 13.

Training and accreditation of expert witnesses

At present, there is no official system of accreditation for expert witnesses who give evidence in the civil courts. It is sufficient for a party to demonstrate to the court that the trial judge will benefit from technical assistance on a particular issue, and that a person with appropriate expertise will give the evidence.

In 2002, one of the expert witness training companies, Bond Solon, along with Cardiff University, introduced an Expert Witness Certificate. The five-day course must be covered within two years, and the modules include report writing, courtroom skills, cross-examination, and law and procedure. The certificate is proving popular and no doubt improves an expert's knowledge and skills.

Many experts attend other ad hoc courses, most frequently on report writing and courtroom skills and this should be encouraged, especially for 'new' experts.

Can training courses provide sufficient quality assurance to meet the needs of solicitors, clients and the courts?

The establishment in 1999 of the Council for the Registration of Forensic Practitioners (CRFP) may however, lead, in due course, to a national system of accreditation that will provide some real assurance that a registered expert is suitable to give evidence. CRFP is a non-profit-making company limited by guarantee. It was set up with support from the Home Office, initially to provide an accreditation scheme for experts who give forensic evidence in the criminal courts. This initiative followed a number of serious miscarriages of justice in the 1980s and 1990s arising from poor forensic scientific evidence. CRFP's central function is to prepare and manage a register of forensic practitioners. The aim is for providers and users of forensic services to come to see the register as a 'definitive indicator of competence'. Applicants are assessed against standards developed for their specialty by experienced peers, and must be revalidated every four years if they are to remain on the register. There is an annual charge to register, and the register must show the practitioner's current fitness to practise in their chosen field.

At the time of writing, there are over 1,600 practitioners on the register in specialties that include:

- Anthropology.
- Archaeology.
- Fingerprint examiners.

- Fire investigation.

- Laboratory science (drugs, firearms, incident reconstruction, toxicology, etc.)

- Odontology (bite marks and identification).

- Physicians, including those working in child abuse and sexual offences.

- Road transport investigation.

- Scene examiners.

Other specialities likely to be added soon include forensic computing, imaging, telecommunications and forensic veterinary surgeons.

The CRFP also has a code of conduct, *Good Practice for Forensic Practitioners*, to which applicants must subscribe. This shares many features with the codes of the expert witness organisations (see above), but also includes that registered forensic practitioners must:

"6. Inform a suitable person or authority, in confidence where appropriate, if you have good grounds for believing there is a situation which may result in a miscarriage of justice.

11. Conduct all work in accordance with the established principles of your profession, using methods of proven validity and appropriate equipment and materials.

12. Make and retain full, contemporaneous, clear and accurate records of the examinations you conduct.

16. Preserve legal professional privilege; only the client may waive this."

While the CRFP's activities currently focus upon experts who work in the criminal courts, it is their intention to offer registration to more categories of experts who practice in civil cases. Moreover, in November 2004, the Legal Services Commission issued a consultation paper, *The Use of Experts*. This encourages solicitors to instruct CRFP-registered experts, and states that it is the Commission's long-term aim to arrive at a position where all experts who are regularly instructed in Commission-funded cases are accredited. However, this could unduly restrict the 'pool' of available experts in publicly funded cases to those willing to undertake the accreditation process.

It is unlikely that the CRFP or any register would ever be sufficiently comprehensive to permit only registered experts to give evidence. Lord Justice Judge, at the 2004 Expert Witness Institute conference, expressed some reservations about accreditation. He said:

- Absence of accreditation cannot be regarded as a disqualification for an individual acting as an expert.

- If there is to be a system of accreditation, it needs to be a system rather than a series of bodies going about it in different ways.

- The success of any accreditation system would depend upon the quality of the accreditors.

- Even the best accreditation system would still leave the occasional fallible or overcommitted expert.

So accreditation is not the complete answer. (See also Chapter 4 on how to select experts.)

CONCLUSIONS

As soon as a solicitor receives instructions from a client, he/she should consider whether an expert may be needed to advise the solicitor, the client, or ultimately, the court. The more experienced a solicitor is in that type of dispute, the less likely it is that an expert's report will be necessary simply to understand the case, unless the matter is very technical. The same may apply when there is ample factual evidence, including from independent witnesses.

However, expert advice will invariably be necessary on liability and causation in areas such as professional negligence, building and IT claims. Experts will often be needed to advise on quantum, but not necessarily at the outset. In all cases, especially potentially low value ones, consideration also needs to be given as to whether the expert might be shared with the other party. Solicitors also need to consider carefully the particular expertise, skills and qualities the particular expert should possess, and whether membership of a professional or experts' body or registration with the CRFP would be advantageous.

The client must be advised whether, in the solicitor's assessment, the court will be likely to permit expert evidence if proceedings become necessary, and the client should be appropriately warned if there is a risk that the costs of instructing the experts may not be recovered. While courts do not very often decide that the proposed expert evidence fails the admissibility test, since the implementation of the CPR a harder look is taken at whether the expert evidence is likely to assist the trial judge and whether the cost of adducing it is proportionate. If the evidence may be of marginal assistance or will be expensive, the case management judge may need some persuading.

Chapter 2
THE CPR AND EXPERTS: WHAT CHANGED?

INTRODUCTION – LORD WOOLF'S VIEW

Lord Woolf's view, in his *Access to Justice* report, was that one of the main generators of unnecessary cost in civil litigation was uncontrolled expert evidence. In *Access to Justice* (HMSO, 1996), he said:

"A large litigation support industry, generating a multi-million pound fee income, has grown up among professions such as accountants, architects and others, and new professions have developed such as accident reconstruction and case experts. This goes against all principles of proportionality and access to justice. In my view, its most damaging effect is that it has created an ethos of what is acceptable which has in turn filtered down to smaller cases."

Lord Woolf considered that many of the problems with expert evidence under the previous regime stemmed from the expert being recruited as part of the team to investigate and advance a party's case. He was aware of the pressure this placed upon experts, who were both advisers to the party instructing them, and independent witnesses giving expert opinion evidence to the court. He was concerned that experts too often acted as partisan advocates for 'their' party instead of neutral fact-finders or opinion givers. He also concluded that experts were instructed when they were not needed, sometimes added to the complexity of a case rather than helping to narrow issues, and that the cost of the expert evidence exceeded the reasonable demands of the case.

Lord Woolf decided that a new approach was required, which would encourage expert's impartiality, and which would give the court greater control. He did not recommend a uniform solution but "a more focused use of expert evidence by a variety of means".

The key features of the CPR regime, developed from Lord Woolf's views on expert evidence, are that:

1. The expert's prime duty is to assist the court.

2. The court can exercise complete control over expert evidence by:

   a) excluding expert evidence unless it is helpful to the court;

   b) limiting the number of experts in a speciality to one per party, unless there is good reason to do otherwise;

   c) directing that expert evidence is to be given by one jointly-instructed expert;

   d) requiring expert evidence to be in written form only;

   e) directing which party will initially pay experts' fees, and limiting the amount of fees that may be recovered.

The other specific innovations of the CPR, in comparison with the previous High and County Court Rules, are:

- Written questions to experts on their reports.

- Experts' discussions.

- Experts' power to apply to the court for directions.

This chapter summarises the main provisions of the CPR relevant to expert evidence, with cross-references to the chapters where particular topics are covered in depth, and also explains how the courts have been applying rule 35.3 (the expert's duty to the court), particularly in relation to what is meant by 'independence'. The chapter concludes with a discussion of the implications of the Human Rights Act 1998 in relation to expert evidence.

CPR BASICS

Parts 1 and 3 of the CPR, on the overriding objective and case management, provide the framework for the court management of expert evidence.

Part 1 – the overriding objective (dealing with a case justly), includes the following principles of particular relevance to expert evidence:

- Ensuring the parties are on an equal footing (there are surprisingly few reported examples of the courts applying this, but see *ES v*

Chesterfield Royal Hospital NHS Trust [2003] EWCA Civ 1284, when the claimant in a clinical negligence claim was given permission for an additional liability expert because the defendants had one expert and two witnesses of fact who were senior doctors from the same specialty – see also Chapter 10).

● Saving expense and dealing with the case in ways which are proportionate to the amount of money involved, the importance of the case, the complexity of the issues and the financial position of the parties (see *Kranidiotes v Paschali* [2001] EWCA Civ 357, when the court rejected a proposed expert accountant on proportionality grounds – see Chapter 6).

● Encouraging the parties to co-operate (for instance in the selection and instruction of a single joint expert)

● Identifying issues at an early stage.

Part 3 – Case Management gives judges wide discretionary powers to give directions and set timetables, including for the disclosure of evidence. The judge can act on paper on his/her own initiative, on application of the parties, or take decisions at case management conferences. Statements of case, issues, or evidence can be struck out or disallowed.

Part 31 – Disclosure of Documents. Only one rule is directly relevant to experts, **CPR 31.14(2)**, which provides that a party may apply for an order for inspection of a document mentioned in an expert's report which has not been disclosed – subject to rule 35.10(4). This apparently innocuous rule added on to a wider rule allowing parties to see documents referred to in statements of case and witness statements has caused some difficulties which are discussed in Chapter 5.

Part 32 – Evidence sets out the court's general powers to control evidence. The most relevant powers in relation to expert evidence are:

● **CPR 32.1** – The court may give directions as to the issues on which it requires evidence, the nature of that evidence and the way in which the evidence is to be placed before the court, and has the power to exclude admissible evidence. These powers work in conjunction with CPR 35.1 and 4 (see Chapter 1 and below). In practice, the case management judge decides whether expert evidence is necessary, whether this will be given by party experts or by single joint experts, by written report only or also by oral evidence.

- **CPR 32.1** – The court can limit cross-examination, and is likely to do so of a single joint expert who is, unusually, called to give oral evidence (see Chapter 9).

- **CPR 32.3** (and the VCF Guidance in the Practice Direction Annex 3) – The court may allow a witness to give evidence by video link. Only selected courts at present have the facility. The power is used mainly for vulnerable witnesses, or those based overseas, but has obvious potential for experts who may only be required to give oral evidence for a limited time on a specific issue.

- **CPR 32.14** – Provides for proceedings for contempt of court to be brought against a person who makes a false statement in a document verified by a statement of truth without an honest belief in its truth. This could apply to an expert – see Chapter 13.

- **The Pre-action Practice Direction and the protocols** – Provide guidance on the use of experts before proceedings are issued (see Chapter 7).

PART 35 – EXPERTS AND ASSESSORS

Part 35 – Experts and Assessors and the Practice Direction provides the specific procedural rules on expert evidence. The main features of Part 35 are:

- **The court's duty and powers to restrict expert evidence (CPR 35.1 and 4).**
  CPR 35.1 imposes on the court a duty to restrict expert evidence to that "which is reasonably required to resolve the proceedings". The practical effect of this was discussed in Chapter 1.

  CPR 35.4 provides that no party can rely upon any expert evidence without the court's permission and, when applying for permission, the party must identify the field of expertise and, where practicable, name the expert (see Chapter 1).

In short, the case management judge may decide that expert evidence is unnecessary, particularly when the trial judge should be able to decide the case on the factual evidence and/or when the value of the claim suggests expert evidence will be disproportionate. The judge can control the numbers and even the identities of the experts who are to be allowed.

CPR 35.4 also gives the court power to limit the amount of experts' fees that are recoverable from another party. This is discussed in Chapter 6.

- **Interpretation (CPR 35.2).**

  This only serves to define an expert as a person "who has been instructed to give or prepare evidence for the purpose of court proceedings" (see Chapter 1).

- **Experts' duty to the court (CPR 35.3).**

  Once proceedings have been issued and the court has given permission to a party, or parties, to rely upon expert evidence, the expert's main duty lies to the court, and not to the party, or parties, instructing and paying him. The CPR did not change the law in this respect but emphasises it. An expert's duty is to help the court on matters within their expertise. The expert remains contractually committed to the instructing party but if there is any conflict between the two duties that to the court takes priority. This duty "overrides any obligation to the person from whom he has received instructions or by whom he is paid".

  The days of the hired gun are definitely over.

  The reasons why the Rules need to emphasise that the expert's duty is to the court is because:

  1. The parties usually choose the expert.

  2. An expert 'creates' their evidence to a greater extent than witnesses of fact through investigations and examinations.

  The implications of this are discussed in more detail later in this chapter and in Chapter 13).

- **General requirement for expert evidence to be in writing (CPR 35.5).**

  The court requires an expert to prepare a **written report** for use in evidence by one or more parties, and to assist the court in deciding the dispute (unless it directs otherwise). In cases allocated to the small claims or fast tracks, and whenever a single joint expert is instructed, expert evidence by written report alone is the norm, and oral evidence from the expert is exceptional (see below). In all cases, the express permission of the court is required to rely upon an expert's written report (see CPR 35.4). The detailed requirements with regard to reports and advice on their preparation are discussed in Chapter 8.

- **Written questions to experts (and answers) (CPR 35.6).**

  This rule provides for **written questions** to be put to experts on their reports, provided this is done once only within 28 days of service of the report, and are for the purpose of clarification only. The questions and answers become part of the report. Questions are discussed in more detail in Chapter 11.

- **Single joint experts (CPR 35.7 & 35.8).**

  The court expects parties to co-operate on selecting and instructing experts and may order a single expert, if the parties have not done so. There are also provisions allowing the court to select the expert, and give directions about the expert's fees. Instruction of a single joint expert is more likely on the small claims and fast tracks (see below) and for technical or quantum issues in multi-track claims. Single joint experts are one of the main innovations of the CPR and are discussed in detail in Chapter 9.

- **The court has power to direct a party to provide information to a party (or expert) (CPR 35.9).**

  This rule gives the court the power to order a party with information to prepare material to assist the other party's expert. The intention could be to prevent the not infrequent problem, in the past, of parties' experts being instructed on very different bases, and to ensure a level playing-field between litigants of unequal resources. The rule is not often relied upon and there is limited case law to assist in its application. (However, see *MMR and the MR Vaccine*

Litigation (No 7) [2003] (unrep), in which the court ordered that scientific studies known to the defendant's experts but not referred to in their reports should be identified and made available for inspection.)

- **Contents of the report (CPR 35.10 and the Practice Direction).** The Practice Direction covers the contents of experts' reports. The rule also requires that:

  1. A report must include a declaration that the expert understands his duty to the court and a statement of truth (rule 35.10(2)).

  2. A report must summarise the expert's instructions and that these "shall not be privileged against disclosure" (rule 35.10(3) and 4)).

  Experts' reports are covered in detail in Chapter 8. Rule 35.10(3) and (4) have proved to be problematic in interpretation, but the Court of Appeal provided helpful guidance in 2003 in *Lucas v Barking NHS Trust* (discussed in Chapter 5).

- **Use by one party of an expert's report disclosed by another (CPR 35.11), and the consequences of failure to disclose an expert's report (CPR 35.13).** These two rules complement one another. CPR 35.11 is based on the principle that "there is no property in a witness", including an expert witness. CPR 35.13 provides that a party who fails to disclose an expert's report may not use the report at the trial or call the expert to give oral evidence, unless the court gives permission. This seems to assume that the party in question has been given permission to rely upon a particular expert's report and has neglected to disclose it on time. It was not an infrequent practice pre-CPR for parties, particularly defendants, to produce late experts' reports, even during the trial – an aspect of the 'litigation by ambush' approach the reforms sought to prevent. The practical consequences of late service of experts' reports and the case law are discussed in Chapters 8 and 10.

- **Experts' discussions (CPR 35.12).** If required by the court, under rule 35.12, experts have to attend a discussion with an expert instructed by the other party, with a view to narrowing the areas of disagreement between the experts and producing an agreed note for the parties and the court. Experts' discussions are considered in detail in Chapter 11.

- **Experts' right to ask the court for directions (CPR 35.14).**
  Experts have the power to apply to the court "to assist them in carrying out their functions". This is a completely new rule, with the intention of giving experts direct access to a case management judge if the expert has problems with those instructing him, or needs guidance. Experts do not make much use of this right (no doubt to the relief of many solicitors) but, notwithstanding this, the rule was amended in 2003 (see below). The issues which may arise if an expert applies are discussed in Chapter 10.

- **The court's power to appoint an assessor to assist the court (CPR 35.15).**
  The power existed under the previous rules. Its present application is discussed in Chapter 3.

The Part 35 Practice Direction is short and mainly covers the duties and responsibilities of an expert witness (see Chapter 1) and the form and content of experts' written reports (see Chapter 8).

PROVISIONS IN RELATION TO EXPERT EVIDENCE ELSEWHERE IN THE CPR

The main provisions relating to expert witnesses included in the other relevant rules and practice directions are summarised below.

Parts 26-29

Parts 26-29 set out the details of the tracking system and the specific rules for each track.

Part 26 provides for cases to be allocated to track, mainly in relation to the likely value of the claim, but complexity and amount of essential evidence are important criteria too. The allocation decision is a matter for the judge (rule 26.5) and is taken on the basis of the information in the parties' statements of case and Allocation Questionnaires (Form N150), possibly at an allocation hearing or case management conference.

The experts' section in the questionnaire merits careful completion, as it is the parties' opportunity to 'make their bids' for the expert evidence they think they require. This is discussed in Chapter 1.

Directions on expert evidence will usually include:

- Whether permission is given to rely upon expert evidence and from which disciplines and in what form (usually by written report).

- Whether the evidence is to be given by a single joint expert or by party-instructed experts.

- The identity of the experts.

- Any specific instructions with regard to the issues to be addressed by the experts.

- The timetable for the disclosure or exchange of reports.

- The timing of written questions and answers.

- The timing of any experts' discussion.

- Any controls the court wishes to impose on expert's fees.

Typical specimen directions on expert evidence are in Appendix 4.

The small claims track (Part 27)

In small claims (up to £5,000, except personal injury and housing disrepair claims when the limit is £1,000), many of the rules of evidence do not apply, including Part 35 (except 35.1, 35.3 and 35.7-8). Specific permission is, nonetheless, required for expert evidence, written or oral (rule 27.5). The advantage of the exclusion of the application of much of Part 35 from small claims is that courts can adopt a flexible approach to expert evidence, perhaps allowing the parties to jointly instruct a local person with the right knowledge and expertise, who can provide a short report or even a letter to help the judge with the essentials at the hearing.

The court may order a losing party to pay a sum for expert's fees (rule 27.14) but this may not exceed the amount specified in the small claims Practice Direction (currently £200 – see paragraph 7.3(2) – which has not been increased since 1999). For proportionality reasons, the courts only give permission for experts in small claims when it is really necessary, usually on a technical issue (e.g. defects in building work, and/or the costs of remedial work), and then only for a single joint expert to prepare a written report. Even then, in the author's experience, the expert's fees will often exceed £200, leaving the successful party, in effect, to pay any balance of the expert's charges out of their damages.

The fast track (Part 28)

The fast track is the normal track for claims with a value between small claims and £15,000, where the court considers the trial is likely to last for no longer than one day. Rule 26.6(5) restricts oral expert evidence at a fast track trial to:

a) one expert per party in relation to any expert field; and

b) expert evidence in two expert fields.

This is somewhat curious wording because, in practice, *oral* expert evidence at a fast track trial is a rarity. (The original draft of the CPR said that no oral expert evidence would be permitted at fast track trials.) Generally, courts will only permit written evidence from single joint experts in fast track cases, or perhaps, in a personal injury claim, from one doctor instructed pre-action by the claimant, with the defendant having permission to put written questions to that expert (see also Chapters 7 and 11).

The usual fast track timetable is 30 weeks from allocation to trial: expert reports are usually ordered to be disclosed 14 weeks from allocation – a tight timescale if a report has not been obtained prior to allocation. Experts should be told the court timetable when they are instructed, and should be sent a copy of the directions. In 2005 a new paragraph 6A was added to the Part 35 Practice Direction which requires parties to serve an expert copies of any orders that require an act to be done by the expert or that otherwise affect him. (See also Chapter 5 and Appendix 1.)

Experts instructed in lower value disputes might need to be reminded about proportionality; very detailed investigations and reports may simply cost too much. A successful party in a fast track case may not be awarded all the costs of their expert report at a summary or detailed assessment (see also Chapter 6).

The multi-track (Part 29)

The multi-track is the usual track for claims over £15,000, or which are not about money.

There are no specific rules in relation to expert evidence for the multi-track, but the Part 29 Practice Direction states, at paragraph 4.10, that the court's general approach will be:

1. To give directions for a single joint expert on any appropriate issue unless there is a good reason not to do so.

2. That like expert's reports will usually be simultaneously exchanged.

3. To direct a discussion between experts if reports are not agreed.

Case management conferences (sometimes more than one) are held in the more complex and high value multi-track claims, and issues in relation to expert evidence are likely to feature strongly. In practice, in claims allocated to the multi-track, the court is more prepared than on the fast track to allow each party to instruct their own expert, particularly on issues of liability if opinion evidence is necessary (as opposed to investigation of facts and background) and on the main heads of quantum, in the interests of justice and on proportionality grounds.

Pre-trial checklist (previously the Listing Questionnaire, Form N170)

(See also Chapter 12)

The second case management questionnaire should be equally carefully completed as the Allocation Questionnaire. At this stage, the court is checking that directions have been complied with, and whether the case is ready for trial. As with the Allocation Questionnaire, the parties should co-operate on completion of the form and copy it to each other. With regard to expert evidence, the following must be identified:

1. The expert reports that have been disclosed, whether they are single joint reports, and if not whether they are agreed, and whether permission has been given for oral evidence.

2. Whether there has been a discussion between the experts and they have signed a joint statement.

3. If oral evidence is considered necessary, and if the trial date is not yet fixed, whether there are dates to avoid for the expert to give that evidence.

At this stage, the difficult issues with regard to expert evidence (these are discussed in more detail in Chapter 10) are likely to be:

● Late service of one or more expert reports.

● Difficulties in arranging for experts to answer questions and/or to meet in sufficient time before the trial.

● A party seeking to persuade the court that additional expert evidence is necessary.

● Problems with availability of an expert to give oral evidence at trial.

These need careful explanation on the form, or in a letter or attachment, and an urgent application or request for a case management conference will be necessary if the trial date will be affected.

SPECIALIST PROCEEDINGS AND EXPERT EVIDENCE

Some of the specific rules on specialist proceedings originally included variations on the main Civil Procedure Rules with regard to expert evidence. However, as the Civil Procedure Rules have been amended since 1999, variations in practice have been removed, leaving only:

Admiralty proceedings (Part 61)

In the Admiralty Court, a judge may sit with assessors when hearing collision claims or other cases involving issues of navigation or seamanship, and the parties will not normally be permitted to call expert witnesses on matters of navigation or seamanship where the court sits with assessors (CPR 61.13). (See Chapter 3 for a discussion on assessors.)

Guides: specialist proceedings

Several of the specialist divisions of the High Court publish guides, which are given effect by practice directions. The contents of the guides supplement the CPR. The most relevant points in relation to expert evidence are summarised below.

The Queen's Bench Guide

Section 7.9 covers experts and assessors. The main additional guidance to the CPR is:

Single experts will often be appropriate to deal with questions of quantum in cases where primary issues are as to liability, and where expert evidence is needed to acquaint the court with matters of fact rather than opinion. However, there remains a body of cases where liability will turn on expert opinion evidence and where it will be appropriate for parties to instruct their own experts; for instance, where the issue is whether a party acted in accordance with proper professional standards, where it will be useful for the court to hear the opinion of more than one expert so as to be exposed to a range of views, enabling the evidence to be tested in cross-examination (paragraph 7.9.5).

An order for a single expert does not prevent a party from having his own expert to advise him, although that is likely to be at his own cost, regardless of the outcome (paragraph 7.9.6).

Parties are expected to co-operate on terms of reference for a single expert, which should include a statement of what the expert is asked to do, identify any documents he is asked to consider and specify the assumptions he is asked to make (paragraph 7.9.7).

Questions put to experts under CPR 35.6 that are oppressive, or which are put without permission for a purpose other than clarification, will usually be disallowed with an appropriate costs order.

When an **expert files with the court a request for directions** under CPR 35.14, he should be careful not to send the court privileged material.

The Chancery Guide

The Chancery Division hears specialist cases such as those relating to companies, land, and contentious probate work.

Chapter 4 of the Guide deals with expert evidence. The points listed above from the Queen's Bench Guide on single experts, questions and directions are repeated. The Guide also says that the court will sometimes order the disclosure of expert reports sequentially rather than by exchange (paragraph 4.14).

The Admiralty and Commercial Court Guide

Section H2 deals with expert witnesses.

While the Guide states that the parties to an action should consider the appointment of an **single expert**, it recognises that cases in the Commercial Court are frequently of a size, complexity or nature such that the use of an single expert is not appropriate, and that therefore there is no presumption in the court in favour of single joint experts (H2.2).

The guide also suggests that:

- A glossary of significant technical terms should be incorporated into an expert's report (H2.7).

- The procedure to be adopted at meetings of experts is a matter for the experts and not for the parties or their legal representatives subject to the direction of the court (H2.14).

- The parties must not seek to restrict the freedom of experts to agree issues at or after a discussion (H2.15).

- Copies of technical documents and unpublished source material relied upon by an expert must be provided with the report (H2.19).

- A party wishing to inspect other documents, particularly published material, referred to in an expert's report, should apply to the court (H2.20).

- At trial, the evidence of expert witnesses will normally be taken as a block, after the evidence of witnesses of fact has been heard (H2.21).

Appendix 11 to the Guide is entitled *Expert Evidence in the Commercial Court: Requirements of General Application*. It recites the principal duties of an expert, which are drawn from the CPR, and from the judgment in the *Ikarian Reefer* case (see Chapter 1).

THE CODES OF GUIDANCE ON EXPERT EVIDENCE AND THE PROTOCOL

At the time of Lord Woolf's enquiry, there was a realisation that it would be necessary to clarify the role of the expert witness in the new civil court procedure: rules and practice directions might not be sufficient. In 1997, Lord Scott (then Sir Richard Scott and the deputy head of civil justice) 'commissioned' an "expert's protocol" from an ad hoc working party established by the Association of British Insurers. Members included lawyers and expert witnesses (including the author). Work on the protocol was halted in 1998 while the working party waited for the publication of the rules.

Unfortunately, the definitive Protocol was not approved and published until 2005. In 1999 two codes of guidance were published, by the Academy of Experts and the reconvened 'official' working party. The senior judges were reluctant to approve either because of disagreements between the Academy and the Expert Witness Institute.

The existence of two codes was a source of confusion. The status and application of both codes suffered as lawyers and experts did not know whether either or both had judicial support. In 2004 the Master of the Rolls, through the Civil Justice Council, asked a High Court Judge and a Circuit Judge to combine the two codes. This was done successfully, and approved by the Council. *The Protocol for the Instruction of Experts* was published in July 2005 and offers guidance to experts and those who instruct them in situations when opinion evidence is to be relied upon in court proceedings. It does not apply to expert advice that parties do not intend to adduce in litigation.

The Protocol is referred to at appropriate places in the book and is reproduced at Appendix 2.

CHANGES MADE TO THE CPR WITH REGARD TO EXPERT EVIDENCE SINCE IMPLEMENTATION

Part 35 has stood the test of time very well and has been changed less often than many other rules. As at May 2005, only the following changes have been made:

1. In 1999, **Practice Direction 35 paragraph 4.3** was amended to require the party who instructs an expert to pay for the expert to answer written questions from other parties. Previously the rule was the other way round. A possible reason was to simplify invoicing arrangements for the expert.

2. In spring 2002, several changes were made:

a) **A new paragraph 1 was added to the Practice Direction**, to spell out in more detail the general requirements of expert evidence from the *Ikarian Reefer* catalogue (see Chapter 1).

b) **Rule 35.10(2)** – the experts' statement of truth – was revised. The old version was:

"I understand that my duty is to the court in preparing this report and giving oral evidence. I believe that the facts stated in this report are true and the opinions are correct."

The revised version is:

"I confirm that insofar as the facts stated in my report are within my own knowledge I have made clear which they are and I believe them to be true and that the opinions expressed represent my true and complete professional opinion."

The new version is certainly more precise – how could opinions be "correct"? (See Chapter 10 for a fuller discussion on the statement of truth.)

c) **Rule 35.12 – Experts' discussions**. There was some minor rewording to make it clear that experts' discussions should only concern issues in relation to the experts' expertise and their opinions in this area. The purpose was to emphasise that It is not appropriate for experts to broaden their discussions to matters outside their expertise and reports, and to discourage experts from trying to reach agreement, even on issues within their remit, if there are genuine differences of opinion which should be aired before the court (see Chapter 11).

d) **Rule 35.14 – Experts applying to the court for directions**. An expert now has to copy any request to the court to his/her instructing party seven days, and to any other party four days, in advance of filing it at court. Previously experts could apply directly without contacting the solicitors. There has been no reported case law on this rule, so what might have prompted the change? The possible reason could be that the courts experienced difficulties with some experts' requests, especially if they arrived in letter form and not as Part 23 applications, and therefore there was an argument for instructing solicitors 'filtering' the requests.

3. In spring 2005 a new paragraph 6A was added to the Practice Direction which requires **parties to serve on an expert copies of any court order** that requires an act to be done by the expert or that otherwise affects him.

EXPERTS' INDEPENDENCE AND DUTY TO THE COURT – GUIDANCE FROM THE COURTS SINCE 1999

The emphasis in the CPR on the independence of experts, and the specific requirement in rule 35.3 that the expert's duty is to the court, has been the focus of a number of important decisions of the senior courts since 1999.

What does independence mean? Generally speaking, an expert witness must be independent of the instructing party to maintain credibility and have no personal 'bias'. One commentator suggested that a useful test of an expert's independence is whether equivalent instructions from the opposing party would yield the same evidence. If an expert witness is not independent because of 'connections' with the instructing party, or fails in the duty to demonstrate objectivity, the court may decide that the party cannot rely on the evidence. Challenges to an expert's independence should be made as soon as possible (see the *Liverpool RC* case below and Chapter 1).

The guidance from the courts has included on whether employees of a party can give expert evidence, possible problems when the client instructs the expert, the positions of close colleagues, friends and business associates of a party acting as an expert, the position of doctors who are treating the claimant, close working relationships between experts and solicitors, and on dealing with experts who display a lack of objectivity by acting as an advocate.

Employees of parties

An employee of a party will usually have difficulty in establishing sufficient independence to act as an expert for their employer. There may be less objection where the expert's evidence will be factual and technical, rather than drawing conclusions from assumptions, or expressing opinions on liability issues, and/or where proportionality is an issue. If the evidence is admitted, the fact of the employment of the expert may affect the weight of the evidence.

In *Field v Leeds City Council* [2000] 17 EG 165, the Court of Appeal said that in a claim for housing disrepair, a local authority employee from the housing claims investigation section could be sufficiently independent, provided he understood his duty to the court and the need for objectivity (for which he might need training). The Court of Appeal also said that the proposed expert's suitability should be demonstrated to the case management judge when seeking permission to instruct him.

Admiral Management Services v Para-Protect Europe Ltd (*The Times*, 26th March 2002), was a dispute between two businesses (in which the claimant alleged that the defendant had "poached" employees and made use of confidential information that they brought with them). The claimant used in-house computer staff to investigate, including searching the defendant's computers (with a court order), and to advise generally. The dispute was settled but the defendant disputed the claimant's claim for expert's fees for their in-house investigator's work. The defendant argued that the work was "fact-finding", that the costs were incurred before solicitors were instructed, and that the claimant should not claim staff time as expert's fees. Burnton J, relying upon *Field*, "saw nothing unjust in reasonable recovery of the costs of in-house experts", provided that overheads and profit were not included, and allowed the claim in principle.

See also *DN v Greenwich London Borough* [2004] EWCA Civ 1659, discussed in Chapter 1, in which an educational psychologist employed by the defendant was allowed to give opinion evidence on his own allegedly negligent actions.

Professional colleague of a party

What about a **professional colleague of a party**? He or she would probably fail the 'appearance of bias' test, even if their expertise and personal qualities suggested they would understand their duty. In *Liverpool RC Archdiocesan Trustees Inc v Goldberg No 2* (*The Times*, 9th March 2001 and *The Times*, 10th August 2001), a claim against a tax barrister for negligent advice, it was held at first instance by Neuberger J that there was no objection in law to the defendant relying upon expert evidence from another tax barrister from the same chambers, who had been a colleague and friend of the defendant for nearly 30 years, i.e. it was not inadmissible evidence (see Chapter 1). He said it would be for the trial judge to decide if the evidence was cogent (the application objecting was made 14 months after the identity of the expert was known and only a few weeks before trial). However, the trial judge, Evans-Lombe J, held that expert evidence from the friend and colleague of the defendant was inadmissible not least because the expert had admitted in his report to his "personal sympathies being engaged to a greater degree than would probably be normal with an expert witness", as a reasonable observer would think that the relationship would affect the views of the expert "however unbiased the conclusions of the expert might probably be".

Experts instructed by the client rather than the solicitor

In principle, there is no difficulty if the client suggests an expert or has already instructed one before involving solicitors in the dispute. However, there are risks, especially if the expert has advised on, or assisted in, steps in the proceedings.

In *Anglo Group plc v Winther Brown & Co Ltd* [2000] 72 Con LR 11, the action arose out of the alleged failure of a computer software system, purchased by the defendants. When the problems began, the defendant consulted a firm, FMC, which acted as a claims consultancy in the computer industry. They advised the defendant generally, including that they should write an adversarial letter to the software suppliers. When proceedings were issued the defendant instructed two individuals from FMC as their computer experts. Toulmin J criticised the experts' lack of independence as one expert admitted that one of his reports for the court had also been written "as a negotiating tool", and the other that part of his evidence was intentionally misleading. Toulmin J also took the opportunity to restate and extend the *Ikarian Reefer* guidance on the duties of an expert witness, now set out in paragraph 1 of the Part 35 Practice Direction (see Chapter 1). The additional guidance he offered included:

- That expert evidence should normally be confined to technical matters on which the court will be assisted by receiving an explanation, or to evidence of common professional practice. The expert witness should not give evidence or opinions as to what the expert himself would have done in similar circumstances or otherwise seek to usurp the role of the judge.

● Experts for opposing parties should co-operate to narrow the technical issues in dispute as early as possible, including at 'without prejudice' meetings.

Hussein v William Hill Group [2004] EWHC 208 QB was a personal injury claim arising from an alleged assault on the claimant at a bookmakers'. The claimant acted in person. Two doctors, a GP and a consultant psychiatrist, who were friendly with the claimant and who had allegedly treated him for his injuries, gave evidence for him. The judge, Hallett J, found that the claimant had greatly exaggerated his injuries. She did not believe most of the evidence from either doctor. The GP had virtually no records of the "consultation and treatment", leading the judge to conclude that he was prepared to say whatever he believed would help the claimant. The psychiatrist, she concluded, had been brought into the case later purely to support it, and she found it "incredible that a Fellow of the Royal College of Psychiatrists could allow himself to give evidence in these circumstances". The judge asked for her judgment and the papers to be referred to the General Medical Council. (See also Chapter 12.)

Other close connections with a party

In *SPE International v Professional Preparation Contractors (UK) Ltd* [2002] WL 499022, the trial judge ruled as inadmissible a report from an 'expert' on the calculation of losses in a very technical dispute in the shot-blasting industry, which he had prepared without any written instructions (he knew nothing of Part 35), and which was outside his expertise – he was an ex-RAF officer, and a management consultant to the claimant. In fact, his wife had carried out most of the work for the report.

Experts who appear regularly for the same party may also be 'tainted', especially if the expert himself, his report or his oral evidence appears not to be objective. In *Cairnstores v Aktiebolaget Hassle* [2002] WL 22612, a patents case, the defendant's expert was criticised by the judge for acting as an advocate when he put forward untenable theories, possibly because of "over-exposure" to the defendant's case, having been involved with that party in similar litigation in several other countries.

In *Helical Bar plc v Armchair Passenger Transport Ltd* [2003] EWHC 367, a market researcher and consultant was allowed to give evidence in a road traffic accident credit hire dispute even though he had worked previously for a company closely involved in the action. It was held that the expert had the relevant expertise (he specialised in surveys of the self-drive car market), the connection was not sufficiently close to question his independence and he was aware of, and was willing to comply with, his duty to the court.

Doctor treating a party

In *Re B (a minor)* (Sexual Abuse: Expert's Report [2000] 1 FLR 871), the Court of Appeal held that the role of an expert who is treating a patient must not be confused with the role of an expert instructed to report to the court, at least in family cases. A father had applied for contact with his daughter. The mother alleged sexual abuse on contact visits. The daughter was referred by her GP to a psychiatrist for treatment. The psychiatrist was then asked to provide a report in the contact proceedings, which concluded that the father had abused the girl and there should be no unsupervised contact. The father applied for an independent expert but the court refused this. The Court of Appeal disagreed and said the mother's solicitors had made an error of judgment, and the treating psychiatrist should not have accepted the instructions.

There has not been a reported case on this subject in personal injury claims, where the issue most commonly arises. Generally, a medical report from an independent doctor on the claimant's condition and prognosis is to be preferred, as a treating doctor may find it difficult to be frank and objective, particularly where the patient remains under his care.

An expert agreeing not to act as a witness for the other party

In *Lilly Icos LLC v Pfizer Ltd* [2000] 23(11) IPD 23089, Jacob J (as he then was) held that a contract in an intellectual property case, under which an expert was said to have agreed with one party that he would not act as an expert witness for the other party, was unenforceable as a matter of public policy, because otherwise a 'rich' party might try to bind a number of experts not to give evidence to limit the other party's choice of expert. It could also deprive the court of valuable evidence.

Expert instructed regularly by the solicitors

Experts who are regularly instructed by a party's lawyers may be less than ideal. In *Smolen v Solon Co-operative Housing Services Ltd* [2003] EWCA Civ 1240, the Court of Appeal upheld the first instance decision to allow the appointment of a second single joint expert when the claimant objected to the first one, even though this was after his report was disclosed, because he had been instructed by the defendant's solicitor many times before. The court found no evidence of impropriety between the solicitor and expert but permitted the instruction of a second expert because the claimant no longer had faith in the first one. But the claimant was ordered to pay half the first expert's fee in the usual way and to pay the fees for the second expert into court (see also Chapter 9).

Experts who act as advocates

Nevertheless, the strongest judicial disapproval is incurred in the courts by experts who take on the role of advocate, particularly if there are also question marks over their independence. *Pearce v Ove Arup* [2002] IPD 25011 centred on an allegation that a leading international architect had dishonestly copied the claimant architects' design for a building. At the trial, these allegations were completely and utterly dismissed by the Honourable Mr Justice Jacob (now Jacob LJ). During the course of the trial, the claimant relied on an architect expert, Mr Wilkey.

Jacob J said:

"In my judgment, Mr Wilkey's 'expert' evidence fell far short of the standards of objectivity required of an expert witness. He claimed to have appreciated the seriousness of what he was saying but made blunder after blunder ... So biased and irrational do I find his 'expert' evidence that I conclude he failed his duty to the court."

Jacob J was particularly critical that the expert came to argue the claimant's case. He decided that Mr Wilkey should be reported to his professional body (see also Chapter 12).

In the matter of *Colt Telecom Group plc* [2002] EWHC 2815 Ch, an accountant insolvency practitioner from a major firm was criticised for giving evidence for one company petitioning for another company's administration, which was strongly opposed. The accountant's firm had recently acted for the 'defendant' company; the firm stood to benefit if his evidence was accepted, as they were proposed as the administrators (which was not brought out in the report). Also he relied on second-hand evidence in valuing the assets, in a field in which he had limited experience. The judge, Jacob J again, concluded that the accountant had failed in his duties to the court and had "espoused his client's cause".

Re C & Re F (children) [2003] EWCA Civ 1148 were disputes between parents concerning the immunisation of their children. The homeopath who gave evidence for the mothers (who were against the immunisation) was criticised by the judge for allowing her deeply-held feelings about immunisation to overrule her duty to the court to give objective evidence and to present "junk science".

In *Phillips & Others v Symes & Others (Costs No 2)* [2004] EWHC 2330 Ch, at a preliminary hearing to decide whether Mr Symes, a bankrupt, had the mental capacity to conduct the litigation, a consultant psychiatrist concluded that he had not had capacity to manage his affairs for the previous 20 years, following a stroke. The judge, Smith J, seriously criticised the psychiatrist for not investigating the issue of capacity adequately (he saw Mr Symes for a total of one hour and only reviewed *some* of the other evidence), for persevering with his opinion for much too long in the face of the other evidence, and for "assuming the role of advocate" for Mr Symes.

In *Great Eastern Hotel Co Ltd v John Laing Construction plc* [2005] EWHC 181 (TCC), a case involving a long delay in the completion of a hotel refurbishment, the trial judge heavily criticised one of the defendant's experts, a programming manager, for asserting the defendant's competence in the management of the project when he had not investigated their terms of engagement, did not know exactly what they had done, and when he had failed to take into account admissions of neglect by one of the defendant's witnesses of fact. His evidence was rejected, as he "had no concept of his duty to the court as an independent witness".

How to guard against instructing a partisan expert is discussed in Chapter 4 and the possible consequences of having done so in Chapter 13.

THE HUMAN RIGHTS ACT 1998 AND EXPERT EVIDENCE

The Human Rights Act came into force on 2nd October 2000, 18 months after the CPR. Article 6(1) of the European Convention on Human Rights (ECHR) (in a schedule to the Act), provides in civil disputes for a "fair and public hearing within a reasonable time by an independent and impartial tribunal established by law".

Equality of arms is an important principle underpinning the ECHR. The European Court of Human Rights (EtCHR) has explained that:

"Equality of arms implies that each party must be afforded a reasonable opportunity to present his case – including his evidence – under conditions that do not place him at a substantial disadvantage vis-à-vis his opponent." (*Dombo Beheer v The Netherlands* [1993] 18 EHRR 213 at paragraphs 32-3.)

Parties also have the right to know and comment upon the evidence and legal submissions of other parties *(Ruiz-Mateos v Spain* [1993] 16 EHRR 505 at paragraph 63).

Generally, the EtCHR has not been prescriptive about contracting states' procedural and evidential rules. Nonetheless, in a number of decisions (several concerning the French system of court-appointed experts), the EtCHR has said that Article 6(1) does not give the parties the right to call expert evidence where that evidence would serve no useful purpose, and that parties in civil disputes must have an adequate and equal opportunity to participate in the instruction of experts and in the process leading to the formation of their opinion, and an opportunity to question and challenge the expert's conclusions (*Mantovanelli v France* [1997] 24 EHRR 370 and *H v France* [1989] 12 EHRR 74). They have also said that the appointment of an expert by the court is not objectionable under Article 6 (*Brandstetter v Austria* [1993] 15 EHRR 578).

CPR Part 35, in general, complies with these requirements. It is perhaps not surprising, therefore, that few challenges have been made to Part 35 on the basis of Article 6. The following might provide potential grounds for challenges:

• A court refusing to allow expert evidence, on admissibility, relevance or proportionality grounds, exercising the power in CPR 35.4 to restrict expert evidence.

• A court directing that expert evidence on a vital issue was to be given by a single joint expert against a party's wishes, or that additional evidence was not to be permitted when a party criticises the single joint expert's report.

• A court refusing to allow an expert to give oral evidence, so preventing testing of the evidence by cross-examination.

• A trial judge considering he is bound by an expert's conclusions, depriving himself of jurisdiction to decide matters crucial to the dispute (see *Terra Woningen v Netherlands* [1997] 24 EHRR 456).

• The role of assessors advising the judge, under CPR 35.15, particularly if in a particular case the advice was given in private without the parties having an opportunity to test it.

• Expert witnesses remaining immune from suit for their work in court proceedings (see Chapter 13), which could deprive a party of a remedy when an expert performs incompetently.

Nevertheless, human rights issues in relation to expert evidence have only been raised in two prominent civil cases since the Human Rights Act came into force.

In *Daniels v Walker* [2000] 1 WLR 1382 CA, a personal injury claim, the issue was the instruction of an additional expert to a single joint expert. The case is discussed in detail in Chapter 9. On receipt of the report of a single joint expert (SJE) occupational therapist, the defendant applied to the court for permission to instruct a second expert, as they considered that the full-time care recommended by the SJE was not justified. The defendants raised two arguments on appeal:

1. That the first instance judge had ignored the overriding objective in refusing the application.

2. That a refusal to permit them to instruct a second expert would

conflict with Article 6 of the ECHR, because it would amount to barring an essential part of the defendants' case.

The Court of Appeal said that the fact that a party has agreed to an SJE being instructed does not prevent that party from being allowed to instruct and rely upon another expert; that, in substantial cases, the instruction of an SJE could be regarded as a "first step", and that the court has discretion to allow a party to obtain further evidence to challenge the SJE report if the reasons were not "fanciful".

The appeal was allowed. However, Lord Woolf, giving the lead judgment, warned against parties raising human rights issues when they were not relevant; even if the Human Rights Act 1998 had been in force (it was not), he considered it undesirable for case management decisions to be made more complicated by introducing arguments under Article 6. He said that the Court of Appeal hoped that judges would be robust in resisting any attempt to introduce such arguments. The decision to allow the appeal was, of course, entirely compatible with Article 6.

In *H v Lambeth Southwark & Lewisham HA* [2001] EWCA Civ 1455, the issue was who should attend an experts' discussion (see also Chapter 11). The case was a complex clinical negligence claim, concerning an alleged failure to diagnose a progressive congenital condition in four children in the same family. The claimant lawyers were concerned about the forthcoming experts' discussion, because the claimant experts were reluctant to discuss the actions of the eminent consultant who was allegedly negligent, and there was a risk that in a closed meeting with colleagues they might be "persuaded to pull their punches". It was argued that in those circumstances, there could be a breach of Article 6 of the ECHR if the meeting went ahead without lawyers present.

The Court of Appeal decided that an experts' discussion does not engage the question of a right to a fair trial under ECHR Article 6, because the court's power to order a discussion is discretionary and any agreement reached at the discussion is not binding on the parties, or on the court. The court declined to order that the claimant's lawyers should attend the discussion on the grounds that their input should be to a "well-crafted agenda". It was also suggested that the meeting might be recorded and, more generally, when time and cost permitted that the appointment of an independent legally-qualified person to chair an experts' discussion might be considered.

A different human rights issue arose in a recent family case, *C-B (a child)*, Lawtel, 7th October 2004, in which the child's guardian ad litem changed her mind about the child living with an aunt (because of a risk that the aunt would be too easily influenced by the mother), shortly before the final hearing to either make a residence order in favour of the aunt, or place the child for adoption. The guardian did not file any evidence to explain the change of mind. The judge placed the child for adoption. The Court of Appeal sent the case back for rehearing, as the aunt had not been given an opportunity to consider and argue against the guardian's changed view, which was a breach of Article 6.

CONCLUSIONS

Lord Woolf's *Access to Justice* report and the CPR have significantly changed the part played by expert evidence in civil disputes (see Chapter 15 for an assessment). While the English civil justice system remains basically adversarial, the greatly increased case management powers of the judges and the introduction of single experts, has moved the English system in the direction of the European inquisitorial systems. Parties and lawyers no longer control when they can rely on expert evidence, sometimes not even from whom it can be obtained, or the form of that evidence. Experts owe a clear duty to the court, on which the courts have given considerable guidance. Part 35 and the Practice Direction have only been amended three times in the six years since the CPR were implemented. Very few challenges have been made to Part 35 on the basis of Article 6 of the Human Rights Act and those that have been made have not succeeded. However, the large number of reported cases on other aspects of expert evidence demonstrates the need for further guidance. The author hopes that the recently published Protocol (see above and Appendix 2) will help to fill that gap.

Chapter 3

THE CHANGING ROLES FOR EXPERTS IN THE POST-CPR CLIMATE

The role of the expert in civil, non-family disputes has changed significantly following the implementation of Lord Woolf's civil justice reforms (which are summarised in Chapter 2). The CPR, in fact, only made subtle, but important, changes to the function of the expert, but the broader climate of changes introduced by Lord Woolf's reforms, and the changes in the way litigation is funded, have encouraged clients, lawyers, experts, judges and others involved in the process to view the role of the expert in a quite different way.

Experts are no longer just expert witnesses engaged by the parties in a civil dispute to provide a report and give oral evidence at trial in support of the case, which the party wants to advance. In the current civil litigation landscape, experts perform a variety of roles, from advising the client with a problem about a potential claim before litigation is even in contemplation, to sitting with and advising a judge in a civil trial.

The various roles played by experts in the new system outlined in this chapter include:

- Advisory experts – a new role outside the court.

- Single joint experts in litigation – the courts' preferred approach, especially in smaller claims.

- 'Conventional' expert witnesses in litigation acting for each party.

- Lead experts who co-ordinate the work of other experts.

- Shadow experts, who are instructed by a party to assist behind the scenes during litigation.

- Assessors, who sit with the judge to assist the court.

- Experts who determine disputes as adjudicators, or who act as mediators facilitating at mediations.

ADVISORY EXPERTS

Solicitors increasingly ask experts, particularly experts advising upon liability and causation, to provide a quick view on a case, for a limited fee, based on one party's information only. The solicitor, or the client, may expect to bear the costs of this advice, regardless of the outcome of any subsequent claim. This is because, in many circumstances, it may be difficult or undesirable for a party to retain that same expert in the litigation, either because the court insists upon a single joint expert instructed by both parties, or because the client and solicitor prefer to keep the advisory expert "behind the scenes" to enable a full and frank discussion to take place with the expert without exposing that discussion, and the expert's views, to the other party and to the court.

Also, the practical effect of the CPR is to create a distinction between:

a) an expert who *advises* a party on a matter within his/her expertise at any stage of a problem, dispute or claim; and

b) an expert witness who is *instructed* by a party during litigation with the permission of the court, to prepare a written report for the court and possibly to give oral evidence.

The former only has a duty to whoever instructs and pays him, the latter has an overriding duty to the court (see Chapter 2).

Thus, an advisory expert retained before the nature and extent of the dispute has been worked out, may not be instructed if the dispute is pursued through litigation, because of the difficulty of demonstrating the independence of the expert when he has been involved in formulating the claim, and the difficulties this may cause with regard to his compliance with the expert's 'duty to the court'.

In conditional fee cases

Since the implementation of the Access to Justice Act 1999 in April 2000, solicitors have been permitted to conduct any civil, non-family litigation on a conditional fee ('no win no fee') basis. Also in April

2000, legal aid was withdrawn from most personal injury claims, and from other classes of disputes, including some of those involving businesses. The current statutory regime for conditional fees allows the successful party to recover from the (losing) party a 'success fee' (charged by the solicitor for accepting the risk that he will not be paid at all if the case is lost) and a 'reasonable insurance premium' (taken out to cover the costs of the client's disbursements and the other party's costs if the case is lost). The relevance of this changed funding climate for the role of experts is that, in many more cases than previously, the solicitor, if not the party, will want early advice on the strengths and weaknesses on liability, in particular to enable the solicitor to carry out a risk assessment before deciding whether to take on the case on a conditional fee basis.

When an advisory expert may be necessary

Advisory experts may be needed to:

1. Look into the background to the dispute, e.g. where a technical person may be best placed to investigate/inspect the scene and appraise what he finds.

2. Provide information on procedures, and standards of practice in a business or profession, e.g. in potential professional negligence claims.

3. Comment upon the strengths and weaknesses of a potential claim against various parties.

4. Be used as a sounding board to test information and assumptions.

5. Advise on lines of inquiry, and upon documents and other evidence likely to be available.

6. Consider the potential value of a claim in different factual scenarios, including making different assumptions about the scope of the legal liabilities.

The duty of an expert adviser

An expert instructed to advise has a duty to exercise all reasonable skill, care and diligence applicable to his professional discipline, in providing advice and opinions. If the client and lawyers rely on the advice, which in the event proves to be incorrect, the expert may be liable in negligence. This is not the case with regard to expert witnesses instructed post the issue of proceedings (see Chapter 13).

Can an adviser be retained as an expert witness for the litigation?

This is not an easy question to answer, as neither the CPR nor the general law are entirely clear about when early advice from an expert may have to be disclosed to the other party and the court. This is discussed in Chapter 5. However, solicitors and clients should err on the side of caution and only plan to retain the same expert for the litigation when the advisory expert's role is largely fact-finding and when the exchanges with the advisory expert, if disclosed, are not likely to compromise the case that it is intended to pursue.

Can the court order disclosure of an advisory report?

In short, the answer is 'no'. A party cannot be compelled to disclose expert advice unless he/she intends to rely upon it. When an expert is engaged purely to advise a client and a lawyer, communications with the expert are privileged e.g. if an expert advises that the client's case is weak, that advice cannot be revealed to a third party unless and until the client decides to waive the privilege.

In *Carlson v Townsend* [2001] WL 273002, the Court of Appeal confirmed that the position has not been changed by the CPR – that the personal injury pre-action protocol does not require a medical expert, selected in accordance with the protocol, to be jointly instructed, or his report to be disclosed to the defendant. Such reports remain privileged and the court cannot order their production, although the claimant would need the court's permission before relying on another expert's report in the proceedings (see also Chapter 7).

Advisory experts will most often be instructed at the beginning of a dispute. If they are (also) instructed later, once proceedings are issued, they are usually described as shadow experts – see below.

Paying advisory experts

Payment arrangements for advisory experts are entirely a matter for the instructing party or solicitor. A fee agreed for this type of work will frequently be a fixed fee on a one-off basis. (For example, in *Sutton v Tesco plc* [2002] 8 *Current Law Digest* 57, the claimant, in a personal injury slipping claim, was allowed to rely upon a report from her treating psychiatrist obtained without discussion with the defendant or the court's permission, to challenge evidence from other experts, including single joint experts, that she was malingering, but not to recover the costs of the report, regardless of the outcome.)

Advisory experts – key questions

1. Does the solicitor or the client need technical advice to understand what happened and why?

2. Is this essential to risk assess the claim, e.g. to decide upon whether to enter into a conditional fee arrangement?

3. Is the advice for the client or the firm's benefit?

4. Might the client want/need to instruct the same expert for any ensuing litigation – if so, how does that affect the choice of expert instructions/discussions?

5. Who should pay for the advice?

SINGLE JOINT EXPERTS (CPR 35.7-8)

(See also Chapter 9)

Lord Woolf originally recommended in his interim *Access to Justice* report that the English courts should adopt the French system of court-appointed experts. This provoked considerable disquiet, particularly from solicitors used to having complete control over expert evidence in their clients' litigation. The compromise adopted in Lord Woolf's final report, and implemented in the CPR, is the single joint expert. (It seems likely that the Rule Committee accepted the very real practical difficulties involved in the courts selecting and instructing appropriate experts, and were alert to the problems that a court-appointed expert system might present in ensuring the courts complied with their obligations under Article 6 of the ECHR to provide a fair trial (now implemented in the Human Rights Act 1998 – see Chapter 2).)

The court has the power, under CPR 35.7 and 8, to direct that evidence on an issue is to be given by one expert only and, when the parties cannot agree who that should be, the court may either decide on an individual from the parties' list, or may appoint an expert in some other manner, e.g. by asking the president of the appropriate professional body to nominate the expert.

Lawyers should be aware that there is a presumption in favour of the appointment of single joint experts in small and fast track claims (see CPR Parts 27 and 28). The objective is to do away with the calling of multiple experts when, given the nature or value of the dispute, this would be disproportionate in cost and might cause delay. The case management judge may also decide in multi-track claims that single joint experts are appropriate when opinion evidence is needed on very technical issues, or to provide reports on some aspects of the damages (except in complex high value claims).

Sometimes one or both parties may have needed, or chosen, to obtain advice from an expert, particularly on liability, before proceedings are issued (see above). If the court decides expert evidence is required, but that evidence from two experts would be disproportionate, the case management judge has a dilemma – whether to impose a new single joint expert on the parties, or to allow the parties to continue to retain their own experts, with the court seeking to narrow the issues in dispute on the expert opinion evidence, by requiring service of written questions on the experts, and/or by ordering an experts' discussion. Frequently the relative cost, or whether involving a new expert will cause delay, will be the deciding factor. The party instructing the expert will usually be required to disclose the expert's instructions.

In a personal injury case, *Sage v Feiven* [2002] 7 *Current Law* 45, the claimant instructed Dr X pre-action (from a list of experts provided by the insurers), but not as a single joint expert. The claimant was not happy with, and did not disclose, the report. After proceedings were issued, the district judge ruled that Dr X should be instructed as a single joint expert to save costs. This was overturned on appeal, as it was not practical that Dr X could leave out of his report any privileged material from his first report and he would be put in an invidious position (*Carlson v Townsend* relied upon.)

Lawyers should also check carefully the guidelines on involvement of experts in any relevant pre-action protocol (discussed in more detail in Chapter 7). The personal injury protocol has specific procedures for the selection and instruction of experts in the investigatory stage – experts do not have to be jointly instructed unless the parties agree (protocol paragraphs 34-42), while the housing disrepair protocol assumes one expert surveyor will be instructed jointly (see protocol paragraphs 3.2 and 3.5). If there is no applicable protocol, the Pre-action Practice Direction says that if parties need an expert pre-action they should if possible engage an agreed expert, and should be aware that if proceedings are issued the court may not allow the use of the expert's report or the recovery of the costs (Pre-action Practice Direction paragraphs 4.9-4.10).

There have been a number of decisions of the Court of Appeal, which provide some guidance on when the appointment of single joint experts is most appropriate. These are discussed in more detail in Chapter 9. It is important to bear these guidelines in mind before instructing an expert:

1. That parties will usually be allowed to instruct their own experts on liability and causation in professional negligence claims – see *S (a minor) v Birmingham Health Authority*, LTL, 23rd November 1999 CA and *Oxley v Penwarden* [2000] WL 1274095.

2. That the courts will, on occasions, permit a party to instruct an additional expert to the single joint expert – see *Daniels v Walker* [2000] 1 WLR 1382 CA and *Cosgrove v Pattison* [2000] WL 1841601.

3. That the court will only rarely allow a single joint expert to give oral evidence – see *Layland v Fairview New Homes plc* [2002] EWHC 1350 Ch and *Austen v Oxford City Council* [2002] AER D 97.

Single joint experts – key points on new role

- SJEs are used to advise the court in low value claims, and on technical and some quantum issues in higher value ones.

- Solicitors should be careful about instructing an SJE pre-action – you will lose privilege on the instructions/report.

- Solicitors should check the protocols for requirements pre-action in particular types of litigation.

- The objective of instructing an SJE is to save time, costs and arguments.

- SJEs will rarely give oral evidence or be cross-examined.

CONVENTIONAL PARTY EXPERT

In higher value, more complex disputes allocated to the multi-track, the courts will usually permit parties to retain their own experts, at least on liability and causation and on the major aspects of quantum. It is important to note, however, that party experts now owe their main duty to the court (under CPR 35.3 – see Chapter 2).

Can an employee of a party be an expert witness?

Perhaps surprisingly, the courts have decided that a properly qualified expert who understands that his primary duty is to the court is not necessarily disqualified from giving evidence by the fact that he is employed by one of the parties. See *Field v Leeds City Council* [2000] 17 EG 165 and *Admiral Management Services v Para-Protect Europe Ltd* (*The Times*, 26th March 2002), discussed in detail in Chapter 2.

LEAD EXPERTS (CPR 35.7)

The court can decide that it would be helpful to the court if one expert, from a 'dominant discipline', co-ordinates the work of other experts and prepares a comprehensive report (see CPR 35 Practice Direction paragraph 5).

The role of a lead expert may include:

● Checking the other experts' reports and assisting with resolving inconsistencies where appropriate.

● Putting the other expert evidence into context and preparing a general covering report or schedule.

Each individual expert will still be required to comply with their duties under the CPR, including attaching a statement of truth to, and taking responsibility for, their individual report. If there are disputes arising from the opinion evidence of the individual experts, these may need to be resolved by written questions to, or oral evidence and cross-examination in court of that expert, not the lead expert.

The role of lead expert is a potentially important one: performed well, it may effect both time and cost savings for the parties and particularly the court. However, an expert should only be willing to accept this role if he is able to make an extensive time commitment, and if he has considerable experience in the type of litigation in question, including familiarity with opinion reports provided by the other professions involved.

This is a role particularly suited to clinicians (when several clinical specialists may need to advise), and to forensic accountants dealing with complex quantum issues, co-ordinating reports from, for example, employment consultants, rehabilitation and care experts, architects or surveyors, and pensions or tax specialists.

However, it would not seem that the courts are not making much use of this provision and there are no reported cases clarifying aspects of the role.

SHADOW EXPERTS

A well-resourced party may decide to retain an expert adviser behind the scenes throughout the litigation, particularly where the court has ordered that there should not be expert evidence in a particular field at all, or that the evidence should be given by a single joint expert. The party and solicitor may conclude that they need continuing advice on technical issues in relation to either liability or quantum or, when a single joint expert has been instructed, they may want assistance with drafting written questions on the single expert's report or preparing questions for cross-examination. There is nothing to prevent a party instructing a shadow expert; the court cannot control the advice that a party receives, only the evidence on which they can rely and the costs which they can recover. Generally, a shadow expert will act as an adviser only, and will not be asked to prepare a written report for the court.

When the CPR was first implemented, it appeared that the role of 'shadow expert' might be rather limited, as the party or solicitor would have to be prepared to bear the costs (as these would not be recovered from the other party even in a successful case). Accordingly, it would only be available to well-resourced parties. Arguably, it is against the spirit of the overriding objective (Part 1 of the CPR) which requires the court to try to "level the playing-field" between the parties. However, increasingly it seems that the courts are prepared to allow a party to introduce additional expert evidence at the later stages of the litigation if there is genuine doubt about the reliability of the opinion of the single joint expert, and may even permit that party to recover at least some of the costs of introducing additional expert evidence. This may encourage more parties to retain shadow experts.

This issue is discussed in more detail in Chapter 9 but see, for instance, *Cosgrove v Pattison* (*The Times,* 13th February 2001), a boundary dispute where one of the parties argued that the single joint expert might be biased, and produced evidence from a witness of fact to support this; he was allowed to call that witness as an expert particularly because this would not cause any delay or greatly increase the costs.

ASSESSORS (CPR 35.15)

The court has the power, under rule 35.15, to appoint an expert as an assessor to "assist the court". This power existed under the previous rules (RSC O.33 rule 2) but was rarely used, except in the Admiralty Court, in patents cases, for taxations (detailed assessment of costs) and for racial discrimination claims in the County Court under section 67 of the Race Relations Act 1976.

The main role of an assessor is to 'educate' the trial judge, especially in a case raising complex technical issues, and to assist him to reach a properly informed decision. The court has to notify the parties of the intention of appointing an assessor, to give the parties an opportunity to object. If the assessor provides a report for the court, this must be sent to the parties. An assessor may also attend the trial "to take such part in the proceedings as the court may direct". This will usually be to advise the judge but not to give oral evidence or be cross-examined. The Rules provide that the fees of an assessor are to be paid by one or both of the parties, depending upon the outcome of the litigation.

Lord Woolf saw a possible wider role for assessors in complex technical litigation, including presiding over meetings between the parties' experts and helping them to reach an agreement. However, to the author's knowledge, this has not been put into practice.

66

Five years after the implementation of the CPR, it seems that the courts are rarely appointing assessors except, as before, in the Admiralty Division in shipping cases. *Owners of the Ship Pelopidas v Owners of the Ship TRSL Concord* [1999] 2 AER (Comm) 737 is a post-CPR example. Steel J emphasised that, in admiralty practice, assessors are not only technical advisers (on nautical science and skills relating to the management and movement of ships), they are also sources of evidence as to the facts. When assessors are appointed therefore, expert evidence on seamanship may not be required from the parties.

The role of assessors was also considered by the Court of Appeal in *Ahmed v University of Oxford and Another* (*The Times*, 17th January 2003 CA), a racial discrimination claim concerning examination marking. Section 67(4) of the Race Relations Act 1976 provides for the judge to be assisted by two assessors, appointed from a list maintained by the Secretary of State of persons with special knowledge and experience of race relations. The Court of Appeal concluded that assessors in this type of case had a specific function – to assist the judge in the evaluation of the evidence, with the judge including the assessors' evaluation, and his view of it, in the reasoning in his judgment. The Court of Appeal said that the position was different when assessors were appointed under CPR 35.15, because then the court has a broad discretion on how to use them – they might have an evidential function, and/or a function involved in assisting on the evaluation of evidence – but they suggested that whatever their function, the principles should be:

● Any directions to the assessors on the law should be given in open court.

● The parties are entitled to respond to any expert evidence given by the assessors.

● The judicial discussion between judge and assessors should remain confidential.

The implementation of the Human Rights Act 1998 in October 2000 could further discourage the appointment of assessors because Article 6, the right to a fair trial, requires transparency in proceedings, including disclosure to the parties of all the evidence taken into account by the judge or tribunal in reaching a decision. France has a system of court-appointed experts. This has prompted a number of successful applications to the European Court of Justice under Article 6 (see Chapter 2).

An application of Article 6 principles could mean that if an English court decided to appoint an assessor, the following would be required:

● Involvement of the parties in the selection of the assessor.

● Disclosure to the parties of any judicial instructions to the assessor and an opportunity for the parties to provide their own instructions.

● Disclosure to the parties of any advice, written or oral, provided by the assessor to the judge prior to the judge reaching a decision on the claim (see *Owners of the Ship Bow Spring v Owners of the Ship Manzanillo II* [2004] EWCA Civ 1007, discussed in Chapter 12).

EXPERT ADJUDICATION

This is a complex subject that is outside the general scope of this book.

An expert or specialist in a particular field may be in a better position than a court or tribunal to decide a particular dispute or aspects of it, particularly when the issues are technical and the parties are commercial organisations. Variations of expert adjudication include:

i) arbitration;

ii) expert determination;

iii) adjudication under a specific scheme, e.g. building disputes under the Housing Grants Reconstruction and Regeneration Act 1996.

All three methods of adjudication are binding. The difference between arbitration and expert determination is that arbitration is subject to some legal safeguards under the Arbitration Acts, and there may be rights of appeal on errors of law and procedure. In expert determination, on the other hand, everything is governed by the agreement between the parties, and the only recourse to the courts for a disgruntled participant might be where there has been a breach of contract by the other party, or a failure to comply with the expert's decision.

The parties may have decided in their original contract that any disputes arising will be determined by one of the above non-litigation solutions. Alternatively, parties in a commercial situation in which a dispute arises may decide on arbitration or expert determination on an ad hoc basis.

In either situation, the agreement should make clear whether the expert is acting as arbitrator or as an expert and should provide for:

a) the means of appointment of the expert, and his fees;

b) the expert's powers;

c) the procedure; and

d) the timetable.

Model agreements for expert determination are available, including from the Centre for Dispute Resolution (CEDR).

The advantage of expert determination is that it can be quick, cheap and is conducted in private. It is most commonly used in disputes concerning:

a) construction;

b) valuation;

c) rent reviews;

d) sale and purchases of businesses;

e) the transfer and valuation of pension rights; and

f) IT.

The court generally will only order resolution of a dispute by one of the alternative means involving experts:

1. If a freely-negotiated contract between the parties specified this (see *Cable and Wireless v IBM* [2002] EWHC Civ 2059, when a clause in a commercial contract providing for disputes under the contract to be referred to mediation, was held to be enforceable and the proceedings were stayed under CPR 26.4).

2. If a pre-action protocol or other legislation required it, e.g. the Housing Grants Reconstruction and Regeneration Act 1996.

3. By consent.

It is important to note that the courts have a specific power under the CPR (Part 1, the overriding objective) and rule 26.4 (power to stay proceedings), to consider whether any form of alternative dispute resolution is more appropriate than litigation and so order.

Litigation on expert determination has tended to concentrate on:

1. Whether the dispute falls within the clause in the agreement (see, for instance, *Rhodia Chirex Ltd v Laker Vent Engineering Ltd* [2003] EWCA Civ 1859) and *Campbell, Chapman and Askaroff v OCE (UK) Ltd* [2005] EWHC 458 Ch).

2. Whether the expert has departed from his instructions (see, for instance, *Veba Oil Supply and Trading Gmbh v Petrotrade* [2001] EWCA Civ 1832, when a finding that he had materially departed was sufficient to render his determination non-binding).

3. The procedure to be adopted by the expert (see, for instance, *Ursa Major Management Ltd v United Utilities Electricity* [2002] EWHC 3041, in which the claimant attempted to resolve matters by issuing Part 8 proceedings, to which the defendant objected – the Master held that a 14-month delay in trying to resolve the dispute through an expert had failed, so the court did have jurisdiction to decide the preliminary issues between the parties. The High Judge agreed)).

The courts will usually enforce experts' decisions without reconsidering the merits except where there has been obvious error.

EXPERTS AS MEDIATORS

Mediators may come from any discipline or background, not just law. If parties to a dispute opt to attempt resolution by mediation, they may also wish to choose a specialist mediator. See Chapter 10 for expert involvement in mediation ancillary to litigation.

CONCLUSIONS

Experts have a variety of roles to play in resolving modern civil disputes. Solicitors need to advise their clients from the outset, not only on whether expert help is necessary but also on the role(s) the expert might play, by choice, or by order of the court.

In particular, lawyers should advise on whether the other parties and the case management judge may prefer single joint or party experts, and whether any costs incurred in obtaining initial advice from an expert is likely to be recoverable.

In commercial or high value disputes, decisions may also need to be taken early on whether to retain advisory experts or shadow experts throughout the dispute, regardless of the court's decisions – so that the costs of this can be built into the case planning and budgeting.

Lead experts could, perhaps, be used more frequently. Many more disputes are suitable for expert determination than are pursued that way.

Chapter 4

SELECTING THE RIGHT EXPERT

Careful selection of the right expert for the case can pay dividends. Involving the right expert at the right time can:

a) prevent a weak case from proceeding too far and incurring costs;

b) help to focus on the key issues in the case;

c) impress the other party;

d) lead to an earlier resolution;

e) eventually make or break the case, or part of it.

In the post-CPR climate, it is particularly important to make the right selection because of:

1. The requirement for experts to be **independent** and to owe their first duty to the court (see Chapter 2).

2. The judicial **preference for single joint experts** – the parties and the court will only have one report and opinion to consider (see Chapter 9).

3. The **reduced scope for multiple experts and 'expert shopping'**, particularly once proceedings are issued. It may be possible to switch experts pre-action before a report on which a party chooses to rely has been disclosed (*Carlson v Townsend* – see Chapter 7). However, once the court has given permission for a named expert in a particular field, the solicitor may not be allowed to change at all or, if he/she can persuade the court there are good reasons to do so, it is likely the court will order that the first report is disclosed. See *Beck v Ministry of Defence* [2003] WL 2149042, discussed in Chapter 10.

4. The **need for transparency** and the impossibility of 'coaching' an expert in what to write and say (see also Chapter 12).

A client might also judge a solicitor by their choice of an expert.

WHAT IS THE EXPERT BEING ASKED TO DO?

The choice of expert should be closely linked to their intended role.

If the party or lawyer is seeking an **adviser** who is unlikely to be retained or relied upon for any litigation, a 'familiar', well-regarded but objective expert is required, with experience of the type of dispute, and of the uncertainties of litigation, especially if advising on liability. He or she may be working to short deadlines, giving opinions on limited information, or on other experts' reports. This is not a role ideally suited to a new expert – new either to those instructing him or to expert witness work. The expert must be independent-minded (advice in support of the case is not necessarily helpful), but you may not need an experienced report writer, or an expert who is good in the witness box.

If an expert is needed **to prepare a report**, ultimately for the court, their expertise in the subject, objectivity and general acceptability to the client, other party and the court are all essential, as is the ability to write clear, jargon-free reports. For a fast track or low value claim, experience in producing short, proportionate reports for a limited fee and answering questions to a tight timetable is also desirable.

The larger or more complex the claim and the more contentious the subject matter of the expert's report, the more likely it is that the case might go to trial, and the more important become the qualities of:

● Senior status and good reputation in their expert field.

● Personal and professional credibility.

● Confidence and robustness, but not arrogance.

● Approachability.

● Reliability, diligence and stamina.

● Experience of acting as an expert witness in sensitive cases.

● Ability to work with other experts and counsel as a team, while maintaining objectivity.

- Meticulous drafting skills for drafting, and perhaps redrafting, complex reports.

- Good oral presentation skills and a courtroom presence.

If there is a choice, performance is more important than reputation.

However, some of the skills that an expert requires can be acquired 'on the job', and an inexperienced expert witness with the required expertise in the relevant discipline is often preferable to the perhaps over-used and over-committed experienced expert.

WHERE TO START

1. **Your own or your firm's 'database'.**

   All litigation law firms and chambers should keep a database of experts who have been found to be satisfactory or better, organised by discipline, geography and experience. The amount of detail stored will depend on the firm's needs, but additional information might include when and by whom in the firm they were last instructed, whether they have been observed at court, and their charges. The database should be reviewed regularly by all fee-earners.

   However, regularly instructing the same few experts has its drawbacks:

   - You are less likely to experience a fresh look at (or obtain new angles on) your cases.

   - You may have difficulty in persuading other parties to accept your recommended expert as a single expert.

   - The court might even decide that your relationship with an expert is too cosy to maintain the experts' independence – see *Smolen v Solon Co-operative Housing Services Ltd* [2003] EWCA Civ 1240, discussed in Chapters 2 and 9.

2. **Experts whose reports and performance at court you have seen.**

   It is useful to keep a supplementary list of this category – usually experts instructed by the other party in a case, who impressed you.

3. **Experts recommended by colleagues in other firms, by counsel's chambers you instruct regularly, or by other experts.**
This category may need more checking in advance of sending instructions (see below).

Secondary sources

1. **Experts recommended by clients**.
This category should generally be viewed with great caution because of the risk that the client may recommend someone they know well, for convenience or for reasons of control. The latter in particular can be dangerous as the expert will, at worst, have difficulty in exerting their independence and at best will ultimately not be regarded by others, especially the trial judge, as complying with their duty to the court under CPR 35.3 (see Chapter 2 for examples, particularly *Hussein v William Hill Group* and *SPE International v Professional Preparation Contractors (UK) Ltd*). Always check with the client and expert the details of their previous working relationship. Client-connected candidates are best rejected by explaining to the client that it is in his interests to instruct someone he has never worked with before.

However, when instructed by large commercial concerns or organisations, on a technical or specialist matter, when your own database does not include the required expertise, obtaining a list of potential candidates from the client may be sensible, provided that you check them carefully (see below).

2. **Expert agencies.**
There has been a mushrooming of agencies providing medico-legal reports for personal injury litigation in the last few years. Some have been and gone, leaving experts owed fees (in one case over £1.5 million). Others are well-established, some with tie-ins to claims organisations or legal expense insurers, some of which require solicitors to obtain their medical reports from a particular agency.

Agencies have some **advantages**:

- Convenience, e.g. when the solicitor is based in a different part of the country to their client and does not have contacts with suitable doctors in the client's area.

- Speed and a fixed price.

- A standardised report format.

However, there are **disadvantages** too:

- There will possibly be no choice in who is instructed unless the solicitor specifically requests this, e.g. to comply with the personal injury pre-action protocol.

- The agency may not have vetting or quality procedures for experts they taken on.

- The agency may control the actual instructions, and the processing and editing of the report, not the instructing solicitor.

- There will be an administration charge for the agency overheads. This should be itemised separately in the invoice. In principle, an agency fee is recoverable, if reasonable (*Stringer v Copley* (unrep) [May 2002] Kingston County Court). The benchmark should be the cost of the time the solicitor would have spent locating selecting and instructing an expert directly (see also Chapter 6).

The Association of Medical Reporting Organisations has been formed with the aim of promoting professional standards in medical reporting (www.amro-uk.co.uk). If using an agency by choice, you may wish to check whether they are a member of the Association.

3. **Directories, databases and professional bodies.**
   These may be useful for specialist experts when the firm's other sources do not produce candidates. Popular and busy experts sometimes do not put themselves forward for commercial directories, especially if a charge is involved. Some directories are merely listings of those who have paid the fee for an entry, others have some quality checks, e.g. references are required from clients or solicitors (as in the Directory published by Sweet and Maxwell, previously with some Law Society involvement).

   Some specialist solicitors' organisations or societies keep databases of experts recommended by members (e.g. the Association of Personal Injury Lawyers).

76

Some professional bodies have separate sections for members who offer expert witness services (e.g. the Royal Institution of Chartered Surveyors (RICS) and the Institute of Chartered Accountants).

The expert witness membership organisations do not offer a specific search service to solicitors but are often prepared to offer names from their membership lists (the Academy of Experts, the Expert Witness Institute and the Society of Experts).

4. **Miscellaneous sources.**

   Other sources may include:

   - Mailshots from experts or advertisements in journals.

   - Articles, other published work or papers for conferences.

   - Meeting experts at seminars and other events.

   - Universities and other academic institutions.

   - Internet or literature searches – some expert witnesses have their own websites.

   - Direct approaches to organisations, trade associations or businesses working in the required field, especially if the type of expertise you are seeking is unusual.

   Obviously, for any source without a reliable recommendation, careful checking of credentials and experience is required.

What to ask a potential new expert to provide

1. Their **qualifications**, a CV and/or brochure.

   Most regular expert witnesses have a CV or brochure. Study it carefully. Questions to consider include:

   - Are they sufficiently senior in their field?

   - Does the case really need a senior person or will a "rising" expert be perfectly adequate and cheaper, i.e. proportionate?

   - Is the CV succinct and well-written? Beware the one 20 pages long.

   - Does the brochure give useful information, or is it purely marketing jargon?

- Does the expert appear to be too 'narrow' for your needs, or hold themselves out as an expert in so many fields that their real 'expertise' may be questionable?

2. **References** from solicitors, barristers or clients.

   Follow them up – if you know the referees, so much the better.

3. **Terms of business**.

   At the very least, these should cover report fees and hourly rates, including for court work and travelling, how expenses and any disbursements will be charged, invoicing arrangements, whether VAT is payable and whether interest is charged for late payment (see also Chapter 6).

4. **Examples of their work**, including expert witness reports for similar litigation if possible.

   Have any reports sent to you been anonymised to protect client confidentiality? Review the reports critically – do they suggest the expert can explain technical issues clearly and persuasively? See the checklist in Chapter 8.

5. **How many expert witness instructions they received** in, say, the last year, how many as a party expert, and for which side, and how many as a single joint expert, and brief details of any court appearances.

   The relative importance of this information will depend on what instructions you intend to send, but be careful of an expert who is always instructed by the same side unless they are new as expert witnesses and are trying to broaden their experience. For a single joint expert, it is always safer to recommend an expert with some experience of instructions from both sides.

6. **What percentage of their working time** they spend on expert witness work.

   This is an important question if you want someone with good current expertise in the 'day-job'. Be wary of experts with limited links to their area of practice, especially if they are retired. Exceptions will be specialist forensic practitioners, e.g. forensic accountants, and where the case requires someone with expertise in a field or industry at a particular date in the past.

7. **How they organise and run their expert witness work** if it is an offshoot of their usual "day-job".

   Do they have a secretary, separate phone line or mobile and e-mail and, if they have a separate office, how often do they visit? Speedy communication with an expert witness is often vital to finalise reports, deal with questions and experts' meetings and find out their availability for trial. It is also important in the run-up to trial.

8. **Whether they are members of one of the expert witness organisations** or are registered with the CRFP.

   Membership/registration may provide some indication that this is a 'professional' expert witness who has some quality assurance and must follow a code of conduct, especially if they are from a discipline that does not have a professional body (see Chapter 1 and below).

What else you might need

1. **Confirmation from the expert that their expertise is appropriate for the task** – particularly if theirs is a technical field with which you are not very familiar. To be meaningful this will have to be based on at least outline instructions.

2. **Confirmation that the expert will not have a conflict of interest** – for this you will need to provide the names of the parties and possibly key witnesses, and any other experts already instructed (see also Chapters 2 and 5). In personal injury claims, it is usually not advisable to instruct a doctor who has been treating the claimant as they will be at risk of breaching patient confidentiality and unable to comment objectively on treatment given or required (see Chapter 2). For professional negligence claims, you may need to know how well the potential expert knows the intended defendant and in what context – have they ever worked together, how long ago, did one train the other? It is not unknown for experts to develop 'cold feet' late into a case when they realise they will be criticising in court in public the most eminent professor in the field who trained them 20 years ago (see, for instance, *H v Lambeth Southwark & Lewisham HA*, discussed in Chapters 2 and 11).

3. If you need advance approval from a funder or client before an expert is instructed, you may want to obtain a **quotation or estimate** for the work. Again, outline instructions will be necessary. Is the estimate proportionate? Will the expert give value for money?

4. **When the work can be undertaken/completed**. Again, outline instructions may be necessary. This will be particularly important to check once proceedings have been issued and a court timetable set. Send the prospective expert the directions (now required by the Part 35 Practice Direction paragraph 6A), and press them on whether they can meet the timetable. Also check whether they appreciate that the work does not always conclude with their report and whether they will be committed to follow-up work, including dealing with questions, discussions with the other expert and, if necessary, attending trial. If you have a trial date, check out their availability before you instruct them, to avoid judicial criticism of you!

What else you might do

Do not only communicate with the expert in writing. Speak to them on the telephone, or meet them to form a view of their interpersonal and communication skills and their understanding of the role of an expert witness.

For significant advice or a report in a case of particular importance to the client, high in value or high profile, you may also want to:

- Hold a **'beauty parade'** with a shortlist of experts, with or without the client, particularly if presentation skills or the ability to cope in the witness box are likely to be vital.

- **Verify the expert's professional qualifications** with their professional body and check whether they have had complaints made against them, or any restrictions imposed on their practise. Bogus experts are not entirely unknown.

- **Check reported judgments** in cases in which they have been instructed for opinions they have given in cases similar to your client's, for comments by judges praising or criticising their evidence, and whether their evidence led to an appeal. However, this is only practicable on judgment websites with advanced search engines.

One senior judge at a public lecture attended by the author suggested solicitors might be negligent for not carrying out such a check!

Discuss the options with the client and possibly counsel, but the decision should be the solicitor's rather than counsel's, as the solicitor is in charge of the litigation team. The chosen party expert for litigation should be someone who generally believes the client's case has merit without being at all 'partisan'!

INEXPERIENCED EXPERT WITNESSES

Training

An expert with real expertise in their subject but with no or limited experience of court work may be perfectly acceptable as an expert witness, but may need more briefing and support. You could suggest they attend some training in report writing, courtroom skills or more generally in law and civil procedure and their duties under the CPR. (Courses are run by the expert witness organisations, the Academy of Experts and the Expert Witness Institute, and by Bond Solon Training (who also run a certificate with Cardiff University – see Chapter 1).) For further details, see www.bondsolon.com.

You may need to send extracts from the rules or specimen reports to a less experienced expert. Certainly, a conference with the expert, client and the advocate will be essential if the case is to go to trial, to see how the expert will stand up to cross-examination (see Chapter 12). Expert witnesses, of course, cannot be 'coached' in how to give their evidence in a particular case (see Chapter 12).

ACCREDITATION FOR EXPERTS

There is some interest, including by senior judges, in establishing a system of official accreditation for expert witnesses. Parties, lawyers and judges would know a particular expert was 'quality assured', which is particularly important for single joint experts.

The potential role of the Council for the Registration of Forensic Practitioners (CRFP) was discussed in Chapter 1.

Membership of one of the expert witness organisations, the Academy of Experts (www.academyofexperts.org) or the Expert Witness Institute (www.ewi.org.uk), is not by accreditation but qualifications are checked and the EWI takes three references from solicitors. Membership may be some indication of an expert witness who is actively interested in keeping up-to-date with issues in expert evidence.

An expert with some accreditation or recognised training may not necessarily be the best expert but they should at least know the basics of the expert witness craft.

CONCLUSIONS

Selecting an expert or group of experts for a claim or dispute is an important step. Relying on regular 'tried and tested' experts is a safe option, but solicitors do need to keep up-to-date on new experts in their fields of work, and it does not always pay to work too closely for too long with a small group of experts. Particular care is needed when selecting new experts and as many checks as is proportionate should be carried out.

Chapter 5
INSTRUCTING THE EXPERT

Instructing the selected expert is a very important step in the working relationship. The initial exchange of letters with the expert will form the contract and it is vital to include all the key ingredients to avoid disputes later, especially over payment, or the timetable for receipt of the report. The specific instructions require particular care, as these form the expert's brief and the expert must summarise them in any report produced for the court.

INITIAL CONTACT

Frequently, a solicitor's initial contact with an expert will be by telephone – particularly with an expert not previously instructed – to check on the suitability and availability of the expert to produce advice or a report to the required timetable and to request their terms of business, CV and references, etc. (see Chapter 4).

An experienced and efficient expert should have a standard package to send you that includes their terms of business. The Expert Witness Institute have model terms of engagement for expert witnesses (available on their website at www.ewi.org.uk); if you receive something similar to this, it is an indication that the business side of your relationship with the expert should run smoothly. If the solicitor has difficulty contacting the expert for an initial discussion, it could be a warning sign that it may not be very easy to have telephone discussions with the expert as the case progresses.

Alternatively, the solicitor may prefer to write to the expert to elicit the basic information on their expertise and charges etc., and to seek an expression of interest from the expert before they enter into a contract and send him the full instructions.

Once preliminaries have been satisfactorily completed, the solicitor should be ready to draft his instructions.

THE LETTER OF INSTRUCTION

It follows from the changing role of experts in civil litigation that experts need to know much more about the background to their instructions than before. Solicitors should ensure that their letter of instruction provides at least the following information:

1. The full name and address of the client(s) and of the other parties to the dispute (and telephone numbers if site visits or examinations are necessary) and their solicitors. This will enable the expert to check for potential conflicts of interest (see below).

2. The same information for other experts who have already been instructed, especially those from the same discipline, including by the other parties, if known.

3. On what basis the expert is being instructed – for initial advice, to prepare a report for the court as an expert witness, and for just one or both parties, or as a lead expert, or for advice only during the proceedings (see Chapter 3).

4. If they are instructed as a single joint expert, whether there will be one or two sets of instructions.

5. If they are being instructed as a shadow adviser during the litigation, the identity of the expert witness(es) already instructed.

6. The approximate value of the claim (and whether it is of particular importance to the client or is a test case) to enable the expert to consider how detailed his report needs to be in the context of proportionality.

7. Whether proceedings have been issued.

8. If so, in which court, whether the case has been allocated to a track and what directions the court has given including:

   a) whether permission has been given to rely upon written (and oral) expert evidence and whether the permission is specific to the named expert;

   b) the timetable for disclosure of the expert report(s) and when you require the report, plus the timetable for questions on the report and for the experts' discussion;

c) any other court directions relevant to the expert evidence;

d) the trial date or window;

e) any court controls or directions on the expert's fees.

9. The specific instructions for the case – see below.

10. Whether the client wants any documents returned at the end of the case.

Remember that your letter of instruction to an expert to prepare a report for court is not privileged against disclosure and that the expert is under a duty to summarise his instructions, written and oral, on which his report is based (CPR 35.10(3) and (4)). Some experts choose to comply with this by simply annexing the solicitor's letter of instruction to their report. The consequences of this rule in the context of privilege are discussed in more detail below, but in short it means in your instruction letter you should avoid:

a) expressing your opinions about the strengths and weaknesses of the case;

b) indicating that either you or the expert is inexperienced in the relevant type of case;

c) inviting the expert to express any concerns about the case in a separate letter to the report (a side letter; see also Chapter 8).

THE SPECIFIC INSTRUCTIONS

The style and detail of the specific instructions will vary considerably depending on what you are asking the expert to do.

Instructions for preliminary advice only, before you have decided whether the client has a cause of action or defence, may be short and may simply enclose the relevant materials. They may be less constrained by concerns that the letter and the expert's reply may have to be disclosed. See *Carlson v Townsend* [2001] (Chapter 7), which decided that an expert's report obtained before proceedings have been issued (and therefore the solicitor's instructions) is privileged until the party decides to rely upon them. However, the law is not clear on whether such a preliminary exchange of correspondence between solicitor and expert might lose its privilege if the same expert was later instructed to act as an expert witness in any ensuing litigation (see below).

If your instructions are to prepare a report which may, or definitely will, be relied upon for court proceedings, then particular care is needed when drafting the specific instructions. It will usually be helpful to the expert if you:

1. Summarise what the case is about.

2. Set out the issues that are in dispute.

3. Explain whether you are instructing the expert to investigate, examine and/or give an opinion on liability, causation or quantum matters.

4. Attach a list, and copies of all relevant documents – see below.

A solicitor can only do this well if he understands the legal matrix of the case and has developed a case theory.

It might seem easier to send the expert a short letter and to enclose relevant documents from the file, e.g. witness statements, but be aware that these documents might become disclosable (see below). If there are disputed facts or scenarios, you may need to ask the expert to work from both, or sometimes from several different, sets of assumptions.

You may want to prepare one or more standard letters to use as a base when instructing an expert – Appendix 3 contains a suggestion – or use a checklist such as the one above. However, each letter of instruction should be individual. It is worth spending the time at this stage of the expert's involvement as an essential investment in the client's case.

Instructions should be a two-way process

You should try to ensure that any specific questions you want the expert to address in the report are framed accurately and neutrally in your letter of instruction and that the expert is comfortable that the real issues in relation to the expert's area of expertise have been identified. An experienced and committed expert should read the letter and all the enclosed papers as soon as possible after receipt to quickly identify:

a) whether he may have a conflict of interest – see below;

b) whether he has the right expertise for the case;

c) that he will be able to produce the advice or report to the timetable indicated;

d) that the instructions are clear;

e) any gaps in the material provided.

If the expert telephones or replies with queries or suggestions on your letter, again you should take it as an indication of a thoughtful and efficient expert.

Oral or subsequent instructions

If possible, include all the instructions to the expert in one comprehensive letter to avoid confusion later on what the instructions were. However, in many cases, particularly more complex ones, the initial letter of instruction will be supplemented by further letters, or by oral instructions in telephone conversations, or at meetings. It is advisable to collect together in one place in the file all the instructions, and to confirm oral instructions in writing as soon as possible, again to avoid confusion. Remember the expert has a duty, under CPR 35.10(3) to summarise in his report the instructions on which his report is based, written and oral.

CONFLICTS OF INTEREST

The emphasis in Part 35 of the CPR on the independence of experts and their duty to the court was discussed in Chapter 2.

Experts clearly should not take on work that might put them in a conflict of interest situation. This could occur if they:

a) are, or have been, instructed by another party in the same case;

b) are regularly instructed by another party and may, therefore, be in possession of confidential or sensitive information; or

c) have a professional or personal relationship with one of the parties or one of the other experts.

To prevent the possibility of a conflict only being recognised at a later stage when the expert has begun work or, even worse, after disclosure of their report, it is good practice to advise the expert of the full names and addresses of everyone involved in the case and to keep this up-to-date if and when additional parties are joined or new experts are instructed.

The risks of conflicts not being picked up early are probably greatest in commercial work, e.g. when large firms of accountants are instructed, or when a sole practitioner expert produces large numbers of similar reports in 'routine' cases and does not have a client database for effective screening.

Attempts to build 'Chinese walls' between groups of experts working on related client business within the same firm may not always be sufficient to preserve the professional duty of confidentiality (see *Bolkiah v KPMG* [1999] 1 AER 517).

One recent example of an expert putting himself in a position of conflict is in the matter of *Colt Telecom Group plc* [2002] EWHC 2815 Ch. An accountant insolvency practitioner from a major firm was criticised by the judge for giving evidence for one company which was petitioning for another company's administration (which was strongly contested), because the accountant's firm had recently acted for the 'defendant' company, and because they stood to gain if his evidence was accepted, as the firm were proposed as administrators (which was not brought out in the accountant's report). The judge concluded that the accountant had failed in his duties to the court and had "espoused his client's cause". He dismissed the petition, which, he said, should never have been brought.

A different type of conflict may arise where the expert has an ongoing professional relationship with 'his' party, as his duty to the court could lead to him breaching confidentiality, or make him reluctant to be in any way critical of his client (see *Liverpool RC Archdiocesan Trustees Inc v Goldberg* and *Cairnstores v Aktiebolaget Hassle*, summarised in Chapter 2). This particularly applies to medical experts who are treating or have recently treated the claimant in a personal injury case, or a child or a parent in a family matter (see *Re B (a minor)* [2000] 1 FLR 871, a contested child contact case in which there were allegations of sexual abuse; the court held that the psychiatrist treating the child was not sufficiently independent to provide opinion evidence).

AGREEING FEES

It is essential to agree the basis on which the expert will be paid, before or on instructions. The expert's terms and conditions and your letter in reply plus the instructions, amount to a contract and if the instructions are yours, rather than the client's, your firm will be liable for the expert's fees under the contract.

Fees are dealt with in more detail in Chapter 6, but the essentials to be agreed on instruction are:

1. The fee for the report or advice and whether this is an estimate, until the expert has received and agreed the instructions.

2. The hourly rate for any subsequent work on the report or for further work on the case.

3. Whether the expert must seek prior authority if the agreed fee is likely to be exceeded or for the costs of any investigation work or tests that he considers are necessary, or for any other disbursements.

4. Daily or hourly fees for trial, including any cancellation fees.

5. When the fees are due to be paid, and whether interest is charged for late payment.

Fees for a single joint expert should also be agreed on instruction – the same details as above, plus how they are to be shared between the parties. If the parties chose to adopt the provisions in CPR 35.8(9), i.e. joint and several liability for the expert's fees, it is prudent to remind the other party and the expert that this means the expert can look to one party to pay the entire fees if the other party defaults on their share.

AVAILABILITY OF THE EXPERT

It will often be critical to obtain a firm commitment from the expert to prepare their report to a timetable, which will enable you to comply with the court directions. It is good practice to ask for the report to be sent to you a minimum of a few weeks before it is due to be disclosed, particularly if you have not previously instructed that particular expert, or you know he is very busy or tends to be late delivering his reports. The few weeks' margin will also give you time to discuss the report with the client, perhaps to ask for some amendments (see Chapter 8), and/or to discuss the report with other experts or with counsel.

When instructing the expert, you should also check that the expert:

a) is committed to carrying out any follow-up work – answering questions on their report and helping to draft questions on the other party's expert's report, attending a conference with counsel, or a discussion with the other expert. It is not unknown for experts to 'lose interest' once their report has been finalised and to appear unwilling to become involved at later stages of the proceedings;

b) is likely to be available for the trial window or trial date, if known, or at least that he does not intend to retire or move abroad by the anticipated trial period.

SENDING MATERIALS TO THE EXPERT

In most cases, the solicitor will need to send some materials to the expert with his instructions. Typically and uncontroversially these will include:

- Documents which have been or will have to be disclosed to the other party in standard disclosure, as they are documents upon which you intend to rely or that may assist the other party.

- Statements of case and schedules of loss.

- Disclosed witness statements and disclosed experts' reports.

- Court orders and directions pertinent to the expert's role.

- Part 35 and the Practice Direction and appropriate guidance on compliance with the rules (some solicitors have produced their own guidance, others may choose to rely upon the protocol for instructing experts).

Do not flood an expert with documents irrelevant to their task – they may charge more for the report because of the extra reading time involved. There is a risk of confusing the expert, and inadvertently encouraging him to comment on matters outside his instructions or expertise.

On the other hand, do not be too economical with what you send him (subject to documents that might be privileged – see below). The risks this time are too narrow a report or one which inadequately covers the issues – and you may only become aware of this when you see the other party's like expert's report. Redrafts or supplementary reports might become necessary. Remember that the court has the power to direct that a party provide information to the other party that an expert needs (CPR 35.9 – see Chapter 2). The rule is not often relied upon, and there is little reported case law to assist in its application.

All material sent to the expert should be specifically listed, either in the letter of instruction, or in an index to the attachments, and the materials should also be paginated for ease of reference. It is essential that both you and the expert have a record of exactly what was sent to him and when, and if you do not prepare the documents yourself, you should look through the bundle before it is sent off.

An expert may need to be reminded that documents that you provide him with should be kept confidential and used only for the purpose of that case. If the expert were to breach this principle, the solicitor might be liable for contempt himself.

PRIVILEGE AND INSTRUCTIONS

As has been discussed earlier, CPR 35.10(3) requires the expert to summarise his instructions in his report, both written and oral, on the basis of which the report is prepared.

Rule 35.10(4) states that instructions to experts are not privileged against disclosure but that the court will not "in relation to those instructions" order disclosure of "any specific document" or allow any questioning in court, "unless [the court] is satisfied that there are reasonable grounds to consider the statement of instruction ... to be inaccurate or incomplete".

91

What does this mean?

- Which instructions must be summarised? Pre-action or only post-action, once the court has given permission to rely upon a report from that expert?

- What does any "specific document" mean? Just the letter of instruction, or other documents sent to the expert? And what if the documents are privileged?

Furthermore, how is this rule consistent with CPR 31.14, which states that a party may apply to inspect a document mentioned in several documents, including an expert's report?

CPR 35.10 was one of two new rules that appeared to change the law with regard to litigation privilege. The other rule, CPR 48.7(3), concerned the disclosure of solicitor/client correspondence on an application for wasted costs. This was declared to be *ultra vires* in *General Mediterranean Holdings SA v Patel* [1999] 3 AER 673.

The EWI and the Academy's codes of guidance (see Chapter 2) offered little guidance on privilege. The protocol only states that "advice which the parties do not intend to adduce in litigation is likely to be confidential. The protocol does not apply in these circumstances".

It is not surprising therefore, that rule 35.10 has caused some problems of interpretation, or that in the early years after the implementation of the CPR the courts were called upon to give guidance on a number of occasions.

In *BCCI SA v Ali (No 3)* [1999] 4 AER 83, the claimant's expert referred in his report (concerning the alleged stigma attaching to ex-employees of the failed bank) to individual employment case histories, which had not been disclosed. The defendant asked to see them. The High Court ordered their disclosure, as the other party was entitled to know the factual premise on which the expert based his report.

In *Morris v Bank of India* (Ch D 15th November 2001) (unreported except on Lawtel), the defendant's expert, in a banking dispute, failed to make clear in his report that he had been sent draft witness statements and other factual information with his instructions. Unusually, experts' reports were exchanged in this case before witness statements. The claimant asked to see the sources of the expert's assertions, as they differed from the pleadings. The defendant claimed the witness statements, in particular, were privileged at that stage. Hart J held that the expert's summary of his instructions was inaccurate or incomplete within rule 35.10(4). The expert had not clarified whether he had been instructed to rely upon the information in the statements but to delete direct references to the statements, in which case they would have lost their privileged status as they did form part of his instructions, or whether he was told to put the draft statements out of his mind. The court held that the lack of clarity, and "the patent defect" in the report, justified ordering disclosure of the actual instructions, including the witness statements.

In *Salt v Consignia plc* [2002] 12 *Current Law* 51, a solicitor's entire letter of instruction to a medical expert was ordered to be disclosed – disclosure of an edited version was not sufficient when the expert had failed to state the substance of his material instructions.

In *Taylor v Bolton Health Authority* [2000] QBD 14/01, Morland J said that, in his judgment, instructions are what an expert is told to do, and what answers he is asked to give to specific questions, but that material he is sent is not part of the instructions. The judge concluded, therefore, that the material had to be disclosed because it was not covered by the privilege extended to the instructions by CPR 35.10.

Dunlop Slazenger International v Joe Bloggs [2003] EWCA Civ 901 decided that if a party chooses to 'deploy in court' documents sent by their expert, which would otherwise be privileged, by referring to them in a witness statement in support of an interlocutory application, the party has waived privilege in the letters and they must be disclosed.

All of these cases pointed firmly in the direction that the court would fairly readily order disclosure of the solicitor's actual letter(s) of instruction and *any material* sent to the expert, whether or not the material would otherwise have been privileged, if the expert's summary of his instructions lacked clarity. Following these decisions, it was this author's practice to advise solicitors to be careful not to send an expert any privileged material, or any other document which might not have to be disclosed.

The most recent decision, and at Court of Appeal level an important authority, *Lucas v Barking, Havering & Redbridge Hospitals NHS Trust*

[2003] EWCA Civ 1102, went further in attempting to clarify the relationship between CPR 31.14 and 35.10(4) and to provide guidance on the difference between 'material' and 'non-material' instructions. This was a clinical negligence case, in which the claimant disclosed with the particulars of claim two medical condition and prognosis reports, one of which referred to an expert's report on liability and causation, and the other to the claimant's witness statement, neither of which had been disclosed at that stage. The defendant applied for their disclosure relying upon CPR 31.14; the claimant resisted disclosure relying upon CPR 35.10(4). It was held that one party might not, as a matter of course, call under CPR 35.10(4) for the immediate disclosure of documents constituting an expert's instructions or referred to in his report, that documents sent to an expert with his instructions are part of those instructions but that they may not all be 'material'; some could be supplied as background only. In any event, the court would only order the disclosure of the actual instructions or any enclosed documents, if there were grounds for believing the statement of the instructions in the expert's report was inaccurate or incomplete. The court also said that the mere mention of a privileged document in an expert's report does not necessarily waive privilege in the document, if the contents of the privileged document are not to be relied upon by the discloser. The Court of Appeal concluded that CPR 31.14 was unlikely to have been intended to change the law of privilege to require "automatic" disclosure of any document referred to in an expert's report.

This overrules the decision by Morland J in *Taylor* and clarifies the position to a large extent. Nonetheless, in the author's view, it is sensible for solicitors to:

- Assume that their instructions to an expert, including oral instructions, may be disclosable.

- Review all documents carefully before sending them to an expert, and be circumspect before sending any privileged material (e.g. counsel's advice), and any statements or reports produced for the case which have not yet been disclosed and which might not be relied upon.

- Consider whether to describe any privileged or undisclosed documents in the list or index as 'for background' only.

- Check carefully, on receipt of an expert's report and before disclosing it, whether the expert's summary of his instructions is accurate and complete (see also Chapter 8).

In 2004, the High Court also decided that drafts of experts' reports remain privileged – see *Jackson v Marley Davenport Ltd* [2004] EWCA Civ 1225, discussed in Chapter 8.

There should be little doubt that post proceedings, *advice* from an expert (as opposed to opinion evidence in a report for the court) does not have to be disclosed, provided that it is not a departure from the evidence in the expert's report or is, for example, a commentary on another expert's report.

The law on legal, professional and litigation privilege seems far from settled – witness the very different approaches taken by the Court of Appeal and House of Lords in the *Three Rivers DC v The Bank of England* litigation (see No 5 [2003] EWCA Civ 474, and 2004 UKHL 48).

INSTRUCTING THE SINGLE JOINT EXPERT

Sometimes one or both parties may have needed, or have chosen, to obtain advice from an expert, particularly on liability, before proceedings are issued. If the court decides expert evidence is required, but that evidence from two experts would be disproportionate, the case management judge has a dilemma – whether to impose a new single joint expert on the parties, or to allow them to continue to retain their own experts, with the court seeking to narrow the issues in dispute on both parties' expert opinion evidence, by requiring service of written questions on the experts, and/or by ordering an experts' discussion.

Frequently, the relative cost, or whether involving a new expert will cause delay, will be the deciding factor.

Both parties can give separate instructions to a single joint expert (CPR 35.8). In *Yorke v Katra* [2003] WL 21491870, the Court of Appeal held that a district judge was wrong to strike out the defence in a small claim because the defendant, a litigant in person, had unilaterally amended the claimant's solicitor's letter of instruction to the single joint expert.

Therefore, it is clearly preferable if the parties co-operate to provide the expert with one set of instructions. This may take some time, as one party will need to take the initiative with a draft, which is sent to the other party to amend and add to. The final letter should be copied to all parties and the expert told that these are agreed instructions.

If separate instructions are given, they must be copied to the other party. A potential difficulty for the expert is that the first party to instruct him may fail to tell him he is a single joint expert. The second instructions from the other party may come as a surprise, and may even cause practical difficulties if the expert has begun work on the first set of instructions, and the two are different. This may be an occasion when the expert may wish to exercise his/her right to apply to the court for directions under rule 35.14 (see Chapter 2 and 10).

In principle, instructions to a single joint expert should be very similar to those to a party expert, but in practice the solicitor/expert relationship is likely to be different in that:

- The expert is not part of the 'team' in the same way as with a party expert.

- You may not have chosen the expert, or worked with him before.

- The expert may even have been instructed previously by the other party as 'their' expert (typically in a fast track personal injury claim where, under the pre-action protocol, the claimant instructs the experts, particularly the medical expert preparing a condition and prognosis report. The court may well adopt this expert as the only one, unless the defendant puts forward cogent arguments for the instruction of a second expert.)

- The court may have ordered expert evidence to be in the form of a single joint expert report to keep costs under control, or to reduce the risk of expert evidence in a low value case or on a technical point being 'used' to bolster a party's case.

- You may be reluctant to tell the expert the potential weaknesses of your client's case: this could mean you are tempted to send shorter instructions and enclose fewer materials from the file. (Certainly, experts have told the author that their instructions as single joint experts are often more bland.)

- You, or your client, may also be tempted to try to give private instructions or information to the expert at a meeting or by telephone. You should avoid the temptation.

There are three important principles to keep in mind when instructing a single joint expert:

1. Fairness and equality of access; the expert must be equally accessible to all the parties and he should be scrupulous to treat all parties equally.

2. Transparency; all instructions to (and responses from) the expert should be equally visible to all parties in the action. To achieve this, all communications should be in writing and should be marked with the names of the persons to whom they are being copied.

3. Agreement; each contact a party has with the expert must be within the terms agreed between the parties.

The President of the Family Division's Ancillary Relief Advisory Group has produced the *Best Practice Guide for Instructing a Single Joint Expert*, which includes useful guidance of general applicability. The guide provides, in Part 6(a), that if a single joint expert has already been instructed, the court may adopt or amend those instructions, as the case management judge thinks fit.

Part 7 of the guide suggests that joint instructions should "reflect the proportionality principle" and should include:

- Basic relevant information.

- Any assumptions to be made.

- The principal known issues.

- The specific questions to be answered.

- Arrangements for attendance at a property or other place.

- Paragraphs 1.1-1.6 of the Practice Direction to CPR Part 35 (on expert's reports) and a copy of this Guide.

- A copy of the relevant parts of the court order concerning the appointment and instruction of the single joint expert.

- Documents necessary for the expert's consideration of the case, sorted and indexed.

Part 8 suggests that upon receiving the letter of instruction, the single joint expert should raise with the solicitors any issues or questions which may arise, including proportionality, lack of clarity or completeness in the instructions and the possible effect on fees of complying with the instructions.

Part 9 proposes that, should a party wish to give supplementary instructions to the SJE, full consideration must be given to proportionality and to the possible effect on the court timetable, and either the other party or the court has to sanction them.

Part 10 provides that all communications by the SJE should be addressed to both parties.

OTHER ISSUES

Expert's contact with the parties or witnesses

In your instructions, you may need to remind the expert that if he meets the client or witnesses, visits the site, etc., without either party's solicitor being present, he should be particularly careful to keep accurate notes of what was said in case of disputes later, and particularly if the client attempts to give him new instructions or a witness imparts new information. In either circumstance, he must inform you and seek further instructions.

Draft reports

Consider whether you want to invite the expert to send you his report in draft in the first instance. This was common practice before the implementation of the CPR, although it is probably less so today, but there is really no reason not to, provided that the solicitor and expert keep on file, and are willing to disclose, the 'audit trail' of their exchanges of letters, notes of telephone calls and the different versions of the report.

Many experts tell the author they receive too little feedback on their reports, and would welcome constructive comments on drafts (or even final reports), see Chapter 14.

Single joint experts may, of their own volition, invite parties to treat their first disclosed report as a draft, particularly if they received very different instructions from the two parties. Letters commenting on the draft should be copied to the other party.

Instructions may be a continuing process

Remember that your first letter of instruction to the expert may not be the last. You may also need to send the expert:

- Further materials he has requested.
- Materials that become available before his report is disclosed.
- The other party's disclosure of documents, or experts' reports.

It is easy to forget to keep 'the expert in the loop' (see Chapter 14).

Be careful that all later instructions are drafted in accordance with the principles described above and discuss with the expert how these might be summarised in any supplementary report.

CONCLUSIONS

The instructions to an expert, like the selection of the expert, are a key stage in the litigation, and repay time and effort.

Experts do not appreciate being asked "to prepare their usual report" – see Chapter 14. Vague or non-specific instructions are less likely to lead to a thorough or thoughtful report. Solicitors should aim to set out the questions and issues for the expert to address in detail but in a neutral way. Brief instructions that mask the weaknesses of the case are a false economy – likely to be discovered when the other party's expert report is disclosed, or when questions are posed to your expert.

Deciding what documents to send to the expert requires particular care in the light of CPR 35.10(4). Notwithstanding the helpful decision of the Court of Appeal in *Lucas*, it is best not to send privileged material, including statements or other experts' reports, which may not ultimately be relied upon.

Remember too that the instructions are part of the contract with the expert, in a similar way to the retainer letter with the client.

Chapter 6

EXPERTS' FEES

Disputes over payment of fees are probably the most common cause of conflict between experts and solicitors, particularly arguments about quotations and estimates, payment for work additional to the report, late or non-payment by the solicitor, disbursements incurred by the expert and cancellation fees. The author has decided a number of County Court small claims made by experts for fees, unpaid or part-paid, in some of which solicitors had not acted very professionally.

The aim of this chapter is to reduce the likelihood of disputes between solicitors and experts occurring, and to set out the provisions of the CPR and the relatively few case law authorities with regard to experts' fees.

AGREEING FEES WITH THE EXPERT PRIOR TO INSTRUCTION

The contract

It is essential to agree the basis on which the expert will be paid before instructions are confirmed. The expert's terms and conditions, your letter in reply (or theirs if they issue terms of engagement) and your letter of instructions form the contract. Ideally, both the solicitor and the expert should sign their acceptance of the terms, including the fees. Some experts will use or adapt the model terms of engagement published by the expert witness organisations. The terms recommended by the Expert Witness Institute and by the Academy of Experts can be found on their websites at www.ewi.org.uk and www.academyofexperts.org. If the expert sends you their terms and you do not respond, the presumption will be that you have agreed them.

If the solicitor sends and signs the letter of instruction, rather than the client, the firm will be liable for the expert's fees under the contract (see also Chapter 13). If it is intended that the client will be responsible for the fees, this must be expressly agreed with the expert. (The client should, of course, agree both to the instruction of the expert and the fees – see below.) The client may need reminding that the expert's duty is to the court and that the expert must be paid in accordance with the contract, even if his report is not favourable to the client's case. Where the contract is with the solicitor, delay or failure by the client or third party funder in putting the firm in funds, will not excuse a breach of contract.

The key terms

The matters that should be agreed with the expert at the outset in relation to fees are:

1. The fee for the report or advice, and whether at this stage this is an estimate until the expert has received and agreed the instructions.

2. The hourly rate for any subsequent work on the case.

3. If other staff are to work under the expert's direction, their fees or hourly rates.

4. Whether the expert must seek prior authority if the agreed or estimated fee is likely to be exceeded, or for the costs of any investigation work or tests that he considers necessary, or for any other disbursements.

5. Daily or hourly fees for attending trial, including any cancellation fees (often charged on a sliding scale according to the period of notice given).

6. Whether travelling time can be charged and at what rate, and mileage rates for car travel and class of rail or airfares (many experts will ask for first class or business class).

7. Whether subsistence (meals and accommodation) are chargeable, in what circumstances, and at what rates).

8. Whether miscellaneous expenses, such as photocopying and printing, can be charged, and at what rate.

9. Whether VAT is to be charged.

10. When the fees are due to be invoiced and paid, including in large cases whether the expert will interim bill, perhaps monthly or quarterly.

11. Where the solicitor has to obtain the funds for the expert's fees and expenses from the client, an insurer, or other party, whether the expert will accept a longer period for payment (see below).

12. Whether interest is charged for late payment (which should be defined) or for deferred payment terms, and at what rate (see below).

13. Whether the expert should keep time records for any work charged at an hourly rate.

Single joint experts

Fees for a single joint expert should also be agreed on instruction – the same details as above, plus how they are to be agreed and shared between the parties and the invoicing arrangements. If the parties choose to adopt the provisions in CPR 35.8(9), i.e. joint and several liability for the expert's fees, it is prudent to remind the other party, and the expert, that this means the expert can look to one party to pay the entire fees if the other party defaults on their share. If one solicitor takes the lead in instructing the expert, he should ensure that the other party also agrees to the expert's terms and conditions.

If the court puts a limit or cap on the expert's fees (see below), the expert should be told especially if the cap was in place prior to instructing him.

Obtaining approval to experts' fees from the client or funder

It is the solicitor's responsibility to ensure that the client or funder, including the Legal Services Commission in publicly-funded cases, grants the necessary prior authority for the estimated or agreed fees, and ensures that increases in those fees are also approved.

If you are instructing an expert pre-action, or before the court has given you permission to adduce a report from that expert, you must warn the client and funder that the costs might not be recoverable (see also Chapter 2). You will also need to do this if you instruct a 'shadow expert' during the proceedings to advise, for example, on a single joint expert's report (see Chapters 3 and 7).

Funding by the Legal Services Commission

With regard to cases funded by the Legal Services Commission (LSC), at the time of writing:

- The expert should be told if this is how the case is to be funded.

- Prior approval of the expert's fees should be sought unless the firm has devolved powers.

- The expert should be told of any LSC limits or restrictions on the fees.

- The solicitor should apply promptly to the LSC for payment of the expert's fees.

- When the money is received, the expert should be paid promptly.

In the past, solicitors frequently excused their delayed payment of experts by claiming delays by the LSC (even when that was not justified). Now that the LSC pays disbursements reasonably quickly on submission of invoices, this 'excuse' is never justifiable.

In November 2004, the LSC published a consultation paper on controlling experts' fees, *The Use of Experts*. The Commission expressed concern that experts' fees had risen faster than lawyers' fees, and that experts were not subject to any quality assurance. The proposal is to introduce new controls on experts' fees through the publication of guidelines which, on assessment, would be accepted as reasonable; Commission granted prior authorities would be abolished.

In civil cases, the proposed guidelines consist of three rate bands for five different categories of experts as follows:

- For medical practitioners, the rates are between £50 and £130 per hour.

- For most other experts, the rates are lower, between £33 and £130 per hour.

In most cases, the rates that the Commission would expect to pay in the above groups are the middle band of £71-£100 and £64-£99 respectively. The highest bands (up to £130 per hour) would only apply to exceptional cases, which would need full justification, and the obtainment of at least three competitive quotes.

These are not generous rates (see the recent surveys of experts' fees, summarised below) and, if implemented, could lead to a reduction in the number of experts willing to accept instructions in publicly-funded cases as has happened with solicitors.

The Commission's proposals for introducing quality assurance for experts through accreditation were explained in Chapter 1.

WHAT EXPERTS CHARGE

At the time of writing, there are no official guidelines on what experts can charge. Given the not insignificant amounts of money paid out in experts' fees in many cases, surprisingly there are no reported cases that give any guidance post implementation of the CPR.

Experts are a very varied breed. Many undertake expert witness work as a 'sideline' to a salaried income or partnership profits from their mainstream work; others virtually run an expert witness consultancy on their own account, and a few are employees or partners in businesses for whom expert witness work is their main livelihood. Not surprisingly, this means that experts' charging rates are wide-ranging. This makes it very difficult for a solicitor to judge the reasonableness of an expert's fee estimate, unless he/she is a specialist in that type of work, and knows the 'going rates'. Some experts in very specialist fields, or where there are few people willing to undertake expert witness work, charge at rates that exceed those of the lawyers!

When an expert decides what to charge, he considers:

a) how much of his work is acting as an expert witness;

b) what overheads he carries for this work;

c) what other experts in the same field charge.

Two surveys of experts' fees were published in 2004.

The first survey, of more than 500 experts, by the legal publishers Sweet and Maxwell, showed that:

● One third of the experts charged less than £100 per hour.

● About a half charged £100-£200 per hour.

104

- 15% charged more than £200 per hour.

Medical experts charged more:

- One third charged over £200 per hour.
- 4% charged over £400 per hour.

The lowest-paid experts in this survey were those advising on consumer issues and engineering production, and forensic experts. Three-quarters of these groups charged less than £99 per hour.

Self-employed experts charged more than those working within organisations.

The second survey, by the training company Bond Solon, found that:

- 26% charged less than £100 per hour.
- 52% charged between £100 and £200.
- 22% charged over £200.

These rates were significantly higher than in a similar survey carried out by Bond Solon in 2002, when 55% of respondents charged less than £100 per hour.

Some experts may be willing to negotiate on their fees, particularly where your firm is able to offer repeat work or for specific cases, e.g. for a not well-resourced private-paying client.

Solicitors should be wary of experts who:

a) charge a high fee for obviously minor adaptations only to a standard report (you will only become aware of this when you have instructed them a few times);

b) charge for amendments only necessary because of their errors or poor drafting;

c) refuse to keep time records or provide breakdowns of invoices.

Other charges

Value added tax

As at 2005, a business should register for VAT when the turnover exceeds £55,000. Many experts will, therefore, charge VAT. Medical experts have been exempt when the service provided is a medico-legal report, but *D'Ambrumenil v Commissioners of Customs & Excise* ([2003] TLR 27) decided that, in principle, VAT is chargeable on medico-legal reports. This is likely to be introduced from April 2005 – the rate has yet to be decided.

Interest

Many experts' standard terms and conditions include the right to charge interest on invoices unpaid after 28 days. Even if there is no specific contractual term, the Late Payment of Commercial Debts (Interest) Act 1998 applies to contracts between solicitors and experts. This allows experts to charge interest at 8%, plus the Bank of England's base rate.

In practice, many experts will only exercise the right to charge interest for very late or persistently late payers.

Witness summonses

If you need to issue a witness summons to secure the attendance of an expert witness at trial (see also Chapter 12), you must pay the expert witness 'conduct money', i.e. travel expenses and their fees under your contract with them. In *Brown v Bennett* (*The Times*, 2nd November 2000), an expert sought to set aside a witness summons because the party instructing him would not pay his fees to appear. The court made the order in the expert's favour.

Cancellation fees

Most experts charge cancellation fees if they are booked for trial and the case settles. It is usual for cancellation fees to be on a sliding scale, starting from a month before trial. Expect to be charged full fees for a cancellation less than seven days before trial.

Martin v Holland and Barrett [2002] 3 Costs Law Reports was a personal injury claim where the defendant objected to paying the claimant's orthopaedic consultant's cancellation fees for trial. The appeal was dismissed on the ground that "it was not unreasonable to expect experts to lay down terms in advance if they are to commit to a day in court".

The reasonableness of cancellation fees will depend upon what the expert does other than his expert witness work; for instance, a hospital consultant (particularly in the private sector) who has to cancel appointments or surgery to be available for trial has a stronger case to charge cancellation fees than a full-time expert witness who returns to his desk to earn fees on other cases when a case settles.

Medical agency fees

In routine personal injury claims, it has become common practice when a medical condition and prognosis report is required for a claimant client to instruct a medical agency, particularly where the client lives in a different part of the country to the solicitors' firm, and the firm does not have a database of doctors who undertake medico-legal work in that area. Also some claims organisations and legal expense insurers have arrangements with particular agencies, and require solicitors handling their work to obtain their medical reports from that source.

Agencies provide a service and need to cover their overheads and make a profit. Most agencies make a charge in addition to the fee paid to the doctor for the report. In principle, this is recoverable between the parties provided that the agency charge does not exceed the reasonable and proportionate costs the solicitor could have charged for the work involved in locating the expert, discussing terms with him, instructing him and checking the report on delivery. (*Stringer v Copley HH Michael Cook*, Kingston-upon-Thames County Court, 17th May 2002 (unrep) but approved by chief costs judge, Master Hurst, in the *Accident Group Test Cases* [2004] EWCA Civ 575.)

The invoice from the agency should show the doctor's and the agency fees separately, and the latter should be sufficiently particularised to enable the instructing solicitor, the other party and the costs officer or judge to be satisfied that they are reasonable, or what part of them can be recovered.

Deferred payment terms

Solicitors may want experts to wait to be paid for their fees when the solicitor does not have an arrangement with the client or funder to pay disbursements as they are incurred, typically in conditional fee or trade union funded cases. You must ask an expert in advance whether he will agree to this. Many will if you instruct them frequently; some will wish to charge an additional fee, perhaps expressed as interest at x%. Do not simply delay paying an expert until it suits you – the relationship will sour which will not encourage the expert to feel committed to the case. A specific deferral fee charged by the expert may not be recoverable from the other party.

Contingency arrangements

It is very clear, however, that the courts will not approve payment of an expert witness' fees on a contingency basis, as this could seriously undermine the expert's independence and credibility (the Law Society Practice Rule 22.11 also outlaws it). The only exception is when the expert is assisting the solicitor and is not providing opinion evidence to the court.

In *R (on the application of Factortame & Others) v SOS for Transport, Environment & the Regions* No 2 [2002] EWCA Civ 932 CA, the claimants were allowed to recover the fees of accountants incurred in connection with the preparation of a claim for an assessment of damages, for which the accountants charged "8% of the final settlement received". The claimants were impecunious and unable to pay fees upfront. The Court of Appeal said this did not conflict with public policy, as the accountants were not involved in the work on liability and were not retained to give expert opinion evidence, but to carry out back-up work for the other accountants who were instructed as expert witnesses, and because the work could have been undertaken by the claimant's solicitors.

COURT CONTROL OF EXPERTS' FEES

The CPR provisions

CPR 35.4(4) gives the court the power to limit the amount of an expert's fee that a party may recover from another party. There was no equivalent in the previous rules. It does not seem that this power is being used extensively; there is little case law giving guidance on when and why it may be appropriate.

However, Lord Woolf and the Rule Committee almost certainly had in mind:

1. Proportionality, as the court now has a duty to try to ensure that the work and expenditure on a case, including experts' fees, are in keeping with what is in issue.

2. The occasional need to prevent a well-resourced party from exercising its financial muscle to out-spend and, therefore, possibly out-play, the less-resourced party to the litigation.

Except by consent, the exercise of this power by the court will not have an impact on the contract between the solicitor and expert.

In *Kranidiotes v Paschali* [2001] EWCA Civ 357, an accountant single joint expert was to be instructed to value a shareholding. The court limited the recoverable fee to £10,000. The expert selected by the parties quoted a fee of £75,000. The court terminated his instructions as the cost was disproportionate, and ordered that another expert should be instructed. The Court of Appeal dismissed the defendant's appeal.

CPR 35.6(4) gives the court the power to order that an expert's fees cannot be recovered if the expert fails to answer valid questions on his report – again, a power that appears to be little-used.

Single joint experts' fees

CPR 35.8(4) gives the court the power, before a single joint expert is instructed to:

1. Limit the amount that can be paid by way of fees and expenses to the expert.

2. Direct that the instructing parties pay that amount into court.

In the author's experience, the first power is used fairly frequently and uncontroversially in low value claims, on proportionality grounds.

In *Smolen v Solon Co-operative Housing Services Ltd* [2003], unusually the court allowed a single joint expert to be replaced when the claimant objected to him after seeing his report, on the ground that the defendant's solicitor worked with him regularly. The claimant was, however, required to pay the fees for the second expert into court, prior to his being instructed. (For a fuller discussion of this case, see Chapter 9.)

CPR 35.8(5) states:

"Unless the court otherwise directs, the instructing parties are jointly and severally liable for the payment of the single joint expert's fees and expenses."

This means that, in a two party case, the parties will pay 50% of the expert's fees each. However, if one party fails to pay their share, the expert can look to the other party to pay the second 50%, rather than having to apply to the court (using the expert's power to do so under CPR 35.14 – see Chapter 10), or to sue the defaulting solicitor for the balance.

Costs estimates and costs capping

The Allocation Questionnaire and Pre-trial Checklist (see Chapters 1, 2 and 12) require the parties to state the costs they have incurred to date, and to provide estimates of their future costs. However, this requirement only extends to base costs, i.e. solicitor's profit costs, not to disbursements, counsel's fees or VAT. It is very arguable how useful this is, either to the court or the other party, in any case in which counsel's or expert's fees are substantial, as the main purpose of estimates is to enable parties to litigation to know what their potential liability will be if they lose the case.

The court does have the power to order estimates to be prepared at any stage and in a specific way for case management purposes, e.g. to assist the judge in deciding what directions to make. The court could require estimates of experts' fees, e.g. when a party was seeking permission to instruct a large number of, or particularly expensive, experts.

This is likely to be a more common practice, following the Court of Appeal's decision in *Leigh v Michelin Tyre plc* [2003] EWCA Civ 1766. Cost estimates, the court said, are an important part of the "machinery of case management", and particularly at Pre-trial Checklist stage, should provide a reasonably accurate estimate of the likely overall costs, especially in "run of the mill" cases. The Court of Appeal then gave the following guidance:

1. Estimates should provide a useful yardstick to measure the reasonableness of the costs finally claimed.

2. The court may take the estimates into account if the other party can show they relied on them, e.g. by not making an offer.

3. The court may take the estimates into account in cases where it decides that it would probably have given different case management directions if a realistic estimate had been given.

4. However, if none of these factors apply, and the costs are otherwise reasonable and proportionate, then the costs should not be reduced simply because they exceed the amount of the estimate.

The Court of Appeal invited the Rule Committee to consider the role played by estimates and costs caps (see below). It is possible, therefore, that in future, parties will be required in all cases to provide estimates of experts' fees and other disbursements in the case management questionnaires. In any case, a party concerned about the likely costs of the other party's experts could invite the case management judge to require estimates of the fees to be filed and served before directions are given permitting reliance on those experts (either the written reports or oral evidence at trial).

In *Leigh*, the Court of Appeal also endorsed costs capping in principle. A full discussion of costs capping is outside the scope of this book, but in *AB v Leeds Teaching Hospital NHS Trust* (in the matter of the Nationwide Organ Group Litigation) [2003] EWHC 1034 and in *Various Ledward Claimants v Kent and Medway Health Authority and East Kent Hospitals Trust* [2003] EWHC 2551 QB, case management judges set costs caps on the claimants' costs, to try to ensure they were kept within reasonable bounds. (A cap is not a fixed fee but an upper limit, which can only be exceeded for costs recovery purposes with the permission of the court.)

The cap in the *AB* case was for just over £500,000 and included a £50,000 cap of the experts' fees. In the *Ledward* case, the parties had agreed that there should be no cap in respect of experts' fees, but the case management judge expressed surprise at this when the claimant's estimates of experts' fees were £172,000. The judge said:

"Permission of the court to instruct experts in particular disciplines is not a licence to instruct them on a whole range of subjects without thought to the costs involved. I wish to know the amount of fees already expended on experts and the parties' estimates for future fees preferably at the next case management conference and also shortly before trial. A copy of those estimates should be sent to the Senior Costs Judge. I further order that any detailed assessment shall be reserved to him."

While cost capping, for the foreseeable future, may only occur frequently in Group Actions or very large claims, where one or both parties' costs appear likely to be disproportionate, it is likely that experts' fees will be included in the cap.

Experts' fees in the small claims track

Paragraph 7.3(2) of the Part 27 Practice Direction limits the amount of fees that can be recovered in the small claims track to £200 per expert. While this might seem to be proportionate for claims worth less than £5,000, in practice reports can rarely be obtained for £200, particularly if an inspection or examination is necessary. The result can be that the successful party has to accept that they cannot recover a significant part of the experts' fees, especially if they alone instruct the expert, rather than the expert being instructed on a joint basis with the fees being shared regardless of the outcome.

Assessors' fees

If an assessor is appointed to assist the court (a rare event outside the Admiralty Division – see Chapter 3), **CPR 35.15(5)** provides that the "remuneration for his services shall be determined by the court and shall form part of the costs of the proceedings", i.e. the unsuccessful party will usually be ordered to pay the fees. As with single joint experts, the court can order any party to pay a specified sum into court before the assessor begins work.

Fees for questions on experts' reports

Either party can raise formal written questions on a disclosed expert's report (under CPR 35.6 – discussed in more detail in Chapter 11). Paragraph 5.3 of the Practice Direction provides that the party who instructed the expert pays those fees, at least initially. This is the reverse of the position when the rules were first implemented; presumably to simplify the expert's invoicing arrangements.

The personal injury pre-action protocol (see Chapter 7) also allows questions to be raised on a disclosed expert's report (usually a medical condition and prognosis report for the claimant with the defendant asking the questions). Paragraph 3.21 of the protocol provides for the questioner to pay the expert's fees. In the author's view this is more logical than the provision in the Part 35 Practice Direction.

Assessment of experts' fees by the court

The court has the power, when assessing costs at the end of litigation (where the parties have failed to agree the amount of costs to be paid by the 'loser' to the 'winner'), to consider, and make decisions upon, the reasonableness of all 'disbursements', including experts' fees. The concept of proportionality is relevant both to reliance upon expert evidence, and upon the cost of obtaining that evidence.

Experts' fees that might be disallowed are listed below:

• For advice or a report which was not relied upon or disclosed.

• For advice or a report obtained without the permission of the court, e.g. for a shadow expert, unless reliance on the report was authorised by a case management judge retrospectively.

• Where the fees were unreasonably incurred for any other reason or are unreasonable in amount.

In *Admiral Management Services v Para-Protect Europe Ltd* (*The Times*, 26th March 2002 (see Chapter 2)), the court allowed fees to be recovered for work carried out by the claimants' in-house investigators, including for the period before solicitors were instructed.

The best ways to avoid experts' fees becoming 'points in dispute' at a costs assessment are as follows:

• Have a clear contract with 'your' experts (see above).

• Ensure estimates provided pre-instructions are firmed up and agreed at a later stage.

• Ensure invoices from experts state clearly the work covered and that disbursements are itemised.

• Require 'your' experts to time record all their work on the case, especially the work additional to the initial report, and either to invoice on that basis, or to provide you with time records for the assessment.

A decision by the court to disallow the recovery of all or part of an expert's fee, on a detailed assessment of costs, will not impact on the contract between the party, lawyer and expert, unless the expert is willing to accept a lesser fee in the circumstances. (Usually any shortfall on fees recovered has to be paid by the person who instructed the expert, generally the solicitor.)

PREDICTABLE COSTS AND EXPERTS' FEES

In 2003 and 2004, the Civil Justice Council successfully brokered:

1. A scheme of predictable solicitors' costs for personal injury road traffic accident claims that settle for less than £10,000 without proceedings having been issued.

2. Fixed success fees in personal injury road traffic and employers' liability funded under conditional fee arrangements.

Both were implemented as amendments to Part 45 CPR (see Chapter 7).

Also in 2004, the Civil Justice Council began to investigate whether predictable or guideline fees for experts' reports, particularly medico-legal reports, in low value personal injury claims, would be feasible. At the time of writing, discussions were in progress with lawyers, experts and judges.

FAILURE TO PAY – THE EXPERT'S REMEDIES

If a solicitor fails to pay agreed reasonable fees on time or after a few reminders, the expert will be entitled to refuse to carry out further work. A solicitor is responsible for paying the proper costs of any professional agents they instruct on behalf of a client, whether or not the solicitor receives payment from the client (see principle 20.01 of the *Guide to the Professional Conduct of Solicitors*, 5th Edition, 1999).

In the survey carried out by Bond Solon in 2004 (referred to above), only 17% of solicitors paid experts promptly, 65% of experts said they were paid late, and 16% said they were paid very late.

There may, of course, be occasions when solicitors will be justified in not paying an expert, at least for part of their fees, including:

● When the expert has completely or seriously failed to comply with instructions or their duty to the court, particularly if that failure has caused you to abandon that expert.

● When the expert's report is received very late (and the expert had been told the importance of the deadline), particularly if that delay incurs costs, e.g. applications to court for extensions of time or to adjourn the trial.

● When the expert's final fees exceed the agreed estimate without authority, provided that the expert knew prior authority was necessary.

An expert may pursue unpaid fees in one of the following ways:

1. Complain to the firm's senior partner (or the Office for the Supervision of Solicitors, although generally because of pressure of work they are unwilling to investigate complaints from experts about fees).

2. Sue the firm in the County Court, ideally after sending a letter of claim.

The Expert Witness Institute's and Academy of Experts' model terms of engagement both provide for disputes on fees to be resolved by mediation or arbitration. The Academy terms also state that if the solicitor fails to pay an invoice within 30 days, the expert is entitled to issue proceedings immediately and to cease work.

An expert disgruntled over badly delayed or non-payment of fees will probably decline to work with you and your firm in future and will tell other experts about their unfortunate experience.

CONCLUSIONS – THE FUTURE

Experts' fees can be a significant proportion of the costs of a dispute, particularly when oral evidence at trial is necessary from a number of experts. Experts' charges for reports and additional work vary greatly, even between experts within the same field. This can sometimes be a source of friction between the parties and makes it difficult for case management judges who are minded to set a recoverability cap. Some official benchmarks for experts' fees would probably be welcomed by solicitors and clients at least, if not by experts, particularly for the more routine types of reports, such as medical condition and prognosis reports in personal injury claims, surveyors' reports in housing disrepair claims, as well as for valuations in applications for the renewal of business leases.

Chapter 7
PRE-ACTION AND THE EXPERT

INTRODUCTION

With the success of the pre-action protocols and early offers to settle, many disputes are resolved without the need for proceedings. "Litigation as a last resort" was one of Lord Woolf's 'mantras', which is clearly being heeded. The number of issued cases has reduced in the High Court, from 9,500 in 1998 to 1,400 in 2003 and in the County Court, from 2 million in 1998 to 1,350,000 in 2003 (money claims only). This means that the majority of most 'litigation' solicitors' work is carried out at the pre-action stage only.

Instructing experts pre-action has the advantage that communication with the expert will probably be privileged (unless the expert is also retained for the proceedings – see below), but has the disadvantage that it may not be certain as to whether the experts' fees can be recovered if proceedings do become necessary.

The Pre-action Practice Direction and pre-action protocols provide guidance, and in some cases procedures, on the use of expert evidence pre-action and are dealt with later in the chapter.

DO YOU NEED AN EXPERT PRE-ACTION?

How to decide

Before deciding to instruct an expert at an early stage of a dispute, you need to answer the following questions:

1. Does your firm need advice from an expert on basic liability issues, to enable you to assess the prospects of success before you decide to take on the case, typically when you are considering whether to run the case on a conditional fee arrangement? (See Chapter 2.)

2. Does the client or funder need advice to consider the cause of action, and the cost/benefit of proceeding with a claim? (See Chapter 2.)

3. Is it likely, if the case proceeds to litigation, that the client will obtain permission from the court to rely upon expert evidence in the field you have in mind? (See Chapter 1.)

4. If the answer to question 3 is 'yes', might the court order that the evidence can only be given by a single joint expert? (See Chapter 9.)

5. Is there an applicable pre-action protocol and, if so, what does it say with regard to expert evidence? (See below.)

6. If the answer to question 1 and/or question 2 is 'yes', but to question 3 is 'no' or 'doubtful', who will pay the expert's fees if they cannot be recovered from another party?

7. If the answer to question 1 and/or 2, and to question 3 and/or 4 is 'yes', will you want to instruct the same expert to advise at the early stage and to prepare a report for the court, or not? If not, refer back to question 5.

Advice from an expert as part of the risk assessment

Obtaining early advice from an expert in a potential conditional fee case is part of the firm's risk assessment. The main risk factors are:

- The facts and evidence in support – the risk that the client and/or lay witnesses will fail to establish what happened.

- Liability – the risk that your client will fail to establish breach of contract, or breach of duty (or the definition of the particular cause of action).

- Delay and limitation – the start date of the limitation period may be uncertain or very soon.

- The opponent – establishing the correct one(s) and their ability to pay damages and costs.

- Causation, particularly in negligence claims.

- Quantum – the risk that damages will be lower than anticipated, including the risk of failing to beat the other party's Part 36 offer.

Expert advice (or later evidence) will often be very important in establishing liability and causation, and in supporting quantum. If expert advice on liability and causation is to be sought as part of the risk assessment process, can it be obtained sufficiently quickly from a reliable expert, and at a reasonable fee? This is not an appropriate stage to instruct an expert new to the firm, but you will also need to consider whether you are likely to retain the same expert throughout the case (will a pre-action protocol effectively require this, particularly if it provides for a single joint expert?), or whether you might want to line up two experts from the same discipline, one to advise now, and the second to write the report for disclosure. It will be relatively uncommon to instruct a quantum expert at a pre-conditional fee agreement/retainer with client stage.

The advantages of retaining the same expert throughout a dispute include:

- Savings in experts' fees, as only one expert will need to read the papers.

- Savings in your time in instructing one expert, and therefore in legal fees.

- Possibly a stronger commitment from the expert if they are part of the 'team' from the outset.

On the other hand, the advantages of changing the expert before any of the formal stages of the dispute are commenced are:

- Greater 'freedom' to have an entirely open 'strengths and weaknesses' discussion with the expert – often vital in a potentially difficult case. The expert may be less likely to give you advice that supports your client's case if they know they are not going to be retained for any litigation.

- That the discussions with the advisory expert will remain privileged, whereas there is always a risk that early exchanges of correspondence and discussions with an expert who is retained for the litigation will not be privileged (see Chapter 5).

- If the protocol or the court will require this expert to be a single joint expert, you and the client will have to accept complete transparency with regard to all communications with that expert. This may not encourage you to be completely open with the expert, which in turn may reduce the value of the advice.

If you do instruct an expert pre-action, make sure to explain the purpose and status of his advice or report – see Chapter 5.

LORD WOOLF'S *ACCESS TO JUSTICE* FINAL REPORT

In Chapter 10 of his final report, Lord Woolf proposed pre-action protocols as codes of sensible practice that the parties would be expected to follow and said:

"Protocols will also be an important means of promoting economy in the use of expert evidence, in particularly encouraging the parties to use a single expert wherever possible. Unless this happens before the commencement of proceedings it will frequently be too late because the parties will already have established an entrenched relationship with their own expert." (Chapter 10, paragraph 6, page 108.)

When the CPR were implemented in April 1999, two protocols were annexed to the rules – for personal injury and clinical negligence claims. Other protocols were approved and annexed between 2000 and early 2004 (see below).

GUIDANCE ON EXPERT EVIDENCE IN THE PRE-ACTION PRACTICE DIRECTION

In February 2003, the Pre-action Practice Direction was extended to provide guidance on how to conduct the early stages of those disputes for which there is no applicable pre-action protocol. With regard to expert evidence, paragraphs 4.9 and 4.10 of the Practice Direction state:

"4.9   The resolution of some claims, but by no means all, may need help from an expert. If an expert is needed, the parties should wherever possible and to save expense engage an agreed expert.

4.10   Parties should be aware that, if the matter proceeds to litigation, the court may not allow the use of an expert's report, and that the cost of it is not always recoverable."

These paragraphs, in effect, do not add any specific advice to that in Part 35, but do serve as a useful reminder for the less experienced solicitor, and for litigants in person. The spirit of the Practice Direction and, indeed of all the protocols, is for parties to co-operate and exchange information and documents pre-action. However, there are risks in disclosing expert evidence pre-action, as you will usually then be obliged to rely on it if proceedings are issued, or the other party would be able to apply to the court for disclosure of the report under CPR 35.9 (see Chapters 2 and 10).

If a party, or their solicitor, is concerned about the court's likely approach to experts in the case, or there is a pre-action dispute between the parties on experts, the court has no specific jurisdiction to resolve the problem before proceedings are issued (as it does with documents under CPR 31.16).

GUIDANCE ON EXPERT EVIDENCE IN THE PRE-ACTION PROTOCOLS

By 2005, there were eight pre-action protocols in place for personal injury, clinical negligence, engineering and construction, defamation, professional negligence, housing disrepair, and occupational illness. Of these, only the protocols for defamation and judicial review make no specific provision for experts, no doubt because experts are rarely instructed in either type of claim, particularly on liability. Parties are expected to comply with the protocols and judges have the power, under CPR Part 3 (Case Management), to impose sanctions for non-compliance.

The personal injury pre-action protocol

(See paragraphs 2.14 and 2.15 of the Notes of Guidance, paragraphs 3.15-3.21 of the protocol and Annex C for a letter of instruction to a medical expert)

The personal injury protocol, which came into force in April 1999, is particularly aimed at fast track claims (up to £15,000), but the principles should be followed in multi-track claims also. This protocol specifically requires the parties to co-operate on the selection of an expert, most frequently a medical expert providing a condition and prognosis report on the accident victim (as this will have to be attached to the particulars of claim), but it also applies to those cases where a liability expert's report is needed.

The protocol requires the claimant to give the defendant the names of one or more suitable experts. If the defendant does not object to at least one of those named, within 14 days, the claimant will then instruct the chosen expert to prepare a report. If the claimant intends to obtain a medical report through a medical agency (see also Chapters 5 and 6), the defendant's prior consent to this should be obtained and, if the defendant so requests, the agency should be asked to provide the names of appropriate doctors in advance.

Provided that the claimant is satisfied with the report, it should be disclosed to the defendant soon after receipt. If the report requires clarification, either party can ask the expert questions (keeping the other party informed of both the questions and the answers). The protocol promotes the practice of obtaining one expert report only.

However, if the defendant objects to all of the experts named by the claimant, or is not satisfied with the report disclosed after raising questions and receiving answers, he may decide to retain his own expert. However, it will be for the court to decide at allocation and directions stage whether the cost of two experts is justified.

The instructing party, usually the claimant, pays the expert's fees for preparing the report. The other party, usually the defendant, pays for the expert to answer 'his' party's questions (the reverse of CPR 35.6, where the party who instructs the expert pays for him to answer questions on his report – see Chapters 6 and 11).

If the defendant admits liability, the claimant should disclose the medical report and delay in issuing proceedings for 21 days, so as to enable a settlement to be explored.

Some points of difficulty

Q1.	Which party initiates the instruction of the expert? (The protocol text refers to the "first" party and "second" party, rather than to the claimant and defendant.)

A1.	The intention is that usually it will be the claimant, partly because it is the claimant who will attach a medical report to the particulars of claim, but the defendant is not precluded from suggesting suitable experts in their letter of response to the claim.

Q2. When should the expert be instructed?

A2. Usually after the exchange of letters of claim and response, because if the defendant denies liability the claimant might discontinue, in which case the costs of the expert report will have been unnecessary. In a claim that is strong on liability, the claimant may sometimes be willing to instruct the medical expert earlier.

Q3. How many names should the defendant be given?

A3. More than one. Three is advisable, so that if the defendant objects to one, the claimant has two experts to choose from.

Q4. Should the expert be jointly instructed?

A4. The protocol does not require it, which the Court of Appeal has confirmed (*Carlson v Townsend* – see below); from the claimant's perspective, there is the disadvantage that the report will automatically be disclosed to the defendant by the expert.

Q5. Does the report have to be disclosed by the claimant?

A5. No, only if he wishes to rely upon it (*Carlson v Townsend* again).

Q6. If the defendants want their own report, can the claimant refuse?

A6. A party can never be prevented from obtaining expert *advice*, but the claimant might reasonably refuse to be examined by another doctor unless the court has given the defendant permission to obtain their own report.

Q7. What else can the defendants do if they are unhappy?

A7. Ask questions on the disclosed report but through the claimant's solicitor, unless the instructions were joint.

The protocol does not state what should happen if the claimant obtains a report under the procedure outlined above, which they do not wish to disclose because it is unsatisfactory or unhelpful. In *Carlson v Townsend* [2001] EWCA Civ 511, the defendants objected to one of the three consultant orthopaedic surgeons nominated by the claimant's solicitor. The claimant obtained a report from one of the other two experts, but decided not to disclose it. Instead, he obtained and disclosed a report from an expert who had not been nominated. The defendants applied to the court for disclosure of the first report, arguing that the first expert had been jointly instructed. The district judge granted the application. On appeal, the circuit judge reversed that decision. The Court of Appeal dismissed the defendant's appeal, confirmed that the personal injury protocol does not require a medical expert who has been selected in accordance with the protocol to be jointly instructed, or the report to be disclosed to the defendant, where the expert's identity has not been revealed.

Lord Justice Simon Browne quoted from Lord Woolf's *Access to Justice* final report:

"Provided at least two names are acceptable to both parties, the claimant may reject a report by the expert of his first choice without letting the defendant know that he has done so." (Paragraph 9 of Chapter 10 at page 109.)

The Court of Appeal decided that pre-action experts' reports remain privileged and the court cannot order their production. (However, the claimant would need the court's permission as usual to rely upon an expert's report in the proceedings and generally the claimant would have to bear the cost of the undisclosed report.)

Lord Justice Brooke said:

"It was not its (the protocol's) aim to deprive a claimant of the opportunity to obtain confidential pre-action advice about the viability of his claim, which he would be at liberty to discard undisclosed if he did not agree with it. There is no hint in the protocol that its authors intended the parties' solicitors to instruct the acceptable expert on a joint basis."

This was an important decision, protecting privilege in a pre-action expert's report, almost certainly not just applicable to personal injury claims. There have been a few other decisions of note on the same subject:

1. In *Sage v Feiven* (APIL Newsletter 2002, Vol 12, Issue 1, page 28), the claimant obtained a report from an orthopaedic surgeon, which was not disclosed (following *Carlson v Townsend*). When proceedings were issued, the defendant invited the district judge

to order a report from the same surgeon as a single joint expert, and the district judge did so, on proportionality grounds. This was overturned on appeal because, inevitably, privileged information would be disclosed to the defendant. The parties were ordered to instruct a new expert.

2. In *Mwamda v East London Bus & Coach Co Ltd* [2002] 8 *Current Law Digest* 66, the claimant was not allowed to rely upon a report obtained from a GP without following the pre-action protocol procedure, and which did not comply with Part 35 in several respects. The court ordered the instruction of a new single joint expert.

3. *Kapadia v Lambeth London Borough Council* [2000] AER D 785 decided that, once a medical expert had been instructed to prepare a personal injury report for the defence, with the claimant's agreement, neither the claimant nor the expert could decide not to release the report because the claimant was not happy with it, as this would defeat the objective of transparency of expert evidence.

Research carried out by the Law Society and Civil Justice Council, published in 2002 (*More Civil Justice? The impact of the Woolf reforms on pre-action behaviour*, Research Study 43, by Tamara Goriely, Richard Moorhead and Pamela Abrams), questioned whether the procedure in the personal injury protocol for agreeing experts' names justifies the delay it causes. The problem identified was that the procedure had led to requests for experts' CVs and to exchanges of correspondence, which prolonged the receipt of medical reports typically by six weeks. To date, no changes have been made to the protocol in this respect.

Pre-action protocol for the resolution of clinical disputes

(See section 4 of the protocol)

The clinical disputes protocol came into force in April 1999. It notes that expert opinion evidence may be needed in clinical negligence disputes:

a) on breach of duty and causation;

b) on the patient's condition and prognosis; and

125

c) to assist in valuing aspects of the claim.

It also notes that the Civil Procedure Rules encourage economy in the use of experts and a less adversarial culture.

However, the protocol is not as prescriptive on the instruction of experts as the personal injury protocol, recognising that expert evidence on liability and causation will often be fundamental to a clinical negligence claim and that requiring parties to share *this* expert evidence would probably not be practicable. The protocol says:

"Decisions on whether experts might be instructed jointly and on whether reports might be disclosed sequentially, or by exchange, should rest with the parties and their advisers. Sharing expert evidence may be appropriate on issues relating to the value of the claim."

The protocol, therefore, does not include any specific procedures for selecting or instructing experts, nor is there a specimen letter of instruction.

In the main, this flexible approach has been welcomed by solicitors and supported by the courts. The pre-action research published in 2002, referred to above, found that district judges occasionally ordered joint reports on liability and causation, but more frequently did so for condition and prognosis and quantum reports.

In *Oxley v Penwarden* [2000] WL 1274095, the first instance judge ordered the parties to a clinical negligence claim (concerning failure to diagnose and treat a vascular condition in O's leg), to agree a single joint vascular surgeon as the sole expert on the issue of causation, against both parties' wishes. He expressed concern that the clinical negligence protocol was not in line with the practice laid down in CPR 35.7 (encouraging the use of single joint experts). However, the Court of Appeal did not agree, supported the flexibility of the protocol with regard to expert evidence, and confirmed that the CPR does not provide a presumption that a single joint expert will be instructed in every case, particularly in negligence claims where the parties "should have the opportunity of investigating causation through an expert of their own choice". The Court of Appeal said that the denial of the opportunity to commission separate expert reports in a case where different schools of thought might exist would require the court, in the absence of agreement, to choose a given school of thought by appointing a particular expert, thereby effectively deciding the issue of causation, without the possibility for challenge.

S (a minor) v Birmingham Health Authority (decided 9th July 1999 QBD but reported in 2001 Lloyd's Rep Med 382) confirmed that single joint experts are not usually appropriate for liability and causation reports in complex clinical negligence claims, particularly at an early stage, to enable each party to present a full case in their statement of case.

The construction and engineering protocol

(See paragraphs 3, 4.3.1 and 5.5)

This protocol came into force in October 2000. It applies to all construction and engineering disputes. It includes professional negligence disputes against building professionals (the personal injury and clinical negligence protocols do not do so). The protocol should be read with CPR Part 60, which covers technology and construction court claims, although Part 60 of course only applies to the larger claims allocated to the multi-track.

The distinguishing features of this protocol with regard to expert evidence are:

- The letter of claim should include the remedy sought and details of how it has been calculated. The claimant must also provide the names of experts already instructed on whom he intends to rely, identifying the issues to which that evidence will be directed.

- The defendant has 14 days to acknowledge the letter and 28 days either to take objections on jurisdiction or to respond and, if doing the latter, he must set out any counterclaim, and provide the names of any experts he has instructed on which he intends to rely, identifying the issues to which that evidence will be directed.

- If the claim is not settled the parties should consider Alternative Dispute Resolution (ADR), whether a joint expert may be appointed, and if so, who that might be, and generally how the dispute is to be progressed.

Perhaps surprisingly, the protocol does not provide for payment of the parties' initial experts' fees: are the parties expected to pay for the advice or report themselves, or is the fee intended to be recoverable if the claim proceeds to litigation, but with a single joint expert providing the report at that stage? To the author's knowledge, there are no reported cases on expert evidence pre-action in construction disputes to assist.

The professional negligence pre-action protocol

(See B2.2, B7 and C6)

This protocol came into force in July 2001, and applies to claims of breach on contract or duty against professionals other than in construction (architects, engineers and surveyors – when the construction and engineering protocol applies) and in healthcare (when the clinical negligence protocol applies). Parties are invited, before working through the protocol, to consider whether their dispute might be resolved through a complaints or arbitration scheme offered by the relevant professional body.

With regard to expert evidence, the main features of the protocol are:

- It is designed to be flexible and does not dictate a standard approach, because some disputes may not need expert evidence at all, whereas in others it will be crucial.

- If the claimant is seeking some form of non-financial redress he should, in his letter of claim, confirm whether an expert has been appointed and, if so, the identity, discipline and date of appointment.

- If the claimant has obtained expert evidence prior to sending the letter of claim, the professional has an equal right to obtain expert evidence prior to sending the letter of response.

- If the claimant has not obtained expert evidence prior to sending the letter of claim, the parties are encouraged to appoint a joint expert and should seek to agree their identity and terms of appointment. If they cannot agree about a joint expert, they are free to appoint their own experts and, expressly, are not precluded from doing so, even if a joint expert is instructed.

Again, there is no provision concerning recoverability of payment to initial party-appointed experts. The final point in the list above is the most interesting, implying approval for the instruction of three experts, one for each party and a single expert. Surprisingly, this does not appear to have given rise to any satellite litigation.

Pre-action protocol for disease and illness claims

(See paragraphs 2.5 and 9.1-12)

This is a variation of the personal injury protocol for disease and illness at work claims and has been in force since 8th December 2003. These claims are often more difficult to pursue than other personal injury claims, as locating the employment(s) where the disease was contracted, and establishing whether there is causation, can be problematic. Limitation may be an issue and, in some cases, the claimant may be so ill by the time the disease is diagnosed that death may be imminent. The claims are often complex and unsuitable for the fast track, regardless of their value.

With regard to expert evidence, the main differences from the personal injury protocol are:

- It is acknowledged that expert opinions will usually be needed pre-action on knowledge, fault and causation, on condition and prognosis, and to value aspects of the claim and that the parties should adopt a flexible approach to obtaining these.

- Claimants are permitted to obtain their occupational health records, GP records and a medical report *before* sending a letter of claim (but none of these are requirements).

- If the claimant has obtained a medical report the defendant becomes entitled to seek their own – it is acknowledged that the defendant will need to see a medical report before they can reach a view on causation.

- Where the parties agree that a single expert in a particular discipline is appropriate, the protocol adopts the procedure for nomination and instruction in the personal injury protocol (see above).

- The cost of a report from an agreed expert will usually be paid by the instructing party, the cost of the expert replying to questions will usually be borne by the party which has asked the questions.

It is too early for there to be any feedback through the courts as to the working of this protocol in practice, but as solicitors on both sides of these types of claims are usually specialists, and drafts of the protocol were in circulation for some years before it was officially adopted, there should be few problems.

Pre-action protocol for housing disrepair cases

(See paragraphs 3.2, 3.5.1b), 3.5.2b)(ii) and 3.6 and Annex C for specimen letters of instruction)

Housing disputes were another type of claim to which Lord Woolf devoted particular attention in *Access to Justice* in 1996 (Chapter 16). On disrepair claims he reported that tenants had told him that taking proceedings was often the only way to get repairs done; while the landlords said that litigation was a form of "queue-jumping" when resources for repairs were limited. The landlords also expressed concern that experts instructed by tenants included in their reports every item of disrepair they could find, not just the items that had prompted the claim or that were very serious. Lord Woolf concluded that it was not realistic for a surveyor to ignore disrepair, which would need to be dealt with in due course. He said:

"I believe that unnecessary litigation might be avoided, and repairs carried out more speedily, if landlord and tenants' representatives could agree a pre-action protocol which sets out a clear procedure to be followed by both sides, and which would be enforceable by the courts in the event of a breach."

This protocol, which eventually came into force on 8th December 2003, took so long to be implemented because the social landlords and the tenant lawyers had great difficulties in reaching a consensus. The protocol applies to claims arising from the condition of residential premises only (not to disrepair raised as a defence and counterclaim to possession proceedings). The protocol reminds tenants to consider other options before using the protocol, including complaints to the Local Government or Independent Housing Ombudsmen.

Expert evidence, in the form of a report from a surveyor and/or environmental health officer, is often crucial to these claims – the report needs to cover the condition of the premises, the disrepair which the landlord ought reasonably to know about, the cause of some items of disrepair, e.g. dampness, the repairs necessary, and their likely costs (in a schedule of works with estimates of costs).

As the value of the claims is usually within the fast track band, the proportionality of expert evidence is often an issue.

The provisions of the protocol with regard to expert evidence are much more detailed than in the other protocols. The main features are:

- The tenant is reminded that expert evidence may not always be necessary, e.g. if the issue relates to the level of damages claimed – tenants are encouraged to take photographs (of defects) before and after any work.

- The tenant should notify the landlord as early as possible that a claim for disrepair is being considered – this letter should propose instruction of an expert (where necessary only), for which there are specimen letters at Annex C, and should request disclosure of the tenancy and repair files for the property.

- In urgent situations, e.g. where the tenant considers there is significant risk to health and safety, the tenant may instruct their own expert at an early stage.

- A full letter of claim should be sent as soon as possible after the early notification letter and should detail the defects in a schedule, their history and the effect on the tenant as well as any special damages claimed.

- Within 20 working days of either letter, the landlord should reply in detail, send the requested relevant documents, and respond to the tenant's proposals with regard to expert evidence, including whether the appointment of a single joint expert and letter of instruction are agreed and if not, why not, and whether the landlord agrees to a joint inspection. Matters to be agreed in the terms of appointment of an expert are itemised in detail (and include charges, and time for delivery of the report and for payment).

- Where possible, experts should be single joint (with the cost shared) and the expert should inspect the property within 20 days. The landlord has 20 working days from receipt of the expert's report to respond. Each party can ask questions of the expert.

- If the landlord does not agree to a single joint expert, the tenant is entitled to instruct their own expert and the court will decide whether either party acted reasonably if proceedings are issued.

131

- Where there is a personal injury element to the claim, the pre-action protocol for personal injury claims should be followed for the personal injury element unless it is sufficiently minor for a GP letter to suffice for the medical evidence. Where the disrepair is urgent, the guidance to the housing protocol suggests that it would be reasonable initially to pursue the disrepair and personal injury claims separately, but that they could later be consolidated and case managed together.

- Where the claim is settled without litigation, the landlord should pay the tenant's costs and out-of-pocket expenses, such as those incurred in small claims track cases, e.g. loss of earnings and experts' fees.

The main areas of practical difficulty are likely to be whether the landlord can provide files within 20 working days and respond to a letter of claim – including proposals to instruct an expert – in the same time frame. Several other protocols have longer and, perhaps, more realistic time scales. With regard to experts, in the past many of the independent surveyors and environmental health officers who specialise in this work were instructed by the tenants. This may lead to similar problems of agreement over the identity of a single expert as has been experienced in personal injury disputes. The final point in the list above seems to be very sensible.

Some guidance on the courts' attitudes to instruction of experts in housing disrepair claims was given in *Field v Leeds City Council* (*The Times*, 18th January 2000). The Court of Appeal said that a disrepair investigator employed by a local authority is not necessarily disqualified by way of his employment from acting as an expert witness for the landlord, provided that the landlord could satisfy the court that the proposed expert understood that his primary duty was to the court, but that in most housing disrepair cases it is preferable for the parties to seek to instruct an independent single joint expert (see also Chapter 2 for a further discussion of this case in the context of experts' duties to the court).

The pre-action research (see above) found that landlord local authorities, in particular, preferred to use their in-house surveyors, as this provided them with an expert they could trust and, they claimed, enabled them to exert greater control over the resolution of the claim and the scheduling of the work to be carried out. It also saved money. Some tenant lawyers agreed, because the in-house surveyors could lean on contractors to make sure the work was done. The researchers suggested this practice by social landlords might continue even if (the then draft) protocol required or encouraged the instruction of single joint experts. If so, there would be few costs savings and the tenant could be disadvantaged, as he would be less likely to have the funding to instruct a second expert to negotiate. The research also suggested that the tenant sending an expert report with the letter of claim helped the landlords to focus more quickly on what repairs were necessary and helped to organise them.

OTHER ASSISTANCE FROM EXPERTS PRE-ACTION

Generally, pre-proceedings, experts will be providing advice and/or a report to the instructing party. The solicitor may not contact them again until proceedings are under way, and permission is obtained from the court to rely upon a written report.

Experts can also be a useful resource pre-action in:

a) advising upon investigations which might be carried out to establish liability, or assist with quantum;

b) advising upon documents which the other party might have, of which disclosure might be sought pre-action, or during the litigation;

c) helping to formulate allegations of breach of contract or negligence for letters of claim or statements of case, or to respond to it.

It is important to bear in mind, however, that if you intend to instruct the same expert for the proceedings, you must respect their duty to the court and be careful not to compromise this by treating the expert too much as 'part of the team' (see Chapter 3).

PREDICTABLE COSTS

In October 2003, the long trailed scheme for fixed recoverable costs in road traffic accident claims, first proposed in 1996 by Lord Woolf in his *Access to Justice* report, came into force. The idea was shelved while the CPR and conditional fees were implemented. It was not until late 2001 that the Civil Justice Council put up its 'Big Tent' to try to resolve the personal injury 'costs war' that had broken out around the payment of success fees and insurance premiums in conditional fee cases. Research on base costs, modelling of options, negotiations between key stakeholders and mediation eventually produced an agreed package, now a new section II in CPR Part 45.

The scheme provides for fixed costs to be recoverable in disputes which are settled prior to proceedings being issued, in respect of road traffic accidents occurring on or after 6th October 2003, where the total agreed value of the damages are outside the small claims limit and do not exceed £10,000. The fixed costs recoverable (before VAT) are calculated by adding:

- £800;

- 20% of the agreed damages up to £5,000; and

- 15% of the agreed damages between £5,000 and £10,000.

To be paid in addition are:

- London weighting of 12.5%;

- A success fee of 12.5% (on base costs before London weighting) in conditional fee agreement cases;

- Disbursements, as specified in the rules, can also be claimed, including fees for expert reports (a medical report and possibly an engineer's report). At the time of writing, May 2005, there are no specified levels of fees but the Civil Justice Council has begun work on this (see below).

The court will consider a claim for more than the fixed costs, but if the assessed costs are less than 20% more than the fixed costs, the claimant will pay both sides' costs of the Part 8 proceedings.

This is a pilot project which is to be reviewed in 2 years' time. The scheme aims to be 'cost neutral' with swings and roundabouts in comparison with actual costs incurred balancing each other out; in any event, claimant solicitors should gain from quicker payments and improved cash flow. The groundwork has already started to extend the scheme to cover costs up to trial and to other types of personal injury and, possibly, other claims.

The next stage is to try to agree fees for experts. In 2004, the Civil Justice Council began to investigate whether predictable or guideline fees for experts' reports, particularly medico-legal reports, in low value personal injury claims, would be feasible. At the time of writing (May 2005), discussions were in progress with lawyers, experts and judges (see also Chapter 6).

CONCLUSIONS

When deciding whether to instruct an expert at an early stage of a dispute, the solicitor and client need to carefully consider the purpose of the expert's advice, whether the same expert may be retained if proceedings are issued, whether the court is likely to give permission for an expert report on that issue, and whether the costs of the advice are likely to be proportionate and will be recoverable. The Pre-action Practice Direction and any applicable protocol should be followed (it seems unlikely there will be many more protocols).

Shortly, there may be statutory guidelines for experts' fees in personal injury cases that settle pre-action.

As disputes between the parties about expert evidence are not uncommon pre-action, it might be helpful if the courts were given the power to hear pre-action applications, as they can in relation to documents under CPR 31.16.

Chapter 8

EXPERTS' REPORTS

INTRODUCTION

The expert's report is often the expert's only contribution to the resolution or determination of a civil dispute. Fewer claims go to trial than pre-CPR and, in those that do, experts (especially single joint experts), are not often called to give oral evidence.

It is therefore important that reports are well crafted and drafted, and comply with CPR Part 35 and any court directions in the case.

Lord Woolf, in his *Access to Justice* report in 1996 (Chapter 13), suggested there was a need to improve the quality of experts' reports. He highlighted the problems as:

● Partisan reports.

● The inclusion of irrelevant material.

● A tendency to stray beyond the expert's field of professional competence.

● Failure to address the real issues.

His solutions to these problems included:

● Court control of experts (see Chapters 1 and 2).

● Training and possibly accreditation of experts (see Chapter 1).

● Improvement in the quality of experts' instructions (see Chapter 5).

While the first has been implemented and some progress has been made with the other two, experts remain critical of many solicitors' instructions (see Chapter 14).

THE PURPOSE OF EXPERTS' REPORTS

A report is written by an expert to help the parties in the preparation and settlement of the case and/or to help the court to decide it. The report is for people who are not experts in the specialist field. The report, whether for the solicitor, client or the court, must address the issues in the case on which the expert has been instructed and contain the facts which the expert has relied upon to reach his or her opinion. It should be a reasoned analysis of the evidence based upon his knowledge, skill and experience in his specialist field.

The expert may be:

a) drafting a preliminary advisory report, i.e. a report to be used by the client and solicitor to decide if the case is worth pursuing, or defending;

b) preparing a report pre-action to assist the parties in valuing or settling the case, or to draft the formal court documents (statements of case). (This type of report, perhaps updated, may be disclosed to the other party and the court at a later stage);

c) writing a report that is to be disclosed to both parties during the proceedings and which may be used to settle the case or at trial.

A preliminary advisory report will usually be privileged from disclosure (see also Chapters 3, 5 and 7) but the expert may not be immune from a claim for damages if he can be shown to have been negligent in its preparation (see also Chapter 13). Where an expert provides advice to a party, and the same expert is then retained to provide a report for the court, it is probably prudent for the expert to set out the position in the report, in case of later queries with regard to his independence. However, this could prompt the other party to ask for the disclosure of the original instructions; it is far from clear whether these remain privileged.

In a report for disclosure to the other party and to the court, the expert has a particular duty to remain independent and to express an objective opinion, but only on issues that are within his expertise and which are part of the dispute before the court. Courts want expert witnesses to cover the strengths and weaknesses of a party's (or both parties') case, and to provide honest unbiased opinions based upon a full appraisal of all the facts and issues relevant to their evidence; not just a partial view based upon what one party wants the court to hear.

If, when drafting the report, the expert feels strongly that a particular matter is essential to his opinion, it is the expert's duty to include this in the report or to withdraw from acting in the litigation. Expert witnesses should include *all* of their relevant opinions in their report for the court. It is not acceptable to set out different views in a separate letter to the client/lawyer (previously referred to as a side letter); at least not once litigation is under way (see below).

THE CPR REQUIREMENTS

General CPR requirement for a report to be in writing (CPR 35.5)

The court requires experts to prepare a written report for use in evidence by one or more parties, and to assist the court in deciding the dispute unless it directs otherwise (**CPR 35.5**). In cases allocated to the small claims or fast tracks, and whenever a single joint expert is instructed, expert evidence by written report alone is the norm and oral evidence from the expert is exceptional.

CPR 35.10 and particularly the Practice Direction set out the detailed requirements for experts' reports. CPR 35.10 provides:

"(2)   At the end of an expert's report there must be a statement that:

a) the expert understands his duty to the court; and

b) he has complied with that duty.

(3)   The expert's report must state the substance of all material instructions, whether written and oral, on the basis of which the report was written.

(4)   The instructions shall not be privileged against disclosure but the court will not, in relation to those instructions –

a) order disclosure of any specific document; or

b) permit any questioning in court other than by the party who instructed the expert, unless it is satisfied that there are reasonable grounds to consider the statement of instructions to be inaccurate or misleading."

The Practice Direction

In one of the leading pre-CPR cases on experts' reports, *National Justice Compania Naviera SA v Prudential Assurance Co Ltd (Ikarian*

Reefer) [1993] 2 Lloyd's Rep 68, Cresswell LJ gave the following general guidance on the contents of experts' reports. In 2003, this was summarised and included in the Part 35 Practice Direction (as a new first paragraph). It states:

- The expert's paramount duty is to the court and this overrides any obligation to the person from whom the expert has received instructions.

- The report should be the independent product of the expert, uninfluenced by the pressures of litigation.

- An expert should assist the court by providing objective and unbiased opinion on matters within his expertise, and should not assume the role of the advocate.

- An expert should consider all material facts, including those which might detract from his opinion.

- An expert should make it clear when an issue falls outside his expertise and when he is not able to reach a definite opinion.

- If an expert changes his view on any material matter after producing his report, he should communicate this to the parties and the court without delay.

The form and content of an expert's court report is also dealt with in the Practice Direction in some detail:

"2.1   An expert's report should be addressed to the court and not to the party from whom the expert has received his instructions.

2.2   An expert's report must:

(1) give details of the expert's qualifications;

(2) give details of any literature or other material which the expert has relied on in making the report;

(3) contain a statement setting out the substance of all facts and instructions given to the expert which are material to the opinions expressed in the report or upon which those opinions are based;

(4) make clear which of the facts stated in the report are within the expert's own knowledge;

(5) say who carried out any examination, measurement, test or experiment which the expert has used for the report, give the qualifications of that person, and say whether or not the test or experiment has been carried out under the expert's supervision;

(6) where there is a range of opinion on the matters dealt within the report –

b) summarise the range of opinion; and

c) give reasons for his own opinion;

(7) contain a summary of the conclusions reached;

(8) if the expert is not able to give his opinion without qualification, state the qualification; and

(9) contain a statement that the expert understands his duty to the court, and has complied and will continue to comply with that duty.

2.3 An expert's report must be verified by a statement of truth as well as containing the statements required in paragraph 2.2(8) and (9) above."

The Protocol for the Instruction of Experts

The Protocol, published in 2005 (see Chapter 2 and Appendix 2), expands upon Part 35 and the Practice Direction in section 13.

The statement of truth (CPR 35.10(2) and PD 35 2.2(9))

Experts demonstrate their understanding of their duty to the court by providing a statement of truth at the end of their reports. This must comply with the CPR.

Final reports must also be signed and dated by the author.

CPR 35.10(2) the experts' statement of truth was revised in March 2002. The old version was:

"I understand that my duty is to the court in preparing this report and giving oral evidence. I believe that the facts stated in this report are true and the opinions are correct."

The new version is:

"I confirm that insofar as the facts stated in my report are within my own knowledge I have made clear which they are and I believe them to be true and that the opinions expressed represent my true and complete professional opinion."

The new version is probably better and is certainly more precise; how could an experts' opinions be "correct"? Check your expert's report to ensure he has used the up-to-date wording. If he has not, it might indicate a more general lack of familiarity with the CPR.

The expert witness organisations have prepared model declarations that include the statement of truth (see the EWI one on their website). The main advantage of an expert including one of these is that it suggests to you, the client, the other party and the court that the expert takes his expert witness work seriously.

Three of the suggested items in the EWI declaration are particularly recommended:

"(viii) At the time of signing the report I consider it to be complete and accurate. I will notify those instructing me if, for any reason, I subsequently consider that the report requires any correction or qualification.

(ix)   I understand that this report will be the evidence that I will give under oath, subject to any correction or qualification I may make before swearing to its veracity.

(x)   I have attached to this report a summary of my instructions."

The consequences of a false statement of truth are serious (see Practice Direction 35 paragraph 2.5 and CPR 32.14 and Chapter 13). A witness, including an expert, may be prosecuted, with the consent of the Attorney General, for contempt of court, the penalties for which include imprisonment. Fortunately, this is a rare occurrence in civil litigation.

Summarising instructions (CPR 35.10)

The requirement in CPR 35.10 for the expert to summarise his instructions in his report was discussed in Chapter 5. It is important that this is done carefully, or the solicitor's letter appended to the report, to avoid the risk of the court ordering the disclosure of the actual instructions, including documents sent with them, although the decision of the Court of Appeal in *Lucas v Barking NHS Trust* (see Chapter 5) somewhat reduces the risk of this.

The author has been told that some solicitors object to experts appending their letter of instruction to the report without permission. This is unwise; solicitors should ensure that the letter of instruction to an expert is self-contained and does not include any statement or comment that would embarrass the solicitor or the client if the other party or the court saw it.

The range of opinion (PD 35 paragraph 2.2(6))

Experts should provide the range of opinion within the profession or expert discipline on a particular issue in dispute, to enable the judge to understand the full spectrum of professional views and not just the opinion of one or two experts. Judges do not want 'opposing' experts to adopt extreme positions on paper, each at opposite ends of a spectrum, and then agree under cross-examination that the most likely position is between the two extremes. The range of opinion is particularly important in a single joint expert report and in a professional negligence dispute.

Reference materials and literature (PD 35.2.2(2))

The Practice Direction requires an expert to give details of any literature or other material on which he has relied for his report. The reason is to enable other experts (and sometimes the lawyers) to read the same material and consider its relevance, if necessary raising written questions on it, or placing it on the agenda for the experts' discussion.

Wardlaw v Farrar ([2003] EWCA Civ 1719) decided that in clinical negligence claims being conducted in the County Courts or District Registries, the judges should adopt the standard direction of the Queen's Bench Masters that any material or literature upon which an expert wishes to rely must be served, either with his report or at the latest one month before trial. Copies of unpublished literature and lists of published literature should be served. Permission is needed from the trial judge before an expert witness can introduce additional material at trial. This decision should be of general application – not just in clinical negligence cases. Indeed, in *DN v Greenwich London Borough* [2004] EWCA Civ 1659, the Court of Appeal specifically suggested that the QB Masters' standard directions on clinical negligence cases should be adapted for education negligence cases.

Breeze v Ahmad [2005] EWCA CW 223 also emphasised that any literature relied upon by one party's expert should be reviewed by the other party's expert and be available for the trial judge.

Experts staying within their expertise

The dangers of experts not staying within their expertise are obvious (see also Chapters 2 and 13).

In particular, if the expert is not providing an opinion on liability, he should avoid describing the events in any detail, especially in a way that suggests his description is 'fact' if aspects of liability are disputed.

In *Pride Valley Foods Ltd v Hall and Partners* [2000] EWHC Technology 106, the trial judge (Toulmin J) was critical of an architect expert in a construction claim whose report was excessively long (200 pages), made findings of fact which were matters for the judge, stated in several places what he would have done in the circumstance in question, and gave opinions on issues of project management which were outside his expertise. The judge said that his report offended "against the established basis on which experts should give evidence" and provided "little or no assistance to the court".

In *SPE International v Professional Preparation Contractors (UK) Ltd* [2002] WL 499022, the trial judge ruled as inadmissible a report from an 'expert' on the calculation of losses in a very technical dispute in the shot-blasting industry, which he had prepared without any written instructions (he knew nothing of Part 35), and which was outside his expertise; he was an ex-RAF officer and a management consultant to the claimant. In fact, his wife had carried out most of the work for the report.

Experts providing liability reports in professional negligence claims should avoid commenting specifically on the 'ultimate issue', i.e. whether the professional in question has been negligent, as that is a matter for the judge (see Chapter 1).

EXPERTS' FAILURE TO COMPLY WITH THE RULES ON REPORTS

Courts are unimpressed with experts who do not appear to be familiar with the rules. In the case of *Stevens v Gullis* [2000] 1 AER 527, an unqualified architectural designer expert prepared his report late, did not include a summary of his instructions, failed to date the report or add a statement of truth, did not relate it to the pleadings or refer to any of the exchanged witness statements, failed to comply with a court order requiring him to rectify the deficiencies of his report, and failed to sign a statement following an experts' discussion. One month before trial, the court (upheld by the Court of Appeal) made an order barring the expert from giving evidence on the ground that he did not understand his duty to the court. The judge said:

"It is essential in a complicated case such as this that the court should have a competent expert dealing with the matters which are in issue between the defendant and third party. Mr Isaac, not having apparently understood his duty to the court and not having set out in his report that he understands it, is in my view a person whose evidence I should not encourage in the administration of justice."

STYLE AND PRESENTATION OF REPORTS

Model report formats

Expert witness organisations and expert witness divisions of some professional bodies have produced model forms of report to assist experts and solicitors. You may wish to send one of the model forms to a new expert or to an expert whose reports could be improved; see those on the websites of the Expert Witness Institute and the Academy of Experts. The UK Register of Experts has published a helpful factsheet on the requirements of reports (www.jspubs.com).

An expert may be very proficient in his field and have carefully analysed the facts of a case, but the impact of his evidence will be greatly weakened if his report is set out poorly. Badly organised reports irritate lawyers and judges; you can take steps to reduce the likelihood of this. Send your expert a copy of CPR 35 and the Practice Direction and perhaps a model report format (see above) when you instruct him, or prepare your own note for experts adapted to your firm's work. There are also report writing courses available for experts from Bond Solon Training amongst others.

Suggestions on presentation

There are no hard rules on the style to be adopted in reports. The following are some suggestions on presentational matters:

1. **Clear headings and sub-headings** are useful for signposting, e.g. in the summary of the facts, the opinion and conclusion.

2. Include a **contents page** also, with reference to page numbers and/or paragraph numbers.

3. **Page numbers** and **paragraph numbers** are required, especially for longer reports.

4. **Short sentences and paragraphs** improve readability.

5. **Headers** on each page are helpful to identify the expert by name and the date of the report.

6. A **front sheet** can provide the essential details – see below.

7. A **synopsis** might be included to help the reader to understand what the case is about, especially if the report is long – 20 or more pages.

8. The report should **differentiate between 'facts'** that are in the expert's own knowledge, and those that he has obtained 'second-hand'.

9. There must be a **clear conclusion**.

10. A **chronology** can help the reader, particularly in complex cases.

11. Reports should be written in the first person, be **signed** by the expert personally, contain the necessary declarations and statements of truth (see above) and be **dated** the day the expert sent the report out.

12. The report should be make clear if **anyone else has carried out tests** or worked on parts of the report.

13. A **glossary** of technical terms might be placed in the appendix if

there are many such terms, or the terms should be explained in the body of the report if they are relatively few.

14. **Graphics**, photographs, diagrams or models will help the solicitor; the client and the judge understand the case.

15. Reports should be printed on A4 good quality **paper,** with good size **margins** around the edges to leave room for the reader to make notes. Double spacing is easier to read than single.

The contents of reports

Reports should be clearly and logically structured, with the structure well signposted, and fact and opinion kept separate. If there are detailed calculations or investigations, they might be included in an appendix to avoid the detail obscuring the key points. The length of a report may vary depending on the circumstances and proportionality, but judges have been known to criticise excessive length.

The front page/the cover sheet

This is essential for identification purposes and should include:

● The status of the report (draft or final version) and to whom it is addressed (the court if proceedings have been issued).

● The court in which the case is being conducted, the case title and case number.

● The parties, and by whom the expert is instructed.

● The instructing party's solicitor's details.

● The expert's full name and details (professional address, telephone number, fax number and e-mail addres).

● The date on which he signed the report.

The main part of the report
1. The introduction

This section might include:

The expert's qualifications (PD 35.2(1))
This should not give too much detail but relate the author's

expertise to the case, to indicate to the court his competence to act as an expert witness in relation to the specific issues. The expert's CV might be included in an appendix.

The identity of any other person who has assisted with the preparation of the report should be given, and whether the author accepts responsibility for their work.

Summary of the case

This should give a *short* synopsis of what the case is about. For example: "This is a condition and prognosis medical report for Miss X concerning the injuries she sustained in a road traffic accident on..."

Summary of conclusions

This should set out in brief the expert's opinions and conclusions and the answers to any specific questions raised in the instructions (PD 35.2.2(7)).

2. **The issues to be addressed (CPR 35.10(3) and PD 35.2.2(3))**

The next section should set out clearly the **summary of the expert's instructions** (written and oral) and the issues or questions that the report addresses. One solution is to annex to the report the solicitor's letter(s) of instruction (see above and Chapter 5 for a fuller discussion on this subject).

The **documents** that the expert has examined and relied upon should be listed, and the details of other sources of evidence given. If there is a long list, it could be provided in an appendix.

3. **The investigation of the facts**

The next section should address the facts. In a complicated case, a chronology can be helpful and can be placed in an appendix.

Experts should identify separately:

a) 'facts' he has observed for himself, e.g. from examining the claimant or the site;

b) 'facts' that are versions of events that he was told by the client or by others, identifying the source;

147

c) 'facts' that he has been asked to assume are correct, again identifying the instruction.

The expert must include all material facts including those which might detract from his opinion (PD 35 1.4). In *Royal & Sun Alliance Trust Co Ltd v Healey and Baker*, Lawtel, 19th October 2000, a claim in negligence against a surveyor, the judge was very critical of a surveyor expert who was "extremely selective" in the material he highlighted in his report to justify his thesis that the rents in the area were falling. His evidence was disregarded.

In a report that deals with very technical issues, it can be helpful for the expert to summarise the technical background. All technical terms should be explained (and, if necessary, cross-referenced to a glossary in an appendix).

It may also be necessary in this section for the expert to refer to the opinions of others, including other experts, which the expert considered in forming his opinion.

Examinations

A description of any examinations and tests, as well as the dates they were carried out and by whom, should be given next. The detail may be put into an appendix.

Research and references (PD 35 2.2(2))

If appropriate, details of any research carried out should be given, and full references should be provided for any literature or works of reference consulted and relied upon. Copies of these papers should appear in an appendix if not too long (see above for a fuller discussion on this subject).

4. **The opinion and conclusions**

In this section, the expert should present his opinion clearly and unambiguously. It is the most important part of the report. The way this is done will vary with the type of report and specialism. The expert should set out each of the issues, then link these issues to the facts and give reasoned argument derived from, and cross-referenced to, the evidence.

If there is a range of professional opinion on an issue, this should be set out (PD 35 2.2(6)) and the expert should explain where his opinion lies within the spectrum, with reasons (see above).

The expert should qualify his opinion if he could not reach a clear conclusion because of insufficient information.

If the expert has seen the report of another expert from the same specialism instructed by the other party, he might comment upon that opinion and the basis for it.

Experts should not:

a) comment on matters outside their instructions, unless they feel very strongly that this is essential to the case;

b) comment on matters outside their expertise, unless expressly asked to do so by the court, and then they should add appropriate caveats and 'health warnings' (see below);

c) try to do the judge's job. In a negligence dispute, the judge decides if someone has been negligent, not the expert. The expert should only say whether, in his opinion, the professional's conduct fell below the standard of a reasonable expert in the field.

Visual material

In the author's view many experts make too little use of plans, photographs and drawings, which can often explain technical matters more easily than words. Originals may need to be inspected for authenticating purposes. Models, videos, CDs and computer simulations can be very helpful too.

Appendices

These might include:

● The expert's experience and qualifications set out in date order (attaching a marketing brochure is not the way to do this).

● The letter(s) of instruction from the solicitors.

● The list of documents examined.

● Results of investigations and tests or calculations.

● A list of reference material referred to and possibly copies of that material.

- A chronology of events.
- A glossary of technical terms in alphabetical order.

Single joint experts' reports

(See also Chapter 9)

A single joint expert's report should not be any different in principle or content to that of a 'party' expert. If the expert received two sets of instructions, they must both be summarised (and possibly annexed), and the report must address both versions of events and issues raised by both parties. It is particularly important for single joint expert reports to keep agreed facts, disputed facts, assumptions and opinion clearly separate, and to give the range of professional opinion on an issue (when that is appropriate).

An SJE should send his report, both draft and final, to both parties at the same time with the same covering letter.

Lead expert's reports (CPR 35 PD paragraph 6)

(See also Chapter 3)

A lead expert co-ordinates the work of other experts and prepares a comprehensive covering report. He must be careful not to edit the other experts' reports more than is strictly necessary, as each individual expert must still take responsibility for his report, and each one must contain a statement of truth. The lead expert's input to the combined report should be to link the other experts' work together and, if practicable, to give an overall opinion.

ON RECEIPT OF AN EXPERT'S REPORT

Key points to check

- Are the client's name and address, etc. correct? Clients get upset if they are not.
- Are the basic facts – dates, places, times and locations – correct? Errors here can mislead and look unprofessional.
- Are the instructions completely and accurately summarised?

- Has the expert listed all the material he has relied upon? Is any of it privileged? Has he attached copies to the report?

- Has the expert commented upon all the specific questions and issues relevant to his expertise? Has he avoided commenting on facts and issues outside his expertise and on the 'ultimate issue'?

- Are the conclusions and statements of opinion clearly set out and based upon supporting evidence?

- Does the expert rely upon very new or untested scientific or technical theories? Is this risky?

- Is the report consistent with other evidence, such as witness statements, documents and the other experts' reports? If not, why not?

- Is the report dated and signed?

- Are there issues raised that the other party is likely to challenge and can answers be supplied in the report now?

Above all, consider how the report affects the strength of the case and, if necessary, discuss this with the expert before the report is finalised for disclosure.

Explaining the report to the client

Each expert's report must be sent to the client soon after receipt, and the conclusions and implications for the case discussed with the client. Some clients will not readily understand when an expert's report does not completely or largely support their case, or when the expert prefers the other party's version of events or states an opinion which appears to be critical of the client. Clients may be upset if an expert raises a new issue. The client must be reminded of the expert's independence and duty to the court, and that it is preferable that the expert's reservations are known at this stage rather than later.

It may also have to be explained to the client why it may not be possible to abandon that expert and instruct another, and why the expert must be paid, despite his seemingly 'unhelpful' report.

Consider also whether:

1. The report suggests amendments that may be necessary to the statement of case.

2. A conference with the advocate, or advice on evidence, is necessary.

3. The report should be sent (as a draft?) to other experts before it is disclosed to the other party.

4. To make or revise a Part 36 offer based on the report.

Remember that the client's instructions are needed before the report is disclosed to the other party or it is filed at court.

DRAFT REPORTS, 'SIDE' LETTERS AND REQUESTING CHANGES TO REPORTS

There is no reason why an expert should not be invited to prepare a report in draft, to enable the instructing solicitor and client to check the report for compliance with instructions, the CPR and any court directions, for factual accuracy, consistency and completeness, and for clarity of presentation. Single joint experts may, on occasions, send both parties a 'draft' and invite comments on matters of fact, before finalising the report and filing it at court.

However, an expert must not be asked to set out his comments on, for example, the weaknesses of the case in a separate 'side' letter (a common practice pre-CPR), as this would be in conflict with the expert's duty to provide his complete and true opinion to the court.

It is perfectly acceptable under the CPR to ask for amendments to an expert's report before disclosure, if:

1. The facts are not accurate.

2. New facts or evidence have come to light since the instructions were sent to the expert.

3. The report does not comply with the CPR formalities, the expert has commented on issues outside his expertise, or has commented too definitively on matters which are for the judge to decide.

4. The expert has not annexed relevant material.

5. The report could be presented in a clearer way.

Solicitors and clients must not, however, ask an expert to amend his report in a way which distorts his true opinion on key issues in the report. This would be a breach of the *Solicitors' Code of Conduct* – see principle 21.10 of the *Guide to Professional Conduct*, 5th edition, 1999. There is a 'grey area' about suggesting to an expert that particular statements in his report might be omitted or rephrased when, perhaps, they do not show the client or the case in the best light, but are not crucial to the evidence or the expert's opinion. The report is the expert's, and he must be the one to decide on its contents: he is entitled to reject suggested amendments if he considers that they materially alter what he wants to say.

In *Robin Ellis v Malwright* [1999] BLR 81, it was made clear that it is not for parties to tell experts what opinions they might hold, and that any interference with the statement of an expert's opinion in a report could lead the court to refuse to allow the expert to give evidence at trial.

In *Carpenter v Pembrokeshire County Council* [2002] EWHC 1968, the dispute concerned negligent construction of a driveway. The claimant's expert was severely criticised by the trial judge because he:

a) allowed himself to be pressurised by the claimant to say that he was concerned about the safety of the driveway, after agreeing with the defendant's expert at an experts' discussion that this was not an issue;

b) argued points of law in the witness box and was an advocate in the claimant's cause.

The judge said he had "abandoned his role as an expert".

Copies of all drafts must be kept on the file in case of queries, together with the letters or attendance notes that explain the reasons for any changes. A court would only very rarely order disclosure of draft versions of expert reports, possibly when the expert's summary of his instructions under CPR 35.10(3) was inaccurate or incomplete (see *Lucas v Barking NHS Trust*, discussed in Chapter 5).

In *Jackson v Marley Davenport Ltd* [2004] EWCA Civ 1225, an expert instructed in a personal injury claim referred in his disclosed report to "having now gained additional information in relation to this case". This caused the other party to want to examine the additional information and to establish what the expert's view was before he received it. The

Court of Appeal held that there was no doubt that, where an expert made a report for legal advisers or for the purposes of a conference, such a report was subject to litigation privilege at the time it was made, and that references to the disclosure of experts' reports in CPR 35.10(2) had to mean references to the actual expert's evidence and not to earlier draft reports. No order for disclosure was made.

Can draft expert reports be relied upon in 'without prejudice' discussions?

UYB v British Railways Board [2000] 1 WL 1629557 CA decided they could not. A draft accountant's report was disclosed in a breach of contract claim for 'without prejudice' settlement discussions, which failed. A final version of the report was disclosed sometime later. The claimant wanted to rely on that disclosure two years after the trial, at a costs hearing when the date of first disclosure was relevant. The Court of Appeal dismissed the application; draft experts' reports disclosed for settlement purposes are not final reports, and so are inadmissible for resolving issues at a costs hearing.

Disclosing the report to the other parties and filing at court

The usual times for disclosing an expert's report are:

- Pre-action, in compliance with a pre-action protocol.

- With the particulars of claim, e.g. a personal injury medical condition and prognosis report.

- In accordance with the court directions. These will often provide for simultaneous exchange of reports, but sometimes one party (often the claimant) will be ordered to disclose their reports first, leaving the second party to decide whether they need their own reports at all, or perhaps whether they only need a report that comments on the disclosed one.

It is vital to check experts' reports carefully prior to disclosure (see above), especially if there are a number of versions on the file. In *Gough v Mummery* [2002] EWCA Civ 1573, one version of the claimant's psychiatric expert's report, in a personal injury case, was filed in the court bundle, and a second version was sent with counsel's brief. One was signed and the other was not. They were both dated the same day. The signed version in the trial bundle attributed the claimant's mental and behavioural problems to drug and alcohol abuse, while the unsigned one in counsel's papers attributed the problems to the accident as well. The confusion only became apparent at trial. The judge refused to adjourn to enable checks to be made, and ordered that the signed version of the report should be relied upon, although this was obviously less favourable to the claimant. The Court of Appeal agreed.

Do inform the expert when his report has been disclosed. This is only courteous; the expert needs to know when the 28-day period for asking written questions under CPR 35.6 commences.

CPR 35.11 AND CPR 35.13

These two rules complement one another. **CPR 35.11** provides that, where a party has disclosed an expert's report, any party may use that expert's report as evidence at the trial. This is based on the principle that 'there is no property in a witness', including an expert witness.

CPR 35.13 provides that a party that fails to disclose an expert's report may not use the report at the trial or call the expert to give oral evidence, unless the court gives permission. This seems to assume that the party in question has been given permission to rely upon a particular expert's report and has neglected to disclose it on time. It was not an infrequent practice, pre-CPR, for parties, particularly defendants, to produce late experts' reports, even during the trial – part of the 'litigation by ambush' approach that the reforms sought to prevent.

Do not wait to disclose a report without good reason. In *Baron v Lovell* [2000] PIQR p20, the defendant failed to disclose a medical report in a personal injury claim for five months, disclosing it only at the pre-trial review. The case management judge and the Court of Appeal refused permission for the defendant to rely on the report. The Court of Appeal found that it was definitely not "in the spirit of Woolf to delay disclosing deliberately as she (one of the defendant's solicitors) intended, until the day a Part 36 Payment was made".

In *Kapadia v Lambeth London Borough Council* [2000] AER D 785, the claimant and the defendant's expert agreed not to disclose the expert's report in a personal injury claim. The court ordered its disclosure (see also Chapter 7).

UPDATING AND SUPPLEMENTARY REPORTS

In some cases, an expert will need to update his report before trial to include evidence disclosed since the report was prepared, and in other situations a second supplementary report may have to be prepared, e.g. on the re-examination of a claimant in a personal injury case, whose prognosis was uncertain at the time of the first report.

Each 'new' report must be dated and signed, and its place in the sequence should be recorded on the front sheet.

LATE REPORTS

It is important for experts' reports to be disclosed in accordance with the court directions. To ensure experts appreciate this, a copy of the directions should be sent with the instructions (the Part 35 Practice Direction now requires this), and a definite date for delivery of the report set, e.g. a month before the disclosure date.

If a report is, nonetheless, 'late', try to reach an agreement with the other party to a slightly later date for exchange or disclosure, or failing agreement, apply to the court. Occasionally the court may decide that a report is so late it cannot be relied upon (see *Baron v Lovell* above), but usually only after making an 'unless' order first. If your late service is challenged retrospectively, you (and the court) will need to consider all the factors listed in CPR 3.9 (relief from sanctions). Before making challenges on the other party's late service, check whether you have complied with all the court directions and have not acted unreasonably in relation to the expert evidence.

In *Meredith v Colleys Valuation Services Ltd* [2001] EWCA Civ 1456, a professional negligence claim arising out of a building survey, the Court of Appeal decided that the judge was wrong to debar the second defendant from relying upon expert valuation evidence served two weeks late, given that the delay was short, there was no 'unless' order, and that the claimant had the report by the time of the hearing in any event. The court said that a costs penalty was a more proportionate sanction.

In *RC Residuals v Linton Fuel Oils Ltd* [2002] EWCA Civ 911, both parties were late serving their expert evidence, and the trial was adjourned. The claimant served expert reports respectively 10 and 20 minutes beyond the time specified in an 'unless' order. The judge struck out the evidence, but the Court of Appeal allowed it, as the defendant had refused service of the reports by e-mail earlier in the day, and because the new trial date would not be affected by so short a delay.

CONCLUSIONS

The CPR are hardly onerous with regard to the form and content of expert reports. However, reports which do not comply, even in minor ways, or which are poorly set out and presented, appear unprofessional and do not aspire confidence in their contents. Most experts would appreciate feedback on their reports (see Chapter 14), and many need guidance on such tricky issues as summarising instructions and providing the range of opinion. The easiest way to improve the basics is to refer the expert to a model report format.

Solicitors have to be careful not to be too prescriptive, particularly when suggesting amendments: the report must remain entirely the expert's work and reflect his unbiased opinion, based on the 'facts' and his investigations.

Chapter 9
SINGLE JOINT EXPERTS (SJEs)

Lord Woolf originally recommended in his interim *Access to Justice* report of 1994 that the English courts should adopt the French system of court-appointed experts. This provoked disquiet, particularly from solicitors used to having complete control over expert evidence in their clients' litigation. Lord Woolf acknowledged this in his final report (*Access to Justice* 1996, Chapter 13, paragraph 16):

"Since the publication of the interim report, resistance to my proposals on single experts has remained particularly strong, and it is clear that the idea is anathema to many members of the legal profession in this country who are reluctant to give up their adversarial weapons."

The compromise adopted in Lord Woolf's final report, which was implemented in the CPR, is the single joint expert. Lord Woolf perceived a need to reduce the cost of expert evidence and the use of experts to bolster a party's case, but accepted that, given the strength of opposition to his initial proposals, it was not realistic to expect a shift towards single experts in the short term, or to specify particular areas of litigation where a single expert should or should not be used. He accepted that:

"In large complex and strongly contested cases, the full adversarial system, including oral cross-examination of opposing experts on particular issues, is the best way of producing a result. That will apply particularly to issues on which there are several tenable schools of thought, or where the boundaries of knowledge are being extended."

On the other hand, he said he thought single experts should be used "wherever the case is concerned with a substantially established area of knowledge and where it is not necessary for the court directly to sample a range of opinions".

In addition, he suggested that SJEs would increase the prospects of

158

settlement and could be an effective way of levelling the playing-field between parties of unequal resources.

Despite Lord Woolf's reassurances that he did not intend that the courts would invariably order SJEs against the parties' wishes, there was concern when the CPR were implemented that the courts would do just that. Commentators said that this would lead parties to appoint 'shadow experts' to advise on the single joint expert's report, which would not effect any saving in costs.

This chapter examines the rules and other guidance on SJEs, how the courts have interpreted the rules and resolved disputes, and aims to give practical advice to parties and their lawyers.

THE CPR PROVISIONS

CPR 35.7-8

CPR 35.7 provides that:

1. Where two or more parties wish to submit expert evidence on an issue the court may direct that the evidence is to be given by one expert only.

2. Where the parties cannot agree the identity of the expert the court may:

   a) select the expert from a list prepared by the parties; or

   b) direct that the expert be selected in such other manner as the court may direct.

CPR 35.8 provides that:

1. Each party may give instructions to the SJE and should copy them to the other party.

2. The court should give directions on the payment of the expert's fee and on any inspection, examination, or experiments which the expert wishes to carry out.

3. The court should limit the amount of fees that can be paid to the single joint expert and direct that the instructing party pays that amount into court.

4. Unless the court directs otherwise, the parties are jointly and severally liable for payment of the expert's fees.

The **Practice Direction** adds no flesh to these relatively bare bones. The only reference to single experts is to a leading expert; where there are a number of disciplines relevant to the issues on which the court has directed, there shall be evidence from a single expert only. He should prepare the general part of the report and be responsible for annexing or incorporating the contents of the reports from experts in other disciplines (see also Chapter 3).

OTHER GUIDANCE

The specialist court guides

The provisions of the specialist court guides on expert evidence were discussed generally in Chapter 2.

The **Queen's Bench and Chancery Guides** both state that single experts will often be appropriate to deal with questions of quantum and where the court needs expert evidence to the facts; but not where liability and causation will turn on expert opinion evidence, when it would be useful for the court to hear the opinion of more than one expert "so as to be exposed to a range of views".

The **Admiralty and Commercial Court Guide** recognises that cases in that court are frequently of a size, complexity or nature to render an SJE inappropriate.

The Pre-action Practice Direction and protocols

These were discussed in Chapter 7. To recap:

- The Pre-action Practice Direction encourages the parties to select one agreed expert when an expert is needed.

- The personal injury and housing disrepair protocols have a procedure for joint selection, but not necessarily joint instruction, of an expert (usually a medical expert in personal injury claims and a surveyor in housing disrepair cases).

- The construction and engineering protocol encourages a joint expert if the claimant has not obtained their own expert evidence before sending the letter of claim.

- None of the other protocols make any reference to single experts.

It is perhaps ambitious to expect parties, especially those not being advised by lawyers, to co-operate on selection and instruction of an expert early in a dispute, when there may be an absence of trust and when the parties are still considering their positions. Moreover, the Court of Appeal has made it quite clear in *Carlson v Townsend* (see Chapters 5 and 7) that advice obtained from an expert pre-action is privileged, thus reducing the incentive to agree to an SJE while a case is still at a formative stage. In *Paul Thomas Construction Ltd v Hyland and Power* (Lawtel, 5th December 2000), the Technology and Construction Court had no hesitation in awarding indemnity costs against a claimant (in a building fees claim for £70,000) who refused to co-operate on the instruction of a joint, or two separate, quantity surveyors, or on an adjudicator, in breach of the construction protocol, and who issued proceedings prematurely.

The expert evidence protocol

(See Chapter 2 and Appendix 2)

The Protocol advises that SJEs are the norm in cases allocated to the small claims and fast tracks. It also suggests that SJEs may be sensible in the early stages of a dispute where examinations, investigations, inspections, preparation of plans or photographs are necessary, especially where such matters are not expected to be contentious.

WHEN MIGHT THE COURT ORDER AN SJE

The objective of CPR 35.7 is to prevent the instruction of multiple experts when, given the nature or value of the dispute, this would be disproportionate in cost and might cause delay. However, the rules give no guidance on when the court is likely to direct that a single expert should give expert evidence against the parties' wishes.

In practice, the courts adopt a strong presumption in favour of SJEs in small and fast track claims. Single experts may also be ordered in larger claims:

a) when the value of the claim is less than about £50,000 and the case is a 'routine' one;

b) when technical assistance to the parties and the trial judge is required on a particular issue, but not where there is a risk that the expert would effectively become the judge of that issue;

c) to provide reports on the less controversial aspects of damages.

It can, however, be difficult for solicitors to anticipate the case management judge's directions in any particular case, as the judges exercise their discretion under CPR 35.7 in very different ways. Certainly, in the early days after the implementation of the CPR, some judges did display considerable enthusiasm for SJEs in situations perhaps not envisaged by Lord Woolf in his report. Since the implementation of the Human Rights Act 1998 in October 2000, there has been a noticeable softening of approach when:

a) technical or professional evidence will be vital or very helpful on liability or causation, or the major part of quantum in a larger case;

b) a report from an SJE could not or does not sufficiently cover the range of opinion to properly advise the trial judge;

c) additional expert evidence can be served and filed without disrupting the trial date and at reasonable cost.

In *Field v Leeds City Council* (*The Times*, 18th January 2000), the Court of Appeal said that an independent single joint expert was more appropriate in a modest value fast track housing disrepair claim than two party-instructed experts (see also Chapters 2 and 7), and in *North Holdings v Southern Tropics* [1999] 2 BCLC 625, an SJE was ordered to value a shareholding.

In *Oxley v Penwarden* [2000] WL 1274095, the first instance judge ordered the parties to a clinical negligence claim (concerning failure to diagnose and treat a vascular condition in Oxley's leg) to agree a single joint vascular surgeon as the sole expert on the issue of causation, against both parties' wishes. However, the Court of Appeal confirmed that the CPR does not provide a presumption that a single joint expert will be instructed in every case, particularly in negligence claims where the parties "should have the opportunity of investigating causation through an expert of their own choice". The Court of Appeal said that the denial of the opportunity to commission separate expert reports, in a case where different schools of thought might exist, would require the court, in the absence of agreement, to choose a given school of thought, by appointing a particular expert and thereby effectively deciding the issue of causation, without the possibility for challenge.

S (a minor) v Birmingham Health Authority [1999] QBD (but reported in 2001 in Lloyd's Rep. Med. 382) also decided that SJEs are not appropriate in high value clinical negligence (or other professional negligence) cases for opinion evidence on liability and causation, as the trial judge will want to hear different views on whether the conduct of the medical staff fell below an acceptable standard. The district judge had ordered an SJE report on liability and causation in a cerebral palsy birth case. This was reversed on appeal.

In *Peet v Mid-Kent Healthcare Trust* [2001] EWCA Civ 1703, a cerebral palsy clinical negligence claim, Lord Woolf took the opportunity to put forward his views on expert evidence in clinical negligence claims generally:

"Litigation of this sort has an adverse effect upon the resources of the health service not only in costs but also in manpower."

He acknowledged that it is difficult to restrict the medical evidence because "there can be difficult issues as to the appropriate form of treatment and problems as to the standard of treatment".

However, he said that in the great majority of cases, non-medical evidence should be given by single experts in the absence of special circumstances.

PERSUADING THE COURT THAT AN SJE IS NOT APPROPRIATE

If solicitors want to argue that a case or issue is not suitable for an SJE, the best time to do so is on the Allocation Questionnaire and/or at the first case management conference. The factors that might influence the case management judge include:

● Whether the value of the claim is sufficiently high so proportionality is not an issue.

● Whether the case, and particularly the issue on which the expert is advising, is complex.

- Whether the expert is to be instructed to advise on liability and causation, or on a significant part of quantum in a substantial case.

- Whether there is a range of professional opinion or different schools of thought on the issues on which the expert is to be instructed, where it will assist the judge to hear from more than one expert.

- Whether each party already has their own expert, and it will be more cost effective for the expert evidence issues to be resolved by parties putting written questions on their reports and/or experts' discussions, rather than by instructing another expert.

WHAT IF THE PARTIES ALREADY HAVE THEIR OWN EXPERTS?

Sometimes one or both parties may have needed, or chosen, to obtain advice from an expert, particularly on liability, before proceedings are issued (see above). If the court decides expert evidence is required, but that evidence from two experts would be disproportionate, the case management judge has a dilemma – whether to impose a new single joint expert on the parties, or to allow them to continue to retain their own experts with the court seeking to narrow the issues in dispute on the expert opinion evidence, by requiring service of written questions on the experts, and/or by ordering an experts' discussion. Frequently the relative cost, or whether involving a new expert will cause delay, will be the deciding factor. The party instructing the expert may be required to disclose the expert's initial instructions (on grounds of openness), but there is no authority on the point and the scope of privilege in relation to instructions to experts is far from clear (as was discussed in Chapter 5). The Protocol suggests that experts who have previously advised a party should only be proposed as SJEs when other parties are given "all relevant information about the previous involvement" (paragraph 17.5).

In a personal injury case, *Sage v Feiven* [2002] 7 Current Law 45, the claimant instructed Dr X pre-action (from a list of experts provided by the insurers) but not as a single joint expert. The claimant was not happy with the report, and did not disclose it. After proceedings were issued, the district judge ruled that Dr X should be instructed as a single joint expert to save costs. This was overturned on appeal as it was not practical that Dr X could leave out of his report any privileged material from his first report and he would be put in an invidious position (*Carlson v Townsend* relied upon – see above and also Chapter 7).

SELECTING AND INSTRUCTING AN SJE

Selecting an SJE

In practice, judges prefer not to select an SJE and will usually give a direction that the parties have 14 days to agree the identity, failing which the president of the appropriate professional body will be invited to nominate someone (see Appendix 4). Such a direction, not surprisingly, often promotes agreement. Where a judge does agree to select an expert from lists drawn up by the parties, CVs for the experts should be provided. The judge may wish to know in particular whether the nominated experts have experience of instructions from both claimants and defendants, and as SJEs. An official system of accreditation of expert witnesses might lead judges to feel more comfortable in making a selection (see Chapter 1).

Challenging the other party's choice of SJE

If you wish to challenge an expert suggested by another party to be the SJE, the following may be legitimate arguments:

- The expert does not have the right expertise for the particular case.

- His expertise is out of date as he has retired from the 'day job'.

- He only has experience of acting for one side.

- He is not sufficiently independent for other reasons (see Chapter 2).

- He was instructed by the other party to advise pre-action (especially if he or the party decline to disclose the instructions).

- He is known always to take a particular approach to an issue in dispute, which other experts (or even better a judge) have questioned.

Be careful not to be defamatory.

Instructing the single joint expert

The *Clinical Disputes Forum Guidelines on Instructing Single Joint Experts* suggests that there are three important principles to keep in mind when instructing a single joint expert. These seem, to the author, to be applicable to all types of claim:

1. **Fairness and equality of access** – the expert must be equally accessible to all the parties and he should be scrupulous to treat all parties equally.

2. **Transparency** – all instructions to (and responses from) the expert should be equally visible to all parties in the action – to achieve this, all communications should be in writing and should be marked with the names of the persons to whom they are being copied.

3. **Agreement** – each contact a party has with the expert must be within the terms agreed between the parties.

CPR 35.8 provides that both parties can give separate instructions to a single joint expert. In *Yorke v Katra* [2003] WL 21491870 CA, the Court of Appeal held that a district judge was wrong to strike out the defence to a small building claim, because the defendant, a litigant in person, had unilaterally amended the claimant's solicitor's letter of instruction to the single joint expert.

However, it is clearly preferable if the parties co-operate to provide the expert with one set of instructions. This may take some time as one party (the claimant?) will need to take the initiative with a draft, which is sent to the other party to amend. The final letter (not the drafts) should be copied to all parties, and the expert should be told that these are agreed instructions. If the parties cannot agree, they might consider whether to invite the court to give directions on the instructions.

All instructions to SJEs should be in writing; if any instructions are given by telephone or in person they should be confirmed in a letter, which should be copied to the other party.

If separate instructions are given, they must also be copied to the other party, along with any enclosures. A potential difficulty for the expert is that the first party to instruct him may fail to tell him he is a single joint expert. The second instructions from the other party may come as a surprise, and may even cause practical difficulties if the expert has begun work on the first set of instructions, and the two are different. The Protocol suggests that the expert might give seven days' notice of a deadline to all instructing parties for the receipt by the expert of any instructions (paragraph 17.10). Alternatively, this may be an occasion when the expert may wish to exercise his/her right to apply to the court for directions under rule 35.14 (see Chapter 10).

In principle, instructions to a single joint expert should be very similar to those to a party expert but, in practice, the solicitor/expert relationship is likely to be different in that:

- They are not part of the same 'team' in the same way as with a party expert.

- The solicitor may not have chosen the expert, or worked with him before.

- The expert may even have been instructed previously by the other party as 'their' expert (typically in a fast track personal injury claim where, under the pre-action protocol, the claimant instructs the experts, particularly the medical expert preparing a condition and prognosis report). The court may well adopt this expert as the only one, unless the defendant puts forward cogent arguments for the instruction of a second expert).

- The court may have ordered expert evidence to be in the form of a single joint expert report to keep costs under control, or to reduce the risk of expert evidence in a low vale case or on a technical point being 'used' to bolster a party's case.

- The solicitor may be reluctant to tell the expert the potential weaknesses of his client's case: this could mean that the solicitor is tempted to send shorter instructions and enclose fewer materials. (Certainly experts have told the author that their instructions as single joint experts are often more bland.)

- The solicitor, or his client, may also be tempted to try to give private instructions or information to the expert at a meeting or by telephone (clearly this must not be done).

GUIDANCE FROM THE FAMILY DIVISION

In November 2002, the President of the Family Division's Ancillary Relief Advisory Group produced a *Best Practice Guide for Instructing a Single Joint Expert*, which includes useful guidance of general applicability. The Guide provides that:

"6. a) if a single joint expert has already been instructed the court may adopt or amend those instructions, as the case management judge thinks fit...

7. Joint instructions should reflect the proportionality principle and include:

a) basic relevant information;

b) any assumptions to be made;

c) the principal known issues;

d) the specific questions to be answered;

e) arrangements for attendance at a property or other place;

f) paragraphs 1.1-1.6 of the Practice Direction to CPR Part 35 (on expert's reports) and a copy of this Guide;

g) a copy of the relevant parts of the court order concerning the appointment and instruction of the single joint expert;

h) documents necessary for the expert's consideration of the case, sorted and indexed.

8. Upon receiving the letter of instruction the single joint expert should raise with the solicitors any issues or questions which may arise, including proportionality, lack of clarity or completeness in the instructions and the possible effect on fees of complying with the instructions.

9. Should a party wish to give supplementary instructions to the SJE, full consideration must be given to proportionality and to the possible effect on the court timetable, and either the other party or the court has to sanction them.

10. All communications by the SJE should be addressed to both parties."

Throughout the life of the case, parties must ensure that the SJE receives copies of all documents relevant to their instructions. This is probably more likely to be achieved if one of the solicitors agrees to do this. A copy of every letter to the expert should be sent to the other solicitor.

SINGLE JOINT EXPERT FEES

(See also Chapter 6)

It is vital that parties agree on what fees are to be paid to the SJE; both an initial report fee and an hourly rate for further work. SJEs should observe any limit on the fees, or seek authority *from both parties* for any increase. Experts' fee notes (sent to each party) should state the total fee charged and the share of the fee each party is to pay.

CPR 35.8(4) gives the court the power, before a single joint expert is instructed, to limit the amount that can be paid by way of fees and expenses to the expert, and to direct that the instructing parties pay that amount into court. In the author's experience, the power in the first part of the rule is used fairly frequently and without controversy in low value claims on proportionality grounds, but the power in the second part is used infrequently.

Kranidiotes v Paschali [2001] EWCA Civ 357 is an example of a higher value case where the power to limit the fee of an SJE was exercised. The court limited the fee of an accountant single joint expert to be instructed to value a shareholding, to £10,000. The expert selected by the parties quoted a fee of £75,000. The court ordered termination of those instructions as the cost was disproportionate, and ordered that another expert should be instructed. The Court of Appeal dismissed the defendant's appeal.

In *Smolen v Solon Co-operative Housing Services Ltd* [2003] EWCA Civ 1240, the court uncharacteristically allowed a single joint expert to be replaced when the claimant objected to him. However, the claimant was required to pay the fees for the second expert into court prior to his being instructed. (For a fuller discussion of this case, see below.)

CPR 35.8(5) provides that the instructing parties are jointly and severally liable for the payment of the single joint expert's fees and expenses unless the court directs otherwise. This means, in a two party case, that they will pay 50% each. However, if one party fails to pay their share, the expert can look to the other party to pay the second 50%, rather than having to apply to the court (using the expert's power to do so under CPR 35.14), or to sue the defaulting solicitor for the balance. The court might direct 'otherwise' where the parties have very unequal resources: there are no reported examples for guidance.

The *Clinical Disputes Forum Guidelines* suggest that if one party does not pay their share of the SJE's fees within three months, the other party should pay.

WILL THE RELATIONSHIP WITH AN SJE BE DIFFERENT FROM A PARTY EXPERT?

Accepting instructions as a single joint expert should not mean a significant change in the way in which the expert investigates the case and prepares the report for the court, but in practice it does involve *some* differences in the expert's role, including in the following respects:

1. The parties may be less willing to share with the expert the potential weaknesses of their case: this could mean you are more likely to be inclined to provide less helpful or detailed instructions – try to resist the inclination.

2. The expert must be very careful not to accept private instructions or information from either party: this means only attending meetings or conferences with a party or their legal advisers with the agreement of the other party and being particularly careful to keep detailed file notes of any important telephone discussions.

3. The expert does carry greater responsibility, as no other opinion evidence on the issue in question generally will be before the court: but this does not mean that the judge is delegating responsibility to the expert, as he/she can still decide to depart from the expert's view in the light of other evidence in the case (see section on SJEs at trial below and Chapter 12).

Parties and their lawyers have to be very careful to act transparently with an SJE at all times. All correspondence must be copied to the other party and telephone contact and meetings kept to a minimum. (It is, of course, permissible for an SJE to meet or examine a party without the other party being present, e.g. in personal injury matters.) It can be a good idea to agree which of the solicitors will be responsible for ensuring the SJE is kept informed of all relevant developments in the case.

THE SJE REPORT AND WRITTEN QUESTIONS (CPR 35.6)

(See also Chapter 8)

A single joint expert's report should not be any different in principle or content to that of a 'party' expert. If the expert received two sets of instructions, they must both be summarised (and possibly annexed), and the report must address both versions of events and issues raised by both parties. It is particularly important for SJE reports to keep agreed facts, disputed facts, assumptions and opinion clearly separate, and for an SJE to give the range of professional opinion on an issue (when that is appropriate).

An SJE should send his report, both draft and final, to both parties at the same time and with the same covering letter.

An SJE report should be discussed with the client in the same way as with a party-instructed expert. If you and your client are not happy with the report because you consider it is inaccurate, the opinions are not justified by the evidence, or the expert appears to be biased, you should put clarification questions to him within 28 days of receipt of the report under CPR 35.6 (see also Chapter 11). Remember that both parties can put questions to an SJE and that you should copy your questions and the expert's answers to the other party. Written questions are not an opportunity to cross-examine the expert by post, although there may be a temptation to do this if you think it is unlikely that the court might agree to further expert evidence on the same issue, or to the SJE being cross-examined at trial (see below).

If you remain unhappy on receipt of the expert's answers to your questions you may wish to consider applying to the court for permission to:

a) change the SJE;

b) instruct an additional expert to the SJE; or

c) call the SJE to give oral evidence at trial.

If you decide to pursue any of these courses of action, you will need to:

1. Give "reasons which are not fanciful" (see *Daniels v Walker* below).

2. Demonstrate why the expert is wrong, or may be so, and that his opinion may be vital to the outcome of the case.

3. Check the costs incurred to date and estimate the possible costs of the further steps proposed, in the context of proportionality, as the court is less likely to allow further steps in a modest claim.

4. Check the timetable to trial, and whether the further work proposed is likely to affect the trial window or date.

ADDITIONAL EXPERTS TO THE SJE

When to use a shadow expert

(See also Chapter 3)

If the SJE evidence is technical, you may need assistance if you wish to challenge it. The best way to do this, if time and funds permit, is to instruct another expert from the same discipline to critically review the SJE report as well as the questions and answers. You will not be able to rely upon any report that the new shadow expert prepares, or to recover the costs even if you succeed at trial, without permission, but you should be able to make a more cogent application to the court for permission to adduce additional evidence.

Changing the SJE

Will the court allow an SJE to be changed after the receipt of their report? The answer is occasionally; either when an SJE has produced evidence that cannot be used, or when one or both parties have completely lost confidence in the SJE.

Perry v Smith [2001] 12 *Current Law Monthly* 57 was a personal injury case, in which a doctor who was instructed as an SJE produced three different supplementary reports. The parties were allowed to instruct a new expert and the judge ruled that the previous one should not be paid.

In *Smolen v Solon Co-operative Housing Services Ltd* [2003] EWCA Civ 1240, the Court of Appeal upheld a case management decision to allow the instruction of a second single joint expert when the claimant (who was acting in person) objected to the first one, after his report had been disclosed, on the ground that he worked regularly with the defendant's solicitor. The court was satisfied that there was no evidence of actual bias but, as the claimant had lost confidence in the expert, the court concluded that another expert might be instructed. The claimant, however, was ordered to make a payment into court on account of the second expert's fees.

When might a second expert be permitted?

If the court orders, or the parties accept, that evidence on a particular issue will be given by a single joint expert, the assumption is that the evidence will consist only of the written report and the expert's answers to any written questions (under CPR 35.6) from either party. If a party has reasonable grounds for concern about the accuracy of the single joint expert's report or the validity of the opinions expressed, a case management judge might be persuaded that an additional report is justified.

In *Daniels v Walker* [2000] 1 WLR 1382 CA, the parties initially accepted an occupational therapy single joint expert to prepare a care report in a high value personal injury claim. Only the claimant's solicitors had instructed the expert. The defendants had expressed dissatisfaction with their letter of instruction, but had not sent their own. On receipt of the report, the defendant applied to the court for permission to instruct a second expert, as they considered that the full-time care recommended by the SJE was not justified. The defendants raised two arguments on the appeal:

1. That the first instance judge had ignored the overriding objective in refusing the application.

2. That a refusal to permit them to instruct a second expert would conflict with Article 6 of the ECHR, because it would amount to barring an essential part of the defendant's case.

The Court of Appeal was more sympathetic to the first argument than the second. They said that the fact that a party has agreed to an SJE being instructed does not prevent that party from being allowed to instruct and rely upon another expert, that in substantial cases instruction of an SJE could be regarded as a 'first step' (but that in most cases it should also be the last step), and that the court has discretion to allow a party to obtain further evidence to challenge the SJE report if the reasons were not 'fanciful'.

In giving guidance, the Court of Appeal stressed the virtue of putting questions to the SJE before making an application to the court, and that if a party or the parties are allowed to obtain their own reports, no decision should be taken as to what oral evidence should be called at trial until there has been a meeting between the experts concerned. Lord Woolf said:

"The great advantage of adopting the course of instructing a joint expert at the outset is that in the majority of cases it will have the effect of narrowing the issues. The fact that additional experts may have to be involved is regrettable, but in the majority of cases the expert issues will already have been reduced. Even if you have the unfortunate result that there are three different views as to the right outcome on a particular issue, the expense which will be incurred as a result of that is justified by the prospects of it being avoided in the majority of cases."

The appeal was allowed. However, the court warned against parties raising human rights issues when they were not relevant; even if the Human Rights Act 1998 had been in force (it was not), they considered it undesirable for case management decisions to be made more complicated by introducing arguments under Article 6. The decision to allow the appeal is, of course, entirely compatible with Article 6 (see also Chapter 2).

Daniels v Walker was the first reported case in which the issue of instructing an expert in addition to an SJE was raised, and some commentators were surprised at the decision. Certainly, it suggested that the courts might be more flexible than was thought to be the case previously.

Cosgrove v Pattison [2000] WL 1841601 was a boundary dispute in which the defendant, who was unhappy with the SJE report, argued that the SJE might be biased, and applied for permission to instruct an expert of his own who was already a witness of fact. The application was refused. On the appeal, Neuberger J held that the following factors should be considered in deciding whether to allow additional expert evidence to that of an SJE:

- The nature of the dispute.

- The number of issues on which the expert evidence was relevant.

- The reason for requesting a second expert.

- The amount at stake.

- The effect of permitting a second expert on the conduct of the trial.

- The delay that might be caused.

- Overall justice to the parties.

In this case, the judge concluded that the disputed matters were mostly factual but did require expert evidence, the admission of a second report from a witness of fact would not delay matters or add much to the costs, and there would be no disadvantage to the claimants because they would also be allowed to instruct a further expert if they wished. The appeal was allowed.

Nonetheless, the courts have certainly not been willing to routinely allow additional experts when SJEs have been instructed, or for their fees to be recovered.

In *Sutton v Tesco plc* [2002] 8 *Current Law Digest* 57, the claimant, in a personal injury slipping claim, was allowed to rely upon a report from her treating psychiatrist, obtained without discussion with the defendant or the court's permission, to challenge evidence from other experts, including single joint experts, that she was malingering, but not to recover the costs of the report, regardless of the outcome.

Popek v National Westminster Bank plc [2002] EWCA Civ 42 was a claim for breach of contract and fiduciary duty, in which an SJE in small business finance was instructed, and reported that the bank had done as much as they could to assist Mr Popek (with loans and mortgages) and had not overcharged him. Questions were put to the expert and answered. At trial Mr Popek, by then acting in person, applied for permission to rely upon the evidence of two additional experts. This was refused. The judge struck out the claim, partly on limitation grounds and partly because there was no sustainable cause of action. The appeal failed, on the basis that the judge was entitled to conclude that the claim was bound to fail, so considering an application made very late in the day to adduce further expert evidence was unnecessary.

In the author's view, the cases are not inconsistent. What the senior courts are saying is that *initially* SJEs are the right approach but if a party has good reasons for wanting additional expert evidence after receipt of the single expert's report, this *might* be allowed depending on the circumstances.

An application for an additional expert to an SJE is more likely to succeed if:

a) the party applying has already put written questions to the SJE under CPR 35.6 and received the answers;

b) the party applying has already obtained advice from another expert in the same field, so cogent arguments can be made on the deficiencies in the SJE's report;

c) the additional report can be filed and served without undue delay or a great increase in costs, particularly if a trial date has been fixed.

SINGLE JOINT EXPERTS AT LATER STAGES OF THE LITIGATION

SJEs and conferences with the advocate

Can an SJE attend a conference with one side's counsel? In *Smith v Stephens*, 26th January 2001 QBD (unrep) and *Peet v Mid-Kent Healthcare Trust* [2001] EWCA Civ 1703, the courts decided not without the consent of the other party. Smith was a personal injury case arising from a road traffic accident in which liability was agreed – the parties had jointly instructed seven experts and the claimant's leading counsel asked for a conference with all seven. Peet was a cerebral palsy clinical negligence claim, in which there were seven SJEs in different non-medical disciplines reporting on aspects of quantum. The claimant wanted the SJEs to attend a conference with counsel to better understand and test their views. The defendant objected. The Master and Court of Appeal refused permission because:

a) Part 35 was designed to ensure an open process;

b) a report by a single joint expert should be *the* evidence from that expert;

c) before trial, a party should not be permitted to test an SJE's evidence, except by written questions, without the consent of the other party.

The *CDF Guidelines* suggest that:

1. If the other party do not object to the SJE attending the conference but cannot be present, they could be sent notes of that part of the conference. (This sounds fine in theory but will it ever happen?)

2. Any discussions with SJEs at court should be treated as conferences.

SJEs and applications to the court under CPR 35.14

SJEs are, perhaps, more likely to use the power available to all expert witnesses, under CPR 35.14, to apply to the court for directions to assist them in their work (see also Chapter 10). This is because it can be more difficult for an SJE to resolve problems than for a party-instructed expert, who can more easily talk issues through with their instructing solicitor.

An SJE might make an application:

a) when instructions from the parties seriously conflict;

b) when there is a dispute over payment of his fees or he considers the work cannot be done for the amount the parties are prepared to pay;

c) when he considers that the written questions on his report are out of time, or otherwise do not comply with CPR 35.6 in that they go beyond questions of clarification.

Since 2002, the rules have provided that an SJE should notify the parties seven days in advance of his intention to apply to the court (see Chapter 2). There are no reported cases of SJEs making applications under CPR 35.14 to give guidance.

SJEs and experts' discussions

The Academy of Experts' *Code of Guidance* suggests (at paragraph 22.2) that where a single joint expert has been instructed but a party has, with the permission of the court, instructed its own additional Part 35 expert, there should normally be a discussion between the single joint expert and the Part 35 expert. Lord Woolf adopted this suggestion in *Daniels v Walker*. The author is not aware of this being a frequent practice, however.

Adjourning trial for a late SJE report

In *Alderson v Stillorgan Sales Ltd* [2001] EWCA Civ 1060, a claim in misrepresentation in the sale of a business, the SJE's report was served only a few days before trial. The claimants applied for an adjournment, as they wanted to obtain advice from their accountant on the report and time to prepare for cross-examination of the expert. This was refused; the court said the claimants should have anticipated that the SJE report might be damaging to their case and taken steps earlier to check on the accountant's availability to advise.

This decision might be explained as the court's general unwillingness to adjourn trial dates, especially in the years immediately after the implementation of the CPR, as on the facts the refusal to adjourn seems harsh and questionably compliant with Article 6 ECHR – the right to a fair trial (see also Chapter 2).

SJE attendance and cross-examination at trial

Single joint experts should only rarely be required to give oral evidence at trial because:

a) the availability of one opinion, rather than two, should encourage settlement;

b) in lower value claims, especially on the fast track, the cost of the expert attending court is often disproportionate.

However, if a single joint expert is called to give oral evidence he/she faces the perhaps daunting prospect of being cross-examined by both parties' advocates.

Lord Woolf, in *Daniels v Walker* and in *Peet* (see above), said, obiter, that usually there should be no need to amplify or test an SJE report by cross-examination of the expert at trial, but that the court has discretion to permit this if it is really necessary, either prior to or at the trial.

Nevertheless, there have been circumstances when case management judges have allowed SJEs to be cross-examined.

Layland v Fairview New Homes plc [2002] EWHC 1350 Ch was a claim concerning the alleged reduction in value of a property located close to an incinerator. On appeal it was held that the circuit judge was not wrong to give summary judgment to the defendant on the evidence before him of an SJE report which said there had been no diminution in value. However, as the claimants had subsequently obtained evidence from two other valuers who disagreed with the SJE, they should be given the opportunity to 'fruitfully exploit' their criticisms of the SJE by cross-examination, as it was for the court to decide upon the valuation issue, not an expert. Neuberger J said:

"The fact that the single expert's view is adverse to the claimants, on whom the burden of establishing a diminution (in value) rests, cannot mean that they are effectively bound by his conclusion. Provided there is a prospect of the expert, through cross-examination, or the court, through submissions, being persuaded to a different conclusion, the claim cannot be dismissed on the basis of the expert's view."

In *Austen v Oxford City Council* [2002] AER D 97, a personal injury case, the trial judge refused permission for the claimant to cross-examine a SJE psychiatrist whose report was unfavourable and hostile to the claimant. The appeal succeeded because the claimant was no longer relying on the SJE report and the judge, not the expert, had to decide whether the claimant's injuries were genuine. Given time, the instruction of a second psychiatrist would have been preferable, but cross-examination of the SJE at trial was an alternative solution.

R and R [2002] EWCA Civ 409 decided that advanced notice of the topics for cross-examination of an SJE was advisable.

The weight to be given to SJE evidence at trial

(See also Chapter 12)

It is for a trial judge to weigh all the evidence, written and oral, including evidence from witnesses of fact and experts. On technical matters, evidence of an expert, including an SJE, is likely to be preferred to that of a lay witness. The following case is a good illustration.

Takenaka (UK) Limited v Frankl (*The Independent*, 11th December 2000) – The case arose out of the admitted publication of defamatory e-mails: the only issue was whether the defendant was the author. The single joint expert analysed the contents of the defendant's computer and concluded that traces of e-mail activity matched the dates and times of the malicious e-mails so it was "most probable" that the defendant's computer was the source. The expert said he was confident that the proof required "on the balance of probabilities" had been reached. The judge commented that:

"A judge tries the case upon the evidence and in this case the expert evidence is of the highest quality in an arcane field in which the judge must be guided by that expert evidence."

Yet, when the disputed matter is one of fact, and the expert is using his experience to interpret events from a distance, the evidence of a lay witness might be preferred, if it is clear and credible. Three recent decisions of the Court of Appeal illustrate the choices very well.

In *Coopers Payen Ltd v Southampton Container Ltd* [2003] AER D 220, a heavy press fell off a delivery trailer that was being towed by a tug. The SJE said this could only have happened if the tug had been travelling at around 9km per hour. However, a witness of fact (for the defendant) said that the trailer had not been travelling any faster than walking pace. The judge at first instance preferred the evidence of the witness of fact. The Court of Appeal disagreed and said it would be unusual to disregard the evidence of an SJE on an issue of fact on which no other direct evidence is called, as "subject to the need to evaluate his evidence in the light of his answers in cross-examination, his evidence is likely to prove compelling".

Where direct evidence is also given on an issue and a witness is credible:

"The judge must consider whether he can reconcile the evidence of the expert witness with that of the witness of fact. If he cannot do so, he must consider whether there may be an explanation for the conflict of evidence, or for a possible error by either witness, and in the light of all the circumstances make a considered choice which evidence to accept."

In this case, the Court of Appeal said that the judge should have accepted the evidence of the expert as there was no alternative explanation for the accident, but that the tug was travelling too fast.

In *Piper v Clifford Kent Ltd* [2003] EWCA Civ 1692, a claim in nuisance for smells emanating from a large egg-producing farm, the judge at first instance awarded damages, but for past nuisance only, based on the report of an SJE who concluded that the smell was not that bad. On appeal, the claimants argued that the smell was bad and was continuing. The Court of Appeal criticised the SJE for failing to note the wind direction when he visited the farm. He was said to be "not really giving expert evidence but simply the evidence of a visitor". The case was remitted back to the County Court for further investigation, as the evidence from the SJE was insufficient to refute the evidence of credible witnesses of fact.

Armstrong and Cannor v First York [2005] EWCA CW 277 was a personal injury claim arising from an RTA. An SJE engineer concluded that the claimants could not have been jolted by the low force of the impact. The trial judge accepted that the engineer, who gave oral evidence, was logical and consistent, but found for the claimants as he accepted that they were honest and had sustained some injuries. The Court of Appeal held that the judge had considered the evidence carefully and directed himself correctly on the law. The defendant's appeal was dismissed.

The importance of SJEs exercising great care cannot be overemphasised. Even at trial or on appeal, it is not too late to challenge SJE evidence if it is plainly wrong or ineptly prepared.

CONCLUSIONS

Decisions of the senior courts since 1999 show that the courts are willing to be flexible about the role of SJEs in the way that Lord Woolf suggested in his *Access to Justice* report, but which is not apparent from the rules and related guidance. Certainly, parties do not have to accept SJEs in every case, and may be permitted to challenge an SJE report if there are good reasons to question the findings or opinions, and this can be done in an efficient and not disproportionate way. Neither the fears of what the courts might do or how parties might react when the CPR were implemented have been realised, but there is some way to go before the place of SJEs in the civil dispute system settles down.

This conclusion was borne out of a survey of litigation solicitors' experiences with SJEs, carried out by the Law Society in 2003. 60% of respondents had no concerns over the frequency of use of SJEs especially in fast track, personal injury and building disputes and 88% were content with the quality of the expert. However, there were concerns about the use of SJEs on complex liability issues, especially in professional negligence claims and in high value quantum cases, and about SJEs effectively making the judge's decision without sufficient understanding of the legal issues. In addition, 55% said they had experienced other difficulties with SJEs, including the wrong choice of expert and the experts' failure to adhere to their instructions and to understand the issues.

Chapter 10
WORKING WITH EXPERTS DURING THE LITIGATION

The main tasks of experts in litigation are summarised here for convenience. They are:

1. To prepare a **written report** for use in evidence by one or more parties and to assist the court in deciding the dispute (rule 35.5).

2. To answer **written questions** on the report, provided these are put once only within 28 days of service of the report, and are for the purpose of clarification only (rule 35.6).

3. To attend a **discussion** with an expert instructed by the other party, with a view to narrowing the areas of disagreement between the experts and producing an agreed note for the parties and the court, if required by the court, under rule 35.12.

4. To give **oral evidence** and be cross-examined on the written report at trial if required by the court.

In addition, experts may be asked to perform many other tasks in relation to a civil dispute, depending upon the parties' resources, proportionality and the needs of the particular case.

Other tasks which an expert may be asked to perform include:

- **Clarifying their instructions** on the dispute – instructions should be a two-way process (see also Chapter 5).

- **Assisting in drafting pre-action letters of claim or response, and statements of case for the litigation**, particularly when acting as a liability expert in professional negligence disputes (see below).

- **Advising upon the documentary evidence**, and particularly the documents which the other party might be expected to disclose (see below).

- **Considering and advising upon other expert opinion evidence** (see below).

- Helping in the **drafting of written questions** on other experts' reports, preparing agendas for **experts' discussions**, and cross-examination questions for trial (see Chapter 11).

- If appointed by one party only, **attending conferences** with the solicitor and trial advocate (see below).

- **Assisting in the settlement of a dispute**, by advising on the other party's approach to liability and quantum and, on occasions, attending settlement conferences or mediations (see below).

This chapter discusses all of the above tasks, except questions on reports and experts' discussions, which are covered in Chapter 11. The chapter also covers when and how solicitors might be allowed to change their expert, assessing and challenging the other party's expert reports, experts and confidentiality, experts changing their opinion, and instructing an expert late in the proceedings.

WORKING EFFECTIVELY WITH AN EXPERT DURING THE CASE

Two of the essential qualities in the relationship between a lawyer and an expert are respect for each other's roles, and good communication. You need to create an effective working relationship with the expert, instructing him carefully and honestly, maintaining a dialogue with him and encouraging him to be pro-active. Too often, solicitors expect experts simply to produce a report to a timetable, preferably a favourable one, and to be available almost instantly to carry out any follow-up work on the case. This is not a recipe for a fruitful relationship (see also Chapter 14).

Remember that experts are not lawyers. Any legal points should be clarified for the expert, as appropriate, and the expert should be discouraged from commenting directly on legal liabilities, in writing or orally.

When each side has their own expert the solicitor may wish to use his expert, particularly an expert working on liability and causation, as an adviser throughout the proceedings (subject to proportionality), although his independence must not be compromised. Making an expert too much 'part of the team' runs the risk that it may be more difficult for the expert to remain completely objective. Single joint experts clearly cannot be asked to advise in the same way. The Civil Procedure Rules provide no guidance on the scope of privilege in relation to experts' general contact with the instructing lawyer or the client during the litigation (see also Chapter 5). A good test might be whether your proposed request to the expert might cause embarrassment to the client, or worse, if the other party or the court became aware of it.

Be aware that whenever an expert is asked to advise, he is likely to charge on an hourly basis. A job that sounds straightforward may, in practice, be complex and time-consuming for the expert. You may want him to estimate the time and costs involved before he does the work, especially if the client, funder or court budget for the case is restricted. A note of all requests to the expert should be kept and preferably confirmed in writing.

Experts appreciate honesty. It is better to raise queries and ask for clarification on a report or other work of an expert when it is received than to do so later. Experts also appreciate feedback – tell the expert how he is doing. Good experts want to learn how to be even better as an expert witness, and you may need to use him again.

THE SPECIFIC TASKS

Experts advising upon drafting

Drafting the key documents in the dispute is mainly the solicitor's responsibility, with assistance from counsel in larger and more complex cases, along with approval from the client. In the more technical cases, however, the liability and causation expert may have a role to play in framing issues and questions, and in checking the technical aspects of drafting. Sometimes quantum experts may usefully have an input too, e.g. in the drafting of a schedule of loss.

An expert may be able to advise upon the drafting of:

- Pre-action letters of claim and response.
- Statements of case.

- Requests for further information.

- Disclosure requests.

- Instructions to other experts.

- Questions to other experts.

- Agendas for experts' discussions.

Experts assisting with documents and disclosure

Again, it is most likely that an expert's help with documents and disclosure will be useful in the more technical type of disputes. You will be sending the documents to the expert that are relevant for the preparation of his report, in any event but, in addition, an expert may be able to:

1. Advise on the documents that your client should have, and may have to disclose. (CPR Part 31 places the responsibility on the client to search for documents and to sign the disclosure statement that he has complied with his obligation.)

2. Advise on the documents the other party should have, and should be disclosing, either pre-action or as standard disclosure during proceedings.

3. Help with applications for pre-action disclosure – what are the key documents in the case which are needed to draft a letter before action or response or the statement of case?

4. Inspect and review the documents disclosed by the other party (perhaps attending on the inspection?) – checking whether they are complete and explaining the more technical ones and their importance.

5. Advise on whether an application for specific disclosure of other documents may be justified and assisting you in responding to an application from the other party.

6. Help with documents and literature which should be annexed to both his own and other experts' reports (see also Chapter 8).

7. Help with the contents of trial bundles and suggested 'reading lists' for the trial.

Timely involvement of an expert in disclosure issues in a complex or very technical case can save time and costs but you must ensure the cost of the expert's work is proportionate and is controlled.

Remember that the court has the power to direct a party to provide information to another party (or expert) (CPR 35.9). The intention appears to be to prevent the not infrequent problem in the past of party's experts being instructed on very different bases, and to ensure a level playing-field between litigants of unequal resources. Also, a party may be reluctant to provide a single joint expert with information that is not helpful to the party's case. The rule is not often relied upon and there is limited case law to assist in its application. In *Re MMR and MR Vaccine Litigation (No 7)* [2003] (unreported), the court ordered that scientific studies, known to the defendant's experts but not referred to in their reports, should be identified and made available for inspection.

If you or your expert considers the other party has information which they have not disclosed, ask for it. If the answer is not satisfactory, make an application to the court.

Experts and witnesses of fact

On occasions, experts will have contact with witnesses of fact, other than the parties, e.g. on a site visit, when carrying out investigations, or by pre-arrangement to obtain further information necessary for their report. Experts should be reminded that they should only talk with witnesses when necessary and should keep notes of the discussions. These may have to be disclosed. If practicable and not disproportionate in cost, it may be preferable for one of the legal team to conduct the interviews, with the expert providing briefing on questions to ask.

In *Bank of Credit and Commerce International SA v Ali (No 3)* 1999 (unreported), one of the experts in his report referred to certain employment case histories, based partly on witness statements provided, and partly on information provided to the expert at interviews he conducted. The defendant applied to see the notes of the interviews; the claimant argued that they were privileged. The court held that no privilege was attached to the notes and that the expert should have annexed his notes of the interviews to his report. (For further discussion of this case, see also Chapter 5.)

Experts assisting with other expert evidence

Perhaps more frequently than assisting with drafting, documents or witnesses, experts will help with the evidence of other experts who have been instructed by both parties.

Other ways in which your expert might assist include:

- Suggesting other experts from related disciplines who may be able to advise on the case.

- Advising upon framing instructions to other experts.

- Commenting upon the reports of other experts, particularly that of their 'opposite number'.

- Advising on drafting questions on other experts' reports, again particularly for their 'opposite number'.

- Drafting agendas for their discussion with their 'opposite number' (see also Chapter 11).

- In a complex case, developing an understanding of the inter-relationship between the different experts' reports at a round table meeting or at a conference with counsel.

- Framing cross-examination questions for other experts at trial.

ASSESSING AND CHALLENGING THE OTHER PARTY'S EXPERT REPORTS

When the other party's expert reports are served, note the date (and the time if there is an 'unless order' deadline) and read the reports thoroughly. You will need to send copies to your client, with your comments and advice, and invite his. You may want 'your' experts to comment upon the reports before advising the client, particularly if the subject matter is very technical. You need to work quickly because of the limited time available to raise questions on the reports under CPR 35.6 – 28 days from service (see also Chapter 11).

You should also check:

- If the report has been served in time in accordance with the court directions.

- That the report is from the specific expert, or type of expert, for which court permission has been given.

- Whether the report complies with the CPR requirements (statement of truth etc) and any specific directions made by the court.

- The summary of the instructions, documents on which the expert relies, and the facts and assumptions set out – do they differ significantly from your expert's and if so why?

- The opinions – are they supported by the evidence, how far do they differ from your expert's?

- Consistency with other disclosed evidence.

- Whether all research and literature is annexed to the report, or suffiently referenced for you and 'your' expert to locate it.

- Whether there is any indication that the expert may have a conflict of interest or not be sufficiently independent.

If you find reasons to challenge the admissibility of the report you need to act quickly. In *Liverpool Roman Catholic Archdiocesan Trustees Inc v Goldberg* (*The Times*, 9th March 2001), in which there was a challenge to the other party's expert on grounds of bias (for a further discussion of this case see also Chapters 1 and 3), Neuberger J criticised a delay of 14 months from when the identity of the expert was known, in making the challenge. He said:

1. Challenges should be made as soon as possible.

2. If a challenge is made, the case management judge should usually decide it unless the trial judge is likely to be in a better position to decide the point.

3. If the challenge is made early and the court has doubts as to its admissibility, where the cost of the expert evidence is high, the court should exclude it.

4. If the objection is raised late the case management judge should be slow in deciding it, especially if the trial is imminent.

Successful challenges (pre-trial) to the other party's expert or report have been made when:

1. The report was served late outside the timescale set by an 'unless order' (but not 20 minutes – see *R.C Residuals v Linton* in Chapter 8).

2. The cost of the report was disproportionate before the costs were incurred (see *Kranidiotes v Paschali* in Chapter 6).

3. An expert failed to comply with his duty to the court and with court directions (see *Stevens v Gullis* – Chapter 8 and below).

4. The expert was not sufficiently independent (see *Re B* and *Liverpool RC* – Chapter 2).

The court also has the power, under **CPR 35.6(4)**, to order that a party may not rely on the evidence of an expert who fails to answer written questions on his report put in compliance with that rule (see Chapter 11). There are no reported cases applying the rule.

In the case of *Stevens v Gullis* [2000] 1 AER 527, an unqualified architectural designer expert prepared his report late, did not include a summary of his instructions, failed to date the report or add a statement of truth, did not relate it to the pleadings or refer to any of the exchanged witness statements, failed to comply with a court order requiring him to rectify the deficiencies of his report, and failed to sign a statement following an experts' discussion. One month before trial, the court (upheld by the Court of Appeal) made an order barring the expert from giving evidence on the ground that he did not understand his duty to the court.

Challenges to a single joint expert report have been made when:

1. A party has lost confidence in the expert – see *Perry v Smith* and *Smolen v Solon Co-operative Housing Service Ltd* (Chapters 3 and 9).

2. The court will be assisted in hearing a second opinion – see *Daniels v Walker* and *Cosgrove v Pattison* (Chapter 9).

Be careful before making an application to the court to challenge admissibility of an expert's report. Ask yourself whether the deficiencies are so serious that they might cause an injustice, whether the costs of instructing another expert can be justified on proportionality grounds and whether, tactically, it might be preferable to allow a very poor report to be put before the trial judge who might decide to disregard it. Losing a 'challenge' application will incur significant costs and may appear to be over-adversarial behaviour, or 'conduct'. Minor deficiencies, e.g. a missing or wrong statement of truth, can be put right by correspondence between the parties, and clarification questions may further expose weaknesses in a report.

Prosser v Castle Sanderson Solicitors (18th April 2000), unreported (except in *Expert Evidence under the CPR*, Day and Le Gat, 2001) is an example of the court criticising the form of an expert's report (here from an estate agent in a professional negligence claim), because it did not identify the instructions or the factual material sent to the expert. The court concluded, however, that these deficiencies were not altogether the expert's fault and allowed the evidence to be adduced. The challenge failed.

Other considerations on receipt of the other party's experts' reports include:

● Whether, and when, you may need advice from counsel.

● Whether, and when, to make an offer to settle or payment into court (see below).

● Whether there are issues to be followed up with the client, witnesses or any of your experts.

Finally, you will need to consider whether and what questions of clarification will arise on the report (this is discussed in more detail in Chapter 11). Usually you will want your expert to assist – invite him to suggest questions. (If the report is from a single joint expert, you will have to rely upon your own knowledge and resources unless you decide to instruct a shadow expert – see also Chapters 3 and 9.) Check what the court directions say about questions and answers. Consider also whether an experts' discussion is likely to be necessary and whether the directions provide for this. Are questions and a discussion both necessary? To decide this, consider proportionality and the time scale.

Judges should allow experts to complete their work

In a care proceedings case, *Re M (children)*, Lawtel, 5th October 2004 CA, an estranged and possibly abusing father had been given permission to obtain expert evidence from an organisation that worked towards reuniting abusers with their children. However, when the expert had started work, the judge ruled they could not interview the children, as their work was experimental, although the judge acknowledged that interviewing the children would not harm them. This was overturned on appeal, as any debate concerning the expert's methodology should have taken place at an earlier stage.

CHANGING AND ADDING EXPERTS

Changing your own expert

When giving directions, the case management judge will always cite the specialty of any expert on whom the parties are being given permission to rely, and will often name the expert(s) if he/they have been identified at that stage. If the latter has been done, you will not be able to adduce evidence from a different expert without obtaining the court's express permission. This will not readily be given unless:

- The named expert had died or is otherwise unavailable.

- His quoted fee far exceeds any limit the court may have placed on the fees (see Chapter 6, and particularly *Kranidiotes v Paschali* [2001] EWCA Civ 357).

- The court is satisfied that the party has lost confidence in the expert for reasons other than that his report is not favourable to that party.

One purpose of the CPR (and enhanced court case management in particular) was to discourage 'expert shopping', a not uncommon practice pre-CPR, when a party would obtain reports from a number of experts in an attempt to find one that supported his case.

Purdy v Cambran [1999] All ER CDJ 1518 was a personal injury claim arising from a road traffic accident in 1990, in which the claimant obtained medical reports from five orthopaedic surgeons and one neurologist over a period of five years. The court struck out the claim for want of prosecution and the judge criticised the claimant for 'expert shopping'. Before the appeal was heard, the defendant's one and only expert died, in their view strengthening the argument for strike-out; the claimant said they could instruct another expert. The Court of Appeal, although accepting that there was some justification for the claimant obtaining a further report in 1995, upheld the strike-out partly because of the substantial prejudice caused to the defendant by the death of their expert witness.

In a more recent case, *Beck v Ministry of Defence* [2003] EWCA Civ 1043, the Court of Appeal took a different approach. This was a high value negligence claim, in which the claimant alleged the RAF's treatment of his psychiatric problems had exacerbated his condition. The parties were given permission to rely on the evidence of one psychiatrist each, on the issues of liability, causation, condition and prognosis. The defendant, the MOD, had never instructed their expert before. They lost confidence in him and asked the claimant to be examined by a second psychiatrist. The claimant refused and the defendant applied to the court for permission to call an alternative expert, on the basis that the expert was not sufficiently familiar with the RAF psychiatric referral system to cover some of the issues in the case, although they said that his report was favourable to their case. The application was granted but the claimant appealed. The Court of Appeal upheld the decision, but this was made conditional upon the disclosure of the first expert's report. The court said:

"I can see no reason for continuing to withhold disclosure of the original report which is now discarded, and every possible reason why such disclosure should be made."

The reason given was that otherwise the claimant would be left wondering whether the report really was favourable to the defendant. The court said that it would not be appropriate to require an applicant in these circumstances to disclose the report before it had been decided whether to allow him to abandon the report because, if it was not granted, the other party could use the weaknesses in the report at trial. It was emphasised also that a party seeking to 'replace' an expert has to provide good reasons to the court (particularly, as here, where a claimant may be subjected to another medical examination), and that 'expert shopping' was to be discouraged.

However, in *Hajigeorgiou v Vasiliou* [2005] EWCA Civ 236, the Court of Appeal held that permission was not needed for the defendant to instruct a different expert than had been canvassed at the case management conference because the judge's directions did not name the expert to be instructed. The decision in *Beck* (above) was confirmed where a proposed expert was named, or a report had been obtained from the intended expert, i.e. that the first instructed expert's report must be disclosed as a pre-condition to instructing a second expert.

As noted above, it may be even more difficult to persuade the court if the expert you seek to change is a single joint expert. Nevertheless, it has been done (see *Smolen v Solon Co-operative Housing Services Ltd* [2003] EWCA Civ 1240 and *Mosedale v Lapwith* [2004] 3 *Current Law Monthly* 50, discussed in Chapter 9). An alternative is to seek permission to instruct an additional expert (see *Daniels v Walker* [2000] 1 WLR 1382 CA and *Cosgrove v Pattison* [2000] WL 1841601, also discussed in Chapter 9).

Adding an expert to level the playing-field

Case management judges will not often be sympathetic to applications requesting more than one expert from a particular discipline per party. 'Strength in numbers' will not usually be an attractive argument on proportionality grounds.

However, in *ES v Chesterfield Royal Hospital NHS Trust* [2003] EWCA Civ 1284, a clinical negligence cerebral palsy claim of high value and complexity, the claimant wanted to instruct two obstetrician experts on liability and causation because the defendant had two obstetricians, who had been involved in her care, as witnesses of fact, plus an obstetrician expert. This, she argued, gave the defendants an unfair advantage. At the case management conference it was held that the evidence of fact from the treating obstetricians could be isolated from the expert evidence on breach of duty, and the claimant was only given permission to call one expert. The Court of Appeal allowed the claimant's appeal, relying upon the overriding objective (CPR 1.1(2)(a)) ensuring the parties are on an equal footing and (c) dealing with a case in a way which is proportionate), on the basis that the defendant's witnesses would inevitably cover a much wider spectrum of medical experience than the claimant's single expert, which could lead to an imbalance at the trial.

Instructing an expert late in the proceedings

Parties are expected to decide upon the expert evidence they consider they need to prove their case at the stage of submission of allocation questionnaires or any early case management conference, so that comprehensive directions can be made, including for expert evidence, through to trial.

However, in a number of situations it can be prudent and more proportionate for a party (and the court) to delay a decision, for instance:

1. When one party only has instructed an expert but not yet disclosed the report and the second party is prepared to await the disclosure before deciding whether to seek permission to instruct their own expert.

2. When liability is very much in dispute and when quantum may be expensive to calculate – a split trial or trial of a preliminary issue may be the right course of action, and instructing experts only in relation to liability.

3. In a complex case, possibly requiring a number of experts, when it is preferable for only the key experts to be instructed initially, leaving the more peripheral ones, especially those dealing with specialist aspects of quantum, to be instructed later as necessary.

Generally, outside the circumstances outlined above, the courts are not very sympathetic to applications for additional expert evidence close to trial (for attempts to adjourn trial for late or unavailable experts, see Chapter 12).

In *Calenti v North Middlesex NHS Trust* (2nd March 2001, New Law 201047002), a clinical negligence claim arising from a viral illness the claimant had suffered, the defendant applied, one month before trial, for permission to adduce evidence from an acknowledged national expert in the viral illness. This was refused because:

a) they had known of this doctor for four years;

b) their expert witnesses had been in touch with him;

c) instructing him so late in the proceedings, when it would be necessary to put questions to him and for him to meet the other experts, would cause unwarranted delay to the trial.

In *Parkin v Bromley Hospitals Trust* [2002] EWCA Civ 478 CA, the claimant's life expectancy had been agreed as 'normal' two years before trial. Five weeks pre-trial and after a care regime had been put in place, the defendant applied to introduce new expert evidence on the life expectancy issue, arguing that the impact of the care regime was a "major change of circumstances" because the value of the claim had changed greatly as a result. This was not accepted.

Similarly, in *Calden v Nunn and Partners* [2003] WL 270906, the Court of Appeal refused to allow the defendant to rely upon an additional expert very late in the proceedings (who had been instructed without permission), after all the other experts had met and largely reached agreement, and when the trial window, already twice-postponed, was imminent. Instead, questions arising from the 'new' expert's report were to be put to the claimant's 'like' expert. Brooke LJ said that a number of aspects of the case "bore all the signs of sloppy pre-CPR practice creeping back".

However, on occasions, so as to 'deal with a case justly', the court will allow an expert to be instructed at a late stage and even allow a party to amend their statement of case based on the expert report. In *Holmes v SGB Services plc* [2001] JPIL 2/01 (p202) CA, no steps were taken by the claimant to obtain expert evidence until nine months after the defendant's witness statements were served, disputing that the personal injury accident could have happened in the way the claimant alleged. The single joint expert advanced a different possible explanation for the accident. The claimant was allowed to amend his particulars of claim and the trial date was vacated. The defendant's appeal was dismissed – the single joint expert's evidence took the case out of the run of ordinary case management decisions and it was for the first instance judge, not the Court of Appeal, to decide what weight to give to the various factors.

Furthermore, in *IPC Media Ltd v Highbury Leisure Publishing Ltd* [2004] EWHC 1967 Ch, a copyright dispute, the parties were given permission only two months before trial to adduce expert evidence on the similarities between the design features of two magazines. The court was persuaded partly because the claimant expressed concern that some of the defendant's witness statements came close to giving opinions on matters that "ought properly to be given by an expert", and partly because the defendant did not argue very strongly against the claimant's application.

EXPERTS AND CONFIDENTIALITY

Experts need to understand that information supplied to them in connection with a potential or actual claim is confidential to those proceedings. Neither parties, nor their solicitors or experts, can make use of information or documents obtained in an action, or documents such as witness statements prepared for use in an action, in other proceedings, without the express consent of the client or other party and of the court case managing the second action (see CPR 31.22). The only exception is documents that have been referred to in open court, usually at a trial.

In *D v C* [2001] EWCA Civ 1511 CA (sometimes reported as *Cornelius v De Taranto*), D (a forensic psychiatrist), sent a medico-legal report prepared for contemplated litigation against E (C's employer), to C's GP and to C's treating psychiatrist, without C's consent and before C had seen the report. C claimed against D for damages for defamation (for the contents of the report) and breach of confidence. The first instance judge ruled that there was a breach of confidence by D; she had no notes to confirm her allegation that she had obtained C's consent to a referral for treatment at their meeting (but the defamation claim was not upheld). £3750 was awarded to the claimant for injury to feelings. The Court of Appeal dismissed the appeal.

EXPERTS CHANGING THEIR OPINION

The Practice Direction to Part 35 paragraph 1.6 provides that:

"If, after producing a report, an expert changes his view on any material matter, such change of view should be communicated to all the parties without delay, and when appropriate to the court."

An expert will sometimes have good reason to change his mind after writing his report:

a) if you or the client provide him with relevant new material;

b) if new research or literature has become available;

c) when a report from the expert for the other party, or counsel at a conference, casts a different light on the case.

Provided that the expert communicates the change quickly, initially to the instructing party's solicitor, he cannot be criticised, even if the revised view is less helpful to the client. However, delay in communicating the new view contravenes Part 35, particularly if it is done shortly before, or at, trial.

197

Will an expert be criticised in court for changing his mind? It depends when and why he has done so. The following two cases illustrate the position well.

Transco plc v Griggs [2003] EWCA Civ 564 was a personal injury case concerning palmar arch disease, allegedly vibration-induced from the excessive use of road drills. There was a dispute on the diagnosis and causation between the medical experts. Both parties' medical experts changed their view to a degree after two discussion meetings. The Court of Appeal said that an expert's willingness to change his opinion in the light of discussion with others, and the evidence as it develops, may be a sign of strength rather than weakness.

In *Carpenter v Pembrokeshire County Council* [2002] EWHC 1968, the claimant's expert changed his mind about the safety of the claimant's driveway (in a dispute about its construction), after reaching an agreement with the other expert that safety was not an issue – he had been pressed by the claimant. The judge disregarded his evidence and said he "had abandoned his role as an expert".

EXPERTS' APPLICATIONS TO THE COURT FOR DIRECTIONS (CPR 35.14)

For the first time, under the CPR, experts have an express power to apply directly to the court for advice and directions "to assist in carrying out the expert's function". This power should be exercised circumspectly: neither the instructing solicitors nor the court take kindly to experts making frequent applications when the problem could be resolved by discussion.

Single joint experts are more likely to need to make use of this power, particularly if the parties or their solicitors are behaving very adversarially.

Experts must notify their instructing solicitor seven days before they apply to the court and the other party's solicitor four days before. Until March 2002, when this rule was changed, the expert could apply to the court directly without contacting the solicitors. Presumably, the reason for the change was to prevent unnecessary applications; but there is certainly no evidence to suggest experts have been making extensive use of their power.

The occasions when an expert might exercise the power could include:

1. When instructions from the parties to a single joint expert are irreconcilable, particularly within an agreed fees framework or court budget.

2. When the expert is concerned that one or both parties are holding back information and/or documents relevant to the preparation of the expert's report and opinion, the court has the power, under CPR 35.9, to order disclosure of information to an expert (also see above).

3. When questions posed by one or more parties on the expert's report are out of time (28 days from service of the report), appear to go further than clarification (e.g. they extend to cross-examination by post, or require substantial additional work), or are disproportionate, given the value of the claim, or the fees agreed with the expert.

4. When the other expert refuses to sign the statement prepared following an experts' discussion.

An expert can make an application to the court by letter. It should not be necessary for the expert to make a formal application, under CPR Part 23. The letter should include the title of the case, the court reference number and details of why directions are sought. The court may decide the application without a hearing.

Unfortunately, the courts have not shown themselves to be well-prepared for applications for directions by experts. Court staff have been known to simply file an expert's letter, rather than refer it to a judge. The letter may not then come to light until another application is made or there is a case management conference. The expert may need to progress-chase the letter if no response is received within a few weeks. This problem may be resolved when parties and experts are able to e-mail requests and applications directly to case management judges; in 2003, a pilot scheme began for e-mails to selected courts.

It is for the court to decide, after considering the expert's request, whether the court's response should be copied to the parties.

There is no reported case law to give guidance on how the courts view CPR 35.14.

EXPERTS AND CONFERENCES WITH COUNSEL

The most common time for experts to attend a conference with counsel is in the final stages of preparation for trial, to 'test' the expert evidence and discuss issues arising from the other party's expert evidence. However, in high value, complex and/or difficult cases, conferences may be advisable before proceedings have been issued (with an expert on liability and causation), or before a report is prepared (perhaps when the expert was instructed to advise pre-action but the case has changed shape significantly since then). When there are a large number of experts instructed by one party, a conference or conferences may be necessary when the main reports have been prepared (to consider gaps and inconsistencies), and when the other party's experts' reports have been served (to consider the differences of opinion and the possibility of a settlement).

Conferences with a 'team' of experts are difficult to arrange and expensive, so ensure the client or funder gives approval. If you have an expert you have not instructed before and/or who is a 'novice' expert, you may need to explain clearly to the expert in advance what will happen at the conference. Otherwise, counsel subjecting him to cross-examination may come as a shock.

At the end of, or after, the conference review the steps to be taken by you and the experts, and make sure dates for completion of any follow-up work are agreed.

Remember that if one or more single joint experts are instructed, attendance at a conference with counsel may not be possible unless the other party agrees – decided in *Peet v Mid-Kent Healthcare Trust* [2001] EWCA Civ 1703. This was a cerebral palsy clinical negligence claim, in which there were seven SJEs in different non-medical disciplines reporting on aspects of quantum. The claimant wanted the SJEs to attend a conference with counsel to better understand and test their views. The defendant objected. The Master and Court of Appeal refused permission because:

1. Part 35 was designed to ensure an open process.

2. A report by a single joint expert should be *the* evidence from that expert.

3. Before trial, a party should not be permitted to test an SJE's evidence, except by written questions, without the consent of the other party.

EXPERTS AND SETTLEMENTS

Experts' reports can be a crucial factor in assisting a settlement. If a report is not particularly favourable, you may want, with the client's agreement, to try to settle the case before the report has to be disclosed. If the report is generally favourable, you may want to make an offer to settle or a payment into court soon after disclosing it.

If one of your expert reports is imminent, you may want to wait before making a Part 36 offer. In *Flynn v Scougall* [2004] EWCA Civ 873, a personal injury claim, the defendant made a payment into court without waiting for a medical report she had commissioned. The report was favourable to the defendant and she wanted to pay in a lesser sum. The claimant accepted the original sum within the 21 days. The court decided that the defendant's application to reduce the payment did not act as a stay on the claimant's ability to accept the offer, as the defendant tried to argue. It was for the court to decide the two issues together.

Experts do not always realise that some of the matters of detail in their reports are important for negotiations (e.g. a% chance that x will occur), and express reluctance to be too specific in case they appear to be too dogmatic. However, it is unwise to press experts too far – over-dogmatic experts may be usurping the judge's role (see Chapter 12).

Experienced experts may be able to advise on issues arising from the other party's like report, to pursue in negotiation. Lawyers should, however, be careful not to draw an expert too far into tactics – their independence could be compromised.

If you are holding a settlement conference or mediation, consider if the expert has a role. Mediation practice is flexible enough to allow experts to attend mediation and even to include testing of the expert evidence in advance of trial. Ensure the experts are comfortable with what is proposed – involving experts as part of the team in a mediation or negotiation might not sit very comfortably with their duty to the court, particularly if the trial will be in the near future. An alternative would be to hold the experts' discussions (CPR 35.12) on the same day as the mediation, with the joint statement from the experts feeding into the mediation. Forensic accountants and similar quantum experts can be very useful in calculating or 'modelling' options to be explored.

When experts from the same discipline hold a discussion, they may assume, incorrectly, that part of the purpose of the discussion is for them to reach agreement or even to 'broker a deal'. Experts' discussions are covered in more detail in Chapter 11, but make sure your expert understands, before he attends a discussion, that the main purpose is to explore whether the areas of disagreement with the other expert can be narrowed.

CONCLUSIONS

In civil proceedings, an expert's main task, and sometimes the only task, is preparing the report for the court. If the case does not settle then the expert may have to answer written questions and/or attend an experts' discussion. It may be sensible also, in larger claims, to ask an expert to consider other experts' reports, and to attend a conference with the advocate, unless he is a single joint expert. Occasionally, experts might attend part of a negotiating meeting or a mediation. Certainly, experts appreciate being involved as a case progresses.

Beyond that, great care is needed. Experts may be able to assist with disclosure of technical or specialist documents, and liability experts might usefully comment upon draft statements of case. Yet, solicitors and counsel should be wary of drawing an expert too much into the case planning, strategy and teamwork, as there is a real risk that the expert's objectivity and duty to the court could be compromised. It should be a rare occurrence for an expert to interview witnesses, or have direct contact alone with the client at later stages of the case.

Challenging the other party's expert evidence, applying to the court to change your own expert or to add an expert late on in the proceedings, are steps to be taken only after very careful consideration as the risk of failure is high. The client needs to be involved in the decision and advised on the possible consequences.

Perhaps surprisingly, experts have only made limited use of their right to apply to the court for directions. Maybe this is because they generally have a good working relationship with solicitors.

Chapter 11
QUESTIONS ON REPORTS AND EXPERTS' DISCUSSIONS

Written questions on experts' reports and experts' discussions in civil cases were CPR innovations. The practice of the court ordering an experts' discussion to explore areas of agreement and disagreement in the experts' reports originated in the Technology and Construction Court (the former Supreme Court Rules Order 36, rules 1-9 and Order 38, rule 38). Lord Woolf frequently adopted examples of good practice from throughout the civil justice system in his *Access to Justice* reports.

The recommendation for experts' discussions in his interim report was widely supported. Only two reservations were expressed, that meetings would be:

1. Futile, if experts were instructed not to agree anything, or if any points of agreement had to be referred back to the lawyers for ratification. Lord Woolf's response was that this would be unprofessional conduct by the lawyers, which could be avoided in heavy cases by the court setting the agenda for the meeting.

2. Expensive, especially if lawyers were to attend. Lord Woolf's response was that, with a clear agenda and an efficient form of meeting (possibly by telephone or video conference), the costs could be contained. Lawyers would not normally attend but might be permitted by the court to do so in some cases 'as observers to ensure fair play'. If the outcome of meetings was to narrow areas of disagreement, and assist settlement or a shorter trial, there would be costs savings.

The Civil Procedure Rules for both written questions and discussions are short and the Practice Direction adds little guidance.

QUESTIONS ON REPORTS (CPR 35.6)

The purpose of the rule is to facilitate a helpful and open exchange of information after expert's reports have been served and prior to trial.

The provisions of CPR 35.6

35.6(2) provides that written questions:

a) may be put once only;

b) must be put within 28 days of service of the expert's report; and

c) must be for the purpose only of clarification of the report; unless the court gives permission or the other party agrees.

35.6(3) provides that an expert's answers to questions shall be treated as part of the report.

35.6(4) provides that where an expert fails to answer questions put in accordance with the rules, the court may order that:

a) the party may not rely upon the evidence of that expert; or

b) the party may not recover the fees and expenses of that expert from the other party.

The Practice Direction provides:

"5.2 that when a party sends written questions to an expert, they must be copied to the other party;

5.3 the party instructing the expert must pay any fees charged by the expert for answering questions put under rule 35.6."

The Protocol covers questions in section 16.

Time for answering the questions

The rules do not prescribe a time limit for the experts' replies to questions but the court will usually do this when giving case management directions. 14-28 days is usual – not unreasonable given that the trial may not be many weeks away, especially in fast track cases. Since April 2005, the Practice Direction requires parties to send the expert a copy of the court's case management directions, so that the timetable and any specific directions in relation to expert evidence are clear to them.

Solicitors and experts should not be too inflexible about either the 28-day period for putting the questions, or the court directed time for the answers. If questions or answers are slightly late, it only matters if this adversely affects the timetable to trial or the trial date itself. Clearly, questions that arrive very late, without agreement, e.g. more than 56 days from service of the report, may not have to be answered. The test is probably whether the trial judge is likely to find the answers helpful.

Experts' duty to answer questions

Experts have a duty to provide answers to questions properly put. Occasionally, an expert will not show commitment to a case once his report has been completed and disclosed, and will be reluctant to deal with questions (or attend an experts' discussion). The solicitor should remind him of CPR 35.6(4), as this gives the rule some teeth (see above).

Experts need to know when their report has been disclosed to the other party, so that they can note when the 28-day period begins and ends. Suggest to the expert also that he tells you when questions are received, in case the other party fails to send a copy to you, either by mistake or deliberately.

Fees for answering questions

In September 1999, the Practice Direction to Part 35 was amended to require the party instructing an expert to pay any fees charged by that expert for answering questions. Previously, it was the party asking the questions who paid the expert's fees. It seems likely that the change was made partly for practical reasons, to facilitate payment of the expert's fees (he only has to invoice one party). (Personal injury practitioners, however, should be aware that the personal injury pre-action protocol requires the party asking the questions to pay for the expert to answer them (see also Chapter 7).)

Working with experts on drafting questions

The number and content of permissible questions should depend upon the clarity of the report and proportionality. Be careful about drafting too many very detailed questions, or about going back with a second set of questions, if you are not satisfied with the first answers. This might prompt the other party or the expert to make an application to the court for an order that the questions do not have to be answered.

The rules say that only questions of **clarification** may be asked without the court's permission. This is not further explained. A common dictionary definition of to clarify is 'to make clear'. The author's impression is that parties and lawyers, however, sometimes interpret clarification as 'cross-examination by post', particularly in fast track claims or any other case when oral evidence at trial from the expert is unlikely.

Solicitors should involve 'their' expert in planning and drafting questions for the other party's expert. 'Your' expert should be able to suggest questions from the specialist or technical perspective, particularly if the report in question contains ambiguities, or there are unexplained omissions, or opinions expressed which do not seem to flow from the evidence. The expert should also check whether the report is self-contained; in particular, whether the results of tests and investigations are included, and whether any literature or research material is annexed or full references given (see *Wardlaw v Farrar* – discussed in Chapter 8).

You will want to check whether the expert's instructions apparently have been summarised accurately, which materials the expert was provided with and has relied upon, and whether copies of these documents have been disclosed (see the discussion on privilege and experts' reports and *Lucas v Barking NHS Trust* in Chapter 5). You will also want to highlight differences from your own expert's report in facts stated as given, assumptions made and particularly opinions and conclusions, and discuss these with your expert. If you are hoping to settle the case, you may want to frame questions that will encourage the other expert to be more precise on particular points.

Do not draft questions that:

a) require the expert to do further work;

b) ask for comments on issues outside the report or the expert's expertise;

c) involve complicated suppositions or hypotheses;

d) directly concern the expert's credibility.

It is not, of course, essential that you do put written questions to the other expert, especially if an experts' discussion is very likely to be held. Questions arising from the report could instead form part of the agenda for the discussion. This can save time and costs.

Do not assume that 'your' expert has to answer questions of the types included in the list above. Suggest to your expert that he checks with you whether questions have been served in time, and whether they comply with rules, before he answers them. You may be able to resolve any problems by discussion with the other party's solicitor. However, it is for the expert to provide the answers – do not be tempted to draft the replies for him, or to redraft his answers to make them more favourable to your client's case. (See also the Court of Appeal's guidance in *Mutch v Allen*, summarised below.)

Single joint experts

Single joint experts may be asked to answer questions from both parties, particularly if the expert is not to be called to give oral evidence, as is usually the case (see Chapter 9).

You should discuss an SJE report with the client in the same way as you would a party-instructed expert. If you and your client are not happy with the report because you consider it to be inaccurate, the opinions are not justified by the evidence, or the expert appears to be biased, you should put clarification questions to him within 28 days of receipt of the report. The questions and the expert's answers must be copied to the other party.

If you remain unhappy on receipt of the SJE's answers, you may wish to consider applying to the court for permission to:

a) change the SJE;

b) instruct an additional expert to the SJE; or

c) call the SJE to give oral evidence at trial.

For a further discussion on these options, see Chapter 9.

If an SJE is concerned that questions put to him are out of time or go further than clarification, he may exercise his power in CPR 35.14 to apply to the court for directions (see Chapter 10).

Questions and answers form part of the expert's report

As the expert's answers form part of his report, they are covered by his statement of truth and form part of his evidence. An expert may need to be reminded of this if his answers are in an over-adversarial style.

The report should not be amended to include the questions and answers, unless the exchange has led to very significant changes to the expert's approach to the issues: whereby a redraft may be necessary to assist the court. It is important to consider whether the cost of this is justified. Also, copies should be kept on file of the disclosed report, the questions and answers, and the amended report.

Guidance on CPR 35.6 from the Court of Appeal

Mutch v Allen ([2001] AER D121 CA) is the only reported case that provides judicial guidance on the use of written questions to experts. This was a personal injury case; the claimant had been badly injured when travelling as a backseat passenger in a car driven by the defendant. He had not been wearing a seatbelt, hence the defendant alleged contributory negligence. The claimant's main medical report noted that he was not wearing a seatbelt, but said nothing as to the consequences of this in relation to his injuries. The medical expert was asked by the defendant, in written questions under CPR 35.6, whether the claimant's injuries would have been materially reduced if he had been wearing a seat belt, and in particular which injuries would have been avoided altogether, and which would have been less severe. The claimant's solicitor objected to the questions and the expert did not reply. The District Judge ordered that the questions should be answered; when the expert did so, he confirmed that the injuries would have been much less severe, which adversely affected the claimant's case.

The dispute before the court was whether the expert's answers should be admitted at trial – the claimant objected on the ground that the questions were not clarification. The case management judge ordered that the answers should not be included, but the Court of

Appeal said that they should, even if the questions were not strictly "clarification"; the court had given permission for them to be put, the claimant had not appealed that decision, and the questions could have been put to the expert in cross-examination, had he attended court. Finally, the Court of Appeal said that one of the purposes of CPR Part 35 is to ensure that experts no longer serve just the interests of those who instruct them, but also contribute to a just resolution of the dispute.

This case suggests that the courts are prepared to be flexible about questions that go beyond clarification, if the answers are very material to the outcome of the case.

EXPERTS' DISCUSSIONS (CPR 35.12)

The CPR provisions

These are notable for their brevity.

1. The court may, at any stage, direct a discussion between experts for the purpose of requiring the experts to:

   a) identify *and discuss the expert* issues in the proceedings; and

   b) where possible, reach *an agreed opinion* on those issues.

2. The court may specify the issues which the experts must discuss.

3. The court may direct that following a discussion between the experts they must prepare a statement for the court showing:

   a) those issues on which they agree; and

   b) those issues on which they disagree and a summary of their reasons for disagreeing.

4. The content of the discussions between the experts shall not be referred to at the trial unless the parties agree.

5. Where experts reach agreement on an issue during their discussions, the agreement shall not bind the parties unless the parties have expressly agreed to be bound by such agreement.

The words in italics above were amended in March 2002 to provide greater clarity on the purpose of meetings (also see below).

The Practice Direction provides no further guidance.

The Protocol

(See Chapter 2 and Appendix 2)

The key points from the Protocol are:

1. The purpose of experts' discussions is to narrow the issues between the experts, identify the extent of agreement and disagreement (and reasons for the latter), and if any action might be taken to further narrow the areas of disagreement (paragraph 18.3)).

2. There should be an agenda prepared between the parties, the solicitors and experts, which should be agreed in advance. The agenda should indicate what matters have been agreed and summarise concisely those which are in issue. It might include questions to be answered by the experts (paragraph 18.5-6).

3. Arrangements for discussions should be proportionate – in small claims and fast track cases telephone discussions or an exchange of letters should suffice.

4. Lawyers will only be present if all parties agree and, if they are present, it will only be to answer questions from the experts (paragraph 18.8).

5. From the discussion, there should be a statement of the areas of agreement and disagreement, which should be copied to the parties and to the court. The summary should also indicate where progress might be made on those matters which cannot be agreed. The summary should be completed and signed by all the participants as soon as is practicable (paragraph 18.10-11).

6. Experts should not agree to attend a 'meeting of experts' if their instructions preclude their reaching agreement; such attendance would be contrary to the spirit of the 'expert meeting' and would merely waste time and money (paragraph 18.7).

The purpose of discussions

Narrowing, at an early stage, the issues to be decided by the court, including issues of expert opinion, is one of the fundamental purposes of judicial case management (see CPR 1.4(2)a)). A judge conducting a case management conference should not only decide whether to direct an experts' discussion, but in many circumstances should also decide, with the help of the parties and the lawyers, the scope and subject matter of that discussion.

Moreover, an important part of the court's case management powers is to set the timetable for the litigation (to prevent cases drifting for want of direction, or one or both parties unduly prolonging the dispute due to inefficiency or for tactical reasons). The court will usually, therefore, direct a timetable for the completion of the experts' discussions.

Experts' discussions can fulfil a number of different purposes, of which the following are probably the most important:

● They act as a check that the experts are working from similar instructions and the same materials.

● They enable the experts to better understand the reasons for their differing views.

● They assist the experts in narrowing, or even resolving, differences in opinion, particularly where these are likely to be material to the outcome of case.

● They assist the experts in agreeing any further work or steps which may be necessary to narrow the areas of disagreement.

● They produce a joint statement for the parties, and if so ordered, for the court, which highlights the areas of agreement and disagreement, to enable the parties and their lawyers to plan subsequent steps in the litigation, and if possible to work towards a settlement of the case.

● Where the action seems likely to proceed to trial, they reduce the issues upon which experts will need to give oral evidence.

While the content of experts' discussions is usually 'without prejudice', and only the statement produced is made available to the parties and to the court it can, nonetheless, be very useful for an expert to see how his 'opposite number' performs at a discussion, particularly his ability to substantiate opinion evidence with reasoned argument, in the face of a different point of view. This will be particularly so when the experts did not know one another prior to their involvement in the case.

Conversely, experts' discussions are not a forum for the experts to seek to resolve the legal issues in the action, or any other matter outside their expertise, unless the experts receive specific instructions to that effect from the parties and their lawyers. Expert witnesses instructed in litigation are not advocates for the parties, and it is not their role to negotiate or to seek to settle the action at an experts' discussion. Solicitors may need to remind experts of this. It is for the parties and their lawyers to consider the effect of any agreement or disagreement between the experts on the future conduct and outcome of the case.

The time and place for a discussion

Sometimes the discussion will be after exchange of reports, sometimes before. There is no reason why a discussion cannot take place even before the experts prepare their reports, for instance, where it would be helpful to agree methodology. The timing needs to be agreed. The usual court direction is that a discussion will take place by a specified date after written questions under CPR 35.6 have been answered.

The practicalities of arranging a date and place for a discussion can be problematic, especially when experts are very committed in their non-expert witness working lives. The solution is often a telephone conference (see below). The venue is also an important consideration. It could be a neutral location, or the experts or solicitors' offices. Access to telephones and a computer (to draft the joint statement) can be useful.

The number of discussions

In the majority of cases, there will only be one discussion but, in larger, more complex and technical cases, as the Academy's *Code of Guidance* suggests, there may be more than one. Perhaps the first will occur before the experts draft their reports, the second after exchange of reports (and possibly questions and answers) and occasionally a third in the run-up to trial or at court. Proportionality and approval by the client are obviously issues if more than one discussion seems necessary.

The type of discussion

The rules refer to 'discussions', not meetings. The discussion can take place:

1. Face-to-face.
2. By telephone.
3. By video conference.

The method chosen will depend on several factors, including:

a) the time scale and the experts' diaries;
b) the value of the dispute – proportionality;
c) the nature of the dispute and how complicated the evidence is;
d) whether documents and graphics need to be considered;
e) the number of attendees;
f) the importance of the expert evidence in question to the outcome of the case.

The principle of proportionality applies. It is good practice to note the reasons why a particular method was selected. This may avoid problems at the assessment of costs.

Discussions can profitably be held **by telephone** when:

- The experts have had previous contact, particularly if they know one another's work very well.

- There are only a few points to discuss arising from the reports, which do not involve checking paperwork, calculations or reference material together.

- The trial timetable makes it very difficult to organise a face-to-face meeting; the courts are not willing to adjourn trials for the convenience of experts (see Chapter 12).

- The claim is of a relatively low value, meaning that a face-to-face meeting would be disproportionate in cost. This is particularly the case if the experts are located at some distance from one another and a meeting would involve at least one day's work.

However, telephone discussions clearly have their limitations:

- They can be exploited by a party or expert who does not really want a discussion. The author was told of a discussion which took place with one expert on a mobile telephone which conveniently cut off each time he had made a point before his opponent could respond.

● It can be much more difficult for the experts to prepare the joint statement which the parties and the court require. It is essential that the experts agree, in advance of the telephone call, who is to prepare the note and preferably that this will be done soon after the call, and that it will be e-mailed or faxed to the other expert for agreement that day.

Conversely, **face-to-face meetings** are much better suited to situations where there are a large number of issues to be discussed between the experts, particularly if they have been working from different instructions and factual evidence, and/or there are major differences in opinion in the reports, based upon the experts' own professional experience, or upon their understanding of established practices in the profession or discipline in question. This is particularly so if the experts do not know one another, or if they will need to look carefully at research or reference material or the paperwork included in their instructions at the meeting.

Of course, an important factor to take into account before arranging a face-to-face meeting is the time and cost involved. Experts should obtain advance approval from the instructing solicitors to the cost of attending a face-to-face meeting and for follow-up work, even where the court has ordered the discussion.

In future, experts' discussions by **video-conferencing** will have distinct advantages, as these could combine the best features of telephone discussions and face-to-face meetings, especially if the experts are able to work on documents on-line simultaneously.

Who should set up the discussion?

There are four possibilities:

1. The **parties** themselves arrange an experts' discussion at an early stage in the dispute, perhaps even before solicitors are instructed. This is most likely to happen in a dispute between businesses, in one which has a high technical content, or where the organisations have in-house lawyers.

2. The **experts** suggest a discussion to plan the methodology of the

work or to narrow the issues in their reports. This is most likely when the opinion evidence concerns highly technical issues and/ or the parties or their lawyers are not particularly experienced in the problem area of the dispute.

3. The **lawyers** suggest a meeting. This is the most frequent scenario because the lawyers conducting the litigation are often in the best position to appreciate the importance of the expert opinion evidence to the case, and are (or should be) aware of proportionality and cost benefit issues.

4. The **court** may order the discussion as a matter of routine (the norm particularly in multi-track cases, or when the court has agreed to each side having their own expert in a fast track case).

If the court directs there shall be a discussion, the experts must comply. In *Stevens v Gullis* [2000] 1 AER 527 (previously discussed in Chapter 8), an expert declined to sign a joint statement following an experts' discussion, despite a specific court order. His evidence was struck out.

Who should be at the discussion?

This is probably the most controversial subject in relation to experts' discussions.

There are two schools of thought. The **generally preferred view** (see Lord Woolf's comments in his final report and the codes of guidance) is that only experts should attend.

The reasons why this is the preferred view include:

1. The role of experts' discussions is to enable expert opinion issues to be debated in a full and frank way, and for the experts to produce a joint statement of the areas of agreement and disagreement. They should not be hindered by the views of others involved.

2. Usually it will be too expensive, and disproportionate, for others to attend.

3. If lawyers attend, they may seek to influence the experts' opinions inappropriately, particularly to prevent agreements that are unhelpful to their client's case.

Other **problems,** which have been mentioned to the author, are:

- Experts of different disciplines may be asked to meet. This suggests poor planning and instruction of experts but, on occasions, may be practicable if there are issues in common covered in the reports.

- Experts can be present who are out of date in their practical experience, and with whom it is difficult or impossible to discuss current professional issues.

- Inexperienced experts, who have been poorly briefed for the discussion, can be present.

The **alternative view** is that it is helpful if lawyers are present, at least in some circumstances, for the following reasons:

1. They can answer questions about the law, evidence or procedures.

2. They can ensure that the experts cover any pre-prepared agenda.

3. They can prevent the experts' discussion trespassing into areas outside their expertise or brief.

4. They can ensure fair play, e.g. to prevent a more senior expert 'pulling rank' or bullying a 'more junior' expert.

5. They can ensure that the experts prepare a joint statement, and preferably at the meeting.

When lawyers do attend, generally their role will be as observers (as Lord Woolf suggested), to ensure fair play and not to participate in, and certainly not to hinder, the discussion. If a lawyer did attempt to unduly influence the outcome of an experts' meeting, this would be counter-productive, as it would devalue the purpose of the meeting, would be apparent to the opposing lawyer and expert, and would run a serious risk of the opposing party making an application to the court, possibly to have the lawyer removed from the record, or for an award of 'wasted costs' against the lawyer at the end of the action.

Lawyers should not turn up to an experts' discussion unannounced – a recipe for an abortive meeting – but the author has been told it happens!

A compromise is for the experts to meet alone but for the solicitors to be available on the telephone to answer questions and deal with problems.

The leading judicial authority on experts' discussions is *H v Lambeth Southwark & Lewisham HA* [2001] EWCA Civ 1455, a complex clinical negligence claim concerning an alleged failure to diagnose a progressive congenital condition in four children in the same family. The claimant lawyers were concerned about the forthcoming experts' meeting, because the claimant experts were reluctant to discuss the actions of the eminent consultant who was allegedly negligent and there was a risk that in a closed environment with colleagues they might be 'persuaded to pull their punches'. They argued that, in those circumstances, it could be a breach of Article 6 of the ECHR if the meeting went ahead without lawyers present.

The Court of Appeal decided that an experts' discussion does not engage the question of a right to a fair trial under ECHR Article 6, because the court's power to order a discussion is discretionary and any agreement reached at the discussion is not binding on the parties, or on the court. The court declined to order that the claimants' lawyers should attend the discussion on the grounds that their input should be to a "well-crafted agenda" and it was also suggested that the meeting might be recorded and more generally, when time and cost permitted, the appointment of an independent legally-qualified person to chair an experts' discussion might be considered.

The **Clinical Disputes Forum** has produced some guidance on experts' discussions in clinical negligence claims. It is the only guide to suggest that lawyers should be present at a discussion unless the parties agree otherwise. For the moment at least, the Court of Appeal does not agree.

Single joint experts and discussions

Self-evidently, SJEs will not often attend discussions! However, on occasions they may be invited to attend a larger discussion of both parties' experts or a discussion with an additional expert in the same discipline permitted by the court (see Chapter 9). The **Academy of Experts'** *Code of Guidance* suggested that, where a single joint expert had been instructed but a party had, with the permission of the court, instructed its own additional Part 35 expert, there should normally be a discussion between the single joint expert and the Part 35 expert. Lord Woolf adopted this suggestion in *Daniels v Walker* (see Chapter 10). The author is not aware of this being a frequent practice, however.

Discussions between experts from different disciplines

Sometimes parties will instruct experts from different disciplines to prepare reports on an aspect of a case (e.g. a nurse and an occupational therapist to prepare a care report, or a building surveyor and a civil engineer to prepare a report on building defects). While not ideal, these 'pairs' may still be required to discuss their reports. Careful agenda preparation is required in these circumstances.

Group discussions

Sometimes meetings may be arranged between a **number of experts**, if their evidence is closely related, particularly in more complex high value claims, or where a **lead expert** has been instructed under CPR 35.7 (see Chapter 3). This type of meeting is much more expensive and difficult to organise. It will generally need a neutral chairman and more sophisticated arrangements for note-taking, and for preparation of the statement for the court.

The agenda

Agendas for most experts' discussions are vital to ensure that the experts confine the discussion to matters of opinion evidence, and especially to those issues which are likely to be particularly relevant to the outcome of the case.

Solicitors perceive the dangers of unplanned meetings as:

a) not advancing the case sufficiently and increasing costs unnecessarily;

b) allowing experts to stray into areas outside their brief or expertise, particularly into matters of legal liability;

c) leading to experts acting as advocates, and attempting to settle the case.

There is certainly merit in these concerns, because the joint statement of the experts' discussion is placed on the court file. Although it is not binding upon the parties (without their consent), or upon the court, in practice it may be very difficult for the parties' advocates to 'unpick' agreements reached by experts at a discussion, unless these are blatantly outside their terms of reference.

As the main purpose of the discussion is to narrow or settle any differences of view between the experts on matters at issue relevant to their opinion evidence, the solicitors should not give instructions as to the precise outcome of the meeting, or on what the experts can or cannot agree, otherwise the meeting serves no purpose except paying lip-service to the idea.

By contrast, some experts have told the author that they prefer not to have an agenda at all, or certainly a flexible one, which they may even draft at the beginning of the meeting. This is because they see the main purpose of the experts' discussions as a full and frank debate on issues in the case.

On occasions, particularly in complex or technical litigation, **the court** may give specific directions and **set the agenda** for an experts' discussion. You should ensure the experts are given copies of any specific directions for the meeting from the court.

On the assumption that at least an outline agenda is desirable, **best practice** suggests that solicitors and experts should draft this together. The most usual procedure will be for the parties' solicitors each to prepare a draft and give 'their' expert sufficient opportunity to comment, before agreeing the final version some days before the meeting.

There is some agreement that the agenda should include a list of **specific questions** arising from the expert evidence, to which the lawyers consider need answers. These will be easier for the experts to answer if they are drafted to invite yes/no responses, and the questions are set out in the form of a schedule, giving adequate space for the experts to give their reasons for the answers. This type of format will invite completion of the joint statement on the spot.

It is also a good idea to permit sufficient time at the meeting to enable experts to raise and discuss other issues, provided they understand that these must be confined to matters strictly relevant to the opinion evidence.

In any event, those arranging the meeting should try to avoid problems, such as one expert arriving at a meeting with an agenda that the other one has not seen before.

The discussion

Experts should have with them:

1. Both experts' reports and any written questions and answers under CPR 35.6.

2. The documents the expert relied upon in preparing the report.

3. The agenda.

4. A laptop, draft schedule or paper to prepare the statement.

5. A telephone to discuss queries with the instructing solicitors.

Experts might tape-record a meeting – but only if they both agree in advance and if they agree that the tape can be listened to by anyone other than the experts. The Court of Appeal, in *H v Lambeth Southwark and Lewisham HA* (see above), suggested tape-recording an experts' discussion as an alternative to the lawyers or clients attending.

The exact format and timetable of the meeting is very much a matter for the experts but the author suggests that in the course of the meeting, the experts:

a) check and agree the agenda;

b) plan the time available;

c) check each other's instructions and the documents the other relied upon (as often differences in reports stem from different instructions);

d) have the general discussion;

e) have a discussion of any specific questions on the agenda;

f) recap on areas of agreement and disagreement;

g) prepare the joint statement and sign it.

The joint statement for the court

An agreed note or statement of the discussion is essential for the parties and their lawyers to use in the next stages of the litigation. If the court has ordered that an experts' discussion should take place, the court will expect a note/statement of the meeting, to be prepared for the benefit of the judge hearing the trial.

In *Plymouth South West Co-operative Society Ltd v ASM* [2004] EWHC 2938 (TCC), the trial judge was critical of the absence of a statement in a case in which there were significant differences between the experts giving evidence. In *DN v Greenwich London Borough* [2004] EWCA Civ 1659, the Court of Appeal was critical when an experts' discussion took place over the weekend before the trial and the joint statement was only delivered on the morning the trial started, which was "far too late for the parties to absorb its significance in an orderly manner".

The preferred view is that the note of the discussion should be prepared on the spot at the meeting while the discussion, the answers to specific questions and any other issues are very fresh in the experts' minds. Preparing the note later, in practice, seems to lead to arguments about what was agreed; the author has been told of cases where delay in preparing the note has prevented one being produced at all.

However, in the following circumstances, delaying completion of the note until after the discussion may be inevitable:

1. When there is extreme time pressure, especially if one or both experts are travelling from a long distance.

2. When experts only discover at the meeting that they have been working from very different instructions and material.

3. When new evidence or a new argument emerges at the discussion, which leads one or both experts to substantially rethink their opinions on key issues.

4. When there is a need to consult reference material not available at the discussion.

5. When it is a meeting taking place by telephone or video link.

If there is a delay, it must be short, and a timetable should be agreed at the discussion for finalising the statement.

The note or statement should be in accordance with the instructions and agenda. Usually, answers to specific questions (along with reasons), will be required, and/or a note on areas of agreement and disagreement. Experts should feel ready to add any other points not specifically raised in the agenda, which they consider are relevant to the expert opinion matters covered in their reports. However, it is essential to bear in mind that:

- It is not the role of the experts to determine legal issues or try to decide the case. It is the court's role to decide upon disputed issues of fact and law, but expert evidence may give support to the issue of whether a legal test has been breached, even if that question is ultimately one that the court has to decide.

- Comments outside the specific expertise of the experts in question are dangerous and should be avoided.

The statement is prepared at least partly for the court and, therefore, needs to be short and confined to the key issues. Hart J in *Morris v Bank of India*, 15th November 2001 (unrep) said of the statement: "it is not intended to be a document of use to the court in deciding which of the experts on those points of disagreement is correct".

The note should be signed by both experts and, perhaps (although the rules do not specifically require this), it should also contain the standard statement of truth (which is a requirement in all experts' reports). Failure to sign the statement can be fatal – see *Stevens v Gullis* [2000] 1 AER 527, discussed above. However, a note not exactly in the right format might be admitted in evidence when the fault was not the experts' – see *Prosser v Castle Sanderson Solicitors* (discussed in Chapter 10).

Experts must not refer the statement to the instructing solicitor for agreement before signing it. Interference by solicitors or parties with the experts, in their complying with the directions given by the court, may amount to a breach of the court's directions – with the result that permission to rely on the expert's evidence at trial may be refused,

In *Robin Ellis Ltd v Malwright Ltd* [1999] BLR 81, 15 Construction Law Journal 14, a trial of a preliminary issue in a dispute concerning a construction contract, the defendant's counsel wished to use the expert's joint statement in cross-examination of the witnesses for the claimant. Counsel for the claimant objected on the ground that it was privileged. The court confirmed that the statement was not privileged, even though the discussion took place 'without prejudice': the statement was a document produced for the court to assist in the management of the litigation and the conduct of the trial.

The fact that the joint statement is not binding was emphasised in *Britannia Zinc v Southern Electric Contracting Ltd* [2002] AER D 68 TCC, in which loss adjusters met and agreed a figure for the losses sustained by the claimant. The claimant argued that the claim was compromised but Seymour J disagreed and said, "it is ludicrous to suggest that merely by appointing a person to act as an expert witness in litigation a party is impliedly clothing that person with authority to enter into a binding (settlement) agreement on its behalf".

A client putting pressure on an expert, following an experts' discussion, is equally bad practice. In *Carpenter v Pembrokeshire County Council* [2002] EWHC 1968, the dispute concerned negligent construction of a driveway. The claimant's expert was severely criticised by the trial judge, because he allowed himself to be pressurised by the claimant to say that he was concerned about the safety of the driveway, after agreeing with the defendant's expert at an experts' discussion that this was not an issue.

After the discussion

Solicitors should check the note, particularly whether:

a) the experts kept to the agenda and to matters within their expertise;

b) all the questions on the agenda have been answered;

c) reasons have been given for any continuing areas of disagreement;

d) any action has been agreed to resolve any outstanding questions.

Solicitors will also want to consider carefully the areas of agreement and what this means for the case. They should send the statement to the client and explain its significance, and possibly discuss it with counsel. The expert may also want a de-briefing discussion with 'their' lawyer, particularly if either expert significantly changed their opinions as a result of the discussion. Solicitors should not be surprised if this happens, as experts may understand the issues better after a meeting and the need to justify one's opinion with one's peer may moderate views.

An expert who changes his opinion as a result of a discussion with another expert may be praised by the court. In *Transco plc v Griggs* [2003] EWCA Civ 564, a personal injury case concerning vibration-induced injury in which both sides' medical experts had changed their minds to a degree following discussions, the Court of Appeal said that an expert's willingness to change his opinions, in the light of discussion with others and the evidence as it develops, may be a sign of strength rather than of weakness.

The note is not binding on the parties, unless they agree otherwise, but as it will be placed on the court file and will be seen by the trial judge, in practice it will be difficult for the parties to argue against views expressed in the statement by the expert whom they instructed. It will be on very rare occasions only that the court will give permission for a party not to rely upon their own expert's opinions, or to introduce new evidence at a late stage to discredit that opinion.

Experts must try to ensure their views are properly and clearly stated in the joint statement. In *Yousif v Jordan* [2003] EWCA Civ 1852, an imprecise statement led the trial judge to dismiss the claim. A retrial was ordered, on the basis that the judge had failed to keep sufficiently in mind the content of the claimant's expert's report which did provide evidence linking the nasal obstruction to the operation (see also Chapter 12 for further discussion of this case). The lessons to be learned from *Yousif* are:

a) to ensure that the advocate is carefully briefed on apparent inconsistencies and ambiguities between your expert's report and the meeting joint statement; or

b) if the case is of sufficient value and complexity, to seek permission for supplemental questions to be put to the experts following the meeting, or to call your expert to give oral evidence.

Sometimes, if the statement is prepared weeks or even months before trial, it may be necessary to prepare an updating statement if other evidence is disclosed in the intervening period. This is most likely to happen in a complex case, where there are a number of pairs of experts who are meeting or discussing their opinion evidence in the run-up to trial.

Experts' discussions at mediation or court

Occasionally, experts are asked to attend mediations or other forms of Alternative Dispute Resolution to assist in settlement. Usually, this involves advising the client and the party's lawyers on strengths and weaknesses or aspects of quantum, but the mediation process is very flexible and sometimes the 'pairs' of experts may be asked to hold discussions within the mediation, to reduce areas of disagreement or to assist with extra-legal options for settlement.

There is still a place for ***ad hoc* experts' discussions at court**, shortly prior to or during the trial, even when the experts have met and discussed the case prior to trial. Inevitably in a trial which is heavily dependent on expert opinion issues, matters will arise from the evidence which need to be discussed by the experts, in the same way that the advocates and solicitors hold periodic discussions and negotiations. These *ad hoc* meetings at court may serve a number of purposes:

a) helping the experts to reach further agreement on issues that arise in evidence which are not really in dispute;

b) helping to narrow down the matters for cross-examination;

c) assisting in settlement.

CONCLUSION

Questions to experts and experts' discussions are probably two of the least controversial aspects of CPR Part 35. In the main, they are being used effectively. Certainly, experts tell the author that they are called to give oral evidence at many fewer trials than pre-CPR. The fears expressed by lawyers to Lord Woolf about experts' discussions – that they would be futile if the experts were instructed not to agree anything, and would be expensive (see the Introduction to this chapter) – do not seem to have materialised.

Chapter 12
EXPERTS AT TRIAL

INTRODUCTION

The majority of disputes now settle well before trial. Therefore, solicitors often have little experience of the steps that need to be taken in the few months before trial, including in relation to expert evidence. Dealing with written questions and answers on experts' reports and arranging experts' discussions are the significant procedural steps at this stage, but filing the pre-trial checklist, instructing counsel, arranging conference(s) with counsel, client and experts, and/or negotiation meetings and preparing the experts for trial are also important.

This chapter gives practical advice on this preparation work, and also looks at how judges weigh up expert evidence at trial from post-CPR reported cases.

THE PRE-TRIAL CHECKLIST (FORMERLY THE LISTING QUESTIONNAIRE)

Permission from the court (a case management judge) is essential for an expert witness to give oral evidence at trial. This will not usually be given until after the pre-trial checklist has been filed, except in large or complex cases where there has been a case management conference after the experts' reports have been disclosed. In the latter cases, an early application for a fixed trial date is essential. As the pre-trial checklist is filed only 8-10 weeks before trial, and final court directions will be received a few weeks later, there may be difficulties in ensuring your experts are available to give oral evidence. This is discussed in more detail below.

The pre-trial checklist requires solicitors:

1. To list the names and fields of expertise of their experts, and indicate for each one whether they are a joint expert, and whether their report is agreed.

2. To state whether there has been a discussion between experts and whether they have signed a joint statement.

3. To give dates to avoid if experts are to be required to give oral evidence, and the trial date is not yet fixed.

If you are seeking permission for the experts to give oral evidence, you may also need to be able to demonstrate that:

a) expert evidence is likely to significantly affect the outcome of the trial;

b) oral evidence from the experts is likely to assist the trial judge;

c) there is a risk of injustice if the expert evidence is not tested at trial; and

d) the cost of the experts' attendance is proportionate.

It is rare for permission to be given for oral expert evidence at one day fast track trials – the first drafts of the rules precluded it entirely and there is no reported authority on when the court might be persuaded it is necessary. If you consider that oral expert evidence really is essential in a case allocated to the fast track, it may be preferable to apply for the case to be reallocated to the multi-track, as the trial is very likely to last more than one day.

It is also uncommon for permission to be given for single joint experts to give oral evidence at trial. However, occasionally case management judges have been persuaded that examining the single joint expert is a preferable solution to instructing a further expert or adjourning the trial (see *Layland v Fairview New Homes plc* [2002] EWHC 1350 Ch) (when the issue in dispute was the value of a property) and *Austen v Oxford City Council* [2002] AER D 97 (when a single joint expert psychiatrist's report in a personal injury case was hostile and unfavourable to the claimant). (These cases are discussed more fully in Chapter 9.)

The European Court of Human Rights has said that a refusal to allow a party to examine witness evidence that may be crucial to the outcome of the case may be a breach of Article 6 of the European Convention of Human Rights. (See for instance *Kostovski v The Netherlands* EHRR (20th December 1989) Series A No 166 and *Saidi v France* ECHR (20th September 1993) Series A No 251C, although these were criminal trials and the point does not seem to have been argued fully in a civil context.)

CPR 35.11 AND CPR 35.13

These two rules complement one another. **CPR 35.11** provides that where a party has disclosed an expert's report, any party may use that report as evidence at the trial. This rule is based on the principle that 'there is no property in a witness', including an expert witness. Therefore, if the opposing party has disclosed an expert's report but subsequently decides not to rely upon that report or call the expert to give oral evidence at trial, you could do so, with permission.

CPR 35.13 provides that a party who fails to disclose an expert's report may not use the report at the trial or call the expert to give oral evidence unless the court gives permission. This seems to assume that the party in question has been given permission to rely upon a particular expert's report, and has neglected to disclose it on time. It was not an infrequent practice pre CPR for parties, particularly defendants, to produce late experts' reports even during the trial – an example of the 'litigation by ambush' tactics the reforms sought to prevent. The practical consequences of late service of expert's reports and the case law were discussed in Chapter 10. The party wishing to rely upon a report served late would need to apply, under rule 3.9, for relief from the sanction in rule 35.13.

ENSURING EXPERT EVIDENCE IS PRESENTED AT TRIAL

Securing experts' availability for trial

This requires good teamwork and planning. The Protocol (see Chapter 2 and Appendix 2) helpfully states that experts have an obligation to attend court if called upon to do so (paragraph 19.1). Experts should be kept advised of the directions and timetable from allocation stage onwards, particularly of the trial window, or likely period in which the trial will take place. They should be invited to provide the solicitor with their specific availability, at the latest before the Pre-Trial checklist is completed or a fixed trial date is applied for. It is prudent not only to obtain information on when the experts *are* available, but also on the reasons *why* they are not available for particular days within the actual or likely trial window.

In *Matthews v Tarmac Bricks and Tiles* (*The Times*, 1st July 1999), junior counsel representing the defendant (attending a hearing to fix the date of the trial) had a list of the dates on which the defendants' experts were not available, but not the reasons. The judge simply fixed the trial for a date that suited everyone else, but on which the two defendant medical experts were not available. The defendants appealed (one expert was going to be on holiday and the other had been subpoenaed to attend court in another case). The appeal failed because the defendants had not made sufficient effort to check whether the first doctor might change his holiday, and whether the second doctor could give evidence in the two cases on the one day, by co-operation between all the parties and the courts.

Moreover, Lord Woolf, giving the lead judgment, said:

"If they hold themselves out as practising in the medico-legal field doctors must be prepared to arrange their affairs to meet the commitments of the courts where this is practical."

While this decision might be explained as the Court of Appeal wishing to appear to be firm about court timetables and trial dates soon after the implementation of the CPR, the message is nonetheless clear – lawyers must provide the courts with the reasons for experts non-availability.

Unavailability of an expert witness will also rarely be justification for an application to adjourn an already fixed trial date, particularly if the expert witness has been instructed relatively late in the case without first checking his availability for trial. This is what happened in *Rollinson v Kimberley Clark Ltd* (*The Times*, 22nd June 1999). In a personal injury case, the Court of Appeal dismissed an appeal by the defendant of a refusal to adjourn a trial date. The defendant had only instructed their expert many months after the parties had agreed that another expert opinion was merited, and only a few months before trial, for which a date was fixed. The Court of Appeal said the defendants should have checked their expert's availability for the specific trial date before they instructed him.

The situation might be different if the type of expertise required is very unusual (see *Great Future International Ltd v Sealand Housing Corp (No 4)* [2001] WL 825214, when the expertise required was in Chinese law. The adjournment application was refused, but for another reason – there had been a long delay in arranging a change of solicitors and the court said that an adjournment to obtain the expert evidence alone might have been permitted).

If late expert evidence has been permitted and this leads to important new lines of inquiry, the court might be persuaded to adjourn the trial. In *Holmes v SGB Services plc* [2001] JPIL 2/01 (p202) CA, the personal injury trial, which was fixed for three weeks ahead, was adjourned to enable the claimant to amend his particulars of claim arising from the report of a single joint expert engineer. His recently served report suggested a possible alternative explanation for how the accident occurred. The defendant appealed but the appeal was dismissed by the Court of Appeal, who were unwilling to disturb a case management decision.

Witness summonses (CPR 34.2)

If there is some doubt about the expert's availability to give essential oral evidence at trial, issue a witness summons under CPR 34.2, particularly if the expert has another trial or commitment in his diary for the same day or period. Many experts do not appreciate being served with a summons, as they perceive it as a hostile act, but a slightly disgruntled expert is better than an order to pay wasted costs for an adjournment, or a claim in negligence if the expert does not attend and the case is lost.

The summons can be issued in the court where the case is proceeding, or in the trial court. Permission from the court is only required if the summons is issued less than seven days before the trial (CPR 34.3(2)). When the summons is served, the witness must be offered, or paid, sums to cover his travelling expenses and to compensate him for his loss of time (known as 'conduct money') (CPR 34.7). The court serves a witness summons by first class post, which may be fast enough when the difficulty is the witness securing time off work, e.g. an NHS consultant. However, in most circumstances it is preferable to arrange personal service of the summons. To be binding, the summons must be served at least seven days before trial (CPR 34.5(1)).

Rule 34.7 was a CPR innovation and certainly applies to expert witnesses. In *Brown v Bennett* (*The Times*, 2nd November 2000), an expert witness sought to set aside a witness summons because the party instructing him could or would not pay his fees for attending court. The court set the summons aside, saying that only in exceptional circumstances would an expert, who could not be paid, be compelled to give evidence.

Depositions (CPR 34.8)

CPR 34.8 provides for a witness to be 'examined' by a judge or examiner of the court before the trial takes place. Permission is required. The witness gives evidence before the examiner and the parties' representatives and can be cross-examined. The evidence is then transcribed and the document is put in evidence at the trial. In theory, this would be a possible solution if an expert is not available for the trial date and an adjournment is not feasible. However, in practice, the provision seems to be rarely used in relation to expert witnesses, probably on grounds of costs.

In the USA, depositions are used frequently, and sometimes scientific and technical expert evidence is tested by the trial judge at a pre-trial hearing (known as a Daubert hearing), to ensure that the evidence is relevant, reliable and can be properly applied to the case in question. The criteria the judges apply include whether any theories put forward by the expert have been published, subject to peer review, or are generally accepted as being valid or can be tested at court. This type of hearing would have its attractions in this jurisdiction when a party wishes to rely upon controversial or experimental expert evidence (see also the section on experts 'theorising' at trial, below).

Evidence by video link (CPR 32.3)

If your expert witness can be available for sufficient time to give evidence on the trial date, but not if he has to travel to the trial court to do so, consider whether he might give evidence by video link. This will only be possible in some courts, and if the expert can attend a suitable video facility. Permission from the court will be required. (See Annex 3 to the Practice Direction Part 32.)

In *Rowland v Bock* [2002] EWHC 692, a party in a debt action successfully appealed an order refusing to allow one of his witnesses to give evidence by video link from Germany (the witness was at risk of being arrested if he returned to the UK). It was held on appeal that the Master, in refusing the request, had failed to give sufficient regard to the need to ensure that parties were "on an equal footing" (under Part 1, the overriding objective), and that his ruling that evidence by video should be limited to cases of illness was too restrictive.

INVOLVING THE ADVOCATE IN THE EXPERT EVIDENCE

Consider in sufficient time whether a conference with the main experts and the advocate is necessary or advisable pre-trial, particularly when you have not instructed the expert(s) before, nor seen them in the witness box. Experts who have not previously given oral evidence will appreciate some advice on likely issues for cross-examination, from you and/or the trial advocate. This can usually be most efficiently achieved at a conference.

It is not, of course, permissible to 'coach' an expert in what they are to say at trial – this would be a breach of the Law Society or Bar Council Professional Conduct Rules. 21.10 of the *Guide to the Professional Conduct of Solicitors* (Eighth Edition, 1999) states that a solicitor must not tamper with the evidence of a witness, or attempt to suborn the witness into changing his evidence, and *R v Salisbury* [2005] EWCA Crim 871, a criminal case against a nurse, in which it was alleged that a number of prosecution witnesses from the NHS had been trained to give evidence. On the facts, after an inquiry, Pitchford J concluded that the witnesses had undergone a process of familiarisation with the pitfalls of giving evidence, which did not invalidate their evidence.

Single joint experts can only attend conferences with counsel with the other party's consent (see *Peet v Mid-Kent Healthcare Trust* [2001] EWCA Civ 1703, discussed in Chapter 9).

Consider whether the advocate might also be sent:

● Copies of the instructions to the expert(s), if they are not annexed to the report(s), and of other key correspondence with the expert.

● Drafts of 'your' experts' reports if they have changed materially before disclosure and/or a note to explain changes that were made and why.

- The comments of the expert(s) on the other party's experts' reports.

- Background on 'your' experts and the other party's experts who will be giving oral evidence. For 'your' experts, any references obtained and their CVs may be useful. For both parties' experts, references to cases in which judges have commented on their evidence, or copies of publications in which they have expressed views relevant to the issues in the instant case, may be useful for cross-examination.

TRIAL PLANNING AND EXPERTS

Practical steps

When you have permission for an expert witness to give oral evidence at trial on a date they can attend, the following steps are still necessary:

1. Ensure that the expert has reserved the date(s) exclusively in his diary – if there is any doubt, serve a witness summons (see above).

2. For trials that are listed for several days, if at all possible plan when the expert needs to attend by discussion with your advocate, the other party and, if there is a pre-trial review, with the court (at diary/listing manager level at least). It is very expensive and unlikely to lead to a good performance by an expert if he attends for several days when it is unnecessary.

3. Ensure that the client and funder have approved the fees for the experts' attendance at court, and that you have agreed cancellation fees with the expert should the case settle (see Chapter 6 for a discussion on cancellation fees).

4. Check that the expert has been kept completely up-to-date with all developments in the case relevant to their evidence – have you sent them any late disclosure documents and the other experts' reports?

5. Check whether the expert has given oral evidence at a trial before and, if not, whether he might benefit from some familiarisation training in courtroom skills, or from a visit to observe a trial at the

court in question. However, do not arrange or endorse specific 'coaching' on the actual case, or use similar scenarios. This was criticised by the Court of Appeal, admittedly in a criminal case, in *Momodou v Limaric* [2005] EWCA Crim 177.

At a minimum, you or the advocate should remind inexperienced experts that when they give evidence they should:

a) address the judge (not the counsel examining them);

b) answer the questions they are asked but no more;

c) keep to the facts and matters within their expertise;

d) avoid being drawn into hypothetical discussions;

e) avoid arguing with the advocate or the judge; and

f) not attempt to win the case.

Expert evidence in the trial bundle

The trial bundle must include all disclosed experts' reports, relevant to matters that remain in dispute on which the parties seek to rely. In a complex case a separate bundle of the expert evidence might be necessary. Further steps to take are listed below:

1. Ensure that you include the correct final served version of the expert's report in the bundle (see *Gough v Mummery* [2002] EWCA Civ 1573 discussed in Chapter 8, in which two different versions of an expert's report were in the trial papers, causing an unfortunate outcome).

2. Note that written questions on the experts' reports, under CPR 35.6, and the experts' replies form part of the reports and should be filed with them in the bundle.

3. Note that the joint statements of experts' discussions under CPR 35.12, are not binding and need not be included in the bundle, although they will be on the court file. If both parties are content to be bound by the statements then they should be included in the bundle.

4. Consider where to locate documents referred to in the experts' reports. Witness statements, statements of case, etc. are best filed

elsewhere. However, you might consider annotating the experts' reports with their location in the bundle for ease of reference by the judge, and by the witnesses at court. Material relied on solely by the expert should be filed with the expert's report, including technical material and publications (see also *Wardlaw v Farrar* [2003] EWCA Civ 1719, discussed in Chapter 8).

EXPERT EVIDENCE AT TRIAL

Ensure that 'your' experts and any single joint experts know exactly when and where to attend, and that someone will meet and greet them. If the solicitor or the advocate decides that an expert should attend to hear the evidence of witnesses of fact or that of other experts, the advocate will need to seek permission from the trial judge for the expert to sit in court. Advise the expert to keep notes of important new points relevant to his evidence, particularly technical matters, and on how to communicate these to the advocate.

Expert evidence will usually follow after the evidence of witnesses of fact for each party, but sometimes the usual trial pattern will be varied by the judge or to accommodate an expert with limited availability. Examination in chief of witnesses is often dispensed with at trial, as the reports have been exchanged and the judge will have read them. Nonetheless, sometimes judges prefer expert witnesses to explain their expertise in relation to the case, and the key points of their opinion, before cross-examination.

Not infrequently, experts from the same discipline instructed by opposing parties will be invited by counsel or the judge to discuss points of continuing disagreement or new points outside the courtroom (see Chapter 11).

In Australia, the Federal Court Rules allow for a practice known as 'hot-tubbing' of expert witnesses. The two experts from the same discipline give evidence immediately after each other and sit before the judge (i.e. not in the witness box), who puts the same questions to each expert in turn, in effect 'chairing' a debate on the differences between their reports. This is probably very effective, but an uncomfortable experience for the experts!

Party withdrawing an expert report at trial

It appears that this is possible. In *Tsavliris Russ (Worldwide Salvage & Towage) Ltd v RL Baron Shipping Co SA (the Green Opal)* ([2003] 1 Lloyd's Rep 523), the defendant served witness statements from Y containing opinion evidence. They were accompanied by a Civil Evidence Act notice (under CPR 33.2) stating that the defendant intended to rely upon the hearsay in the statements but would not call the expert at trial. However, after discussions between the parties, the trial began on the assumption that the witness would, in fact, be called to give oral evidence. On the second day of the trial, however, the defendant's counsel said that the witness would not be testifying. The claimant applied for permission to cross-examine him, under CPR 33.4. The defendant's counsel then said that the statements were being withdrawn from evidence. The claimant objected, as they had been "put in evidence". The judge dismissed the claimant's application and said, "As any experienced litigator well knows, a trial is a dynamic process. Many, if not most, trials throw up unanticipated surprises."

This decision does not sit very comfortably with CPR 35.11 (see above).

Experts changing their mind at trial

Chapter 10 discussed the importance of experts communicating any changes of opinion to the parties and the court without delay, and some reported instances where they had failed to do this. Changing their mind or admitting a mistake in the witness box at trial can be a disaster.

Deveron Joinery Co Ltd v Perkins, Lawtel, 30th July 2003 concerned the supply of windows to a house. The parties' experts agreed that there were problems with the windows, but not on how they should be resolved. The claimant's expert was criticised by the judge for admitting a mistake under cross-examination, "He should clearly have corrected his witness statement before that point in time, indeed, before he went into the box, or at latest in chief."

However, the Court of Appeal overturned the first instance decision because the judge had "developed his own theory" about the reason for the defects in the windows instead of recalling the claimant's expert to deal with the unsatisfactory elements of his evidence.

Similarly, in *C-B (a child)* (Court of Appeal, Lawtel, 7th October 2004), a public law childcare case, the child's guardian ad litem changed her mind about the child living with an aunt (because of a risk that the aunt would be too easily influenced by the mother), shortly before the final hearing, to either make a residence order in favour of the aunt or to place the child for adoption. The guardian did not file any evidence to explain the change of mind. The judge placed the child for adoption. The Court of Appeal sent the case back for rehearing, as the aunt had not been given an opportunity to consider and argue against the guardian's changed view. There had been a breach of Article 6 ECHR.

The best way to guard against an expert changing their stance at trial is for the expert to attend a conference with the solicitor and advocate pre-trial (see above), but that may not always be proportionate or possible.

Experts pursuing theories at trial

Experts who are not independent or whose evidence, written and oral, appears to be partisan inevitably lose credibility with the judge. Their evidence will be disregarded entirely or very little weight attached to it. See Chapter 2 for a discussion of the civil case authorities in this area.

Experts should also work within the parameters of the case and the law for the benefit of the judge. They should not put forward radically new or untried theories or methods. This is what happened in *Cooke v United Bristol Health Care* ([2003] EWCA Civ 1370; *The Times*, 23rd October 2003), when an accountant promoted a novel method of stepped multiplicands to calculate the cost of future care. The judge concluded that this was an "illegitimate assault" on the Lord Chancellor's discount rate set under section 1 of the Damages Act 1996.

In *Environmental Technologies Inc v Symphony Plastic Technologies plc* [2004] EWHC 2945 Ch, a case concerning the alleged copying by the defendants of the claimant's formula for an additive used in the manufacture of thin film plastic products, the judge reviewed the witness evidence (including that of the experts) in a confidential part of his judgment, but commented that judges are "very rarely helped by competing expert reports which express opinions which are not tested, or are not maintainable by reference to supporting material".

The risks stemming from highly speculative expert evidence are well illustrated by the sudden infant death criminal cases of *R v Sally Clark* [2003] EWCA Crim 1020 CA and *R v Angela Cannings* [2004] EWCA Crim 01 CA In both cases, convictions of the mothers for the alleged murder of two babies each were based largely on the disputed evidence of expert witnesses for the prosecution. In particular, in the *Sally Clark* case, a Home Office pathologist failed to disclose relevant microbiological tests on one of the children, and departed from 'mainstream medicine' in forming his view of the likely cause of death. A second expert, a professor of paediatrics, previously highly-regarded and a regular expert witness for the Crown in infant death cases, presented very graphic 'statistics' of the likelihood of two infant 'cot' deaths occurring in one family, which were not evidence-based. The professor also appeared as an expert for the Crown in the *Cannings* case. Both convictions were overturned on appeal. The Court of Appeal said that the professor's evidence in the *Clark* case was over-dogmatic and his reputation may have influenced the jury in the *Cannings* case.

These decisions, and the related disciplinary investigations by the General Medical Council into the conduct of the professor and another paediatrician who involved himself in the *Sally Clark* case after watching Mr Clark on television, caused unprecedented criticism of the use and interpretation of expert evidence in the criminal courts.

A working party of the Royal Colleges of Pathologists and Paediatrics and Child Health subsequently carried out a thorough review of how sudden infant death cases are investigated and presented at court. Their report (of September 2004) said:

"Those who give medical evidence to courts have a duty to ensure that the foundation of that evidence is sound. Unfortunately doctors are occasionally drawn into error because they base their testimony on medical belief rather than scientific evidence. There is also the temptation, particularly in the very adversarial arena of the criminal courts, to be pushed into certainties when there are none. Unfortunately there is insufficient training emphasis on the necessity of a scientific foundation for expert testimony ... It is also important that the courtroom is not a place used by doctors to fly their personal kites or

239

push a theory from the far end of the medical spectrum ... Lawyers often try to press the professional expert to expand their testimony into areas where they have no expertise and he or she can end up expressing a hunch with alarming certainty. Doctors should be willing to say 'I don't know' without shame or inhibition."

In *Re U (Serious Injury: Standard of Proof)* and *Re B* [2004] 2 FLR 263, two public law cases, the Court of Appeal gave further guidance of general applicability on medical issues:

- Particular caution is needed in any case where medical experts disagree.

- The court must be on guard against very dogmatic experts.

- Courts must not forget that science moves on and that today's medical certainty may be discarded by the next generation of experts.

The lessons for lawyers practising in the civil court from these cases and this report are listed below:

- There is a need to select expert witnesses carefully.

- Experts should be instructed to provide the *range* of opinion in their profession on key and contentious issues in the case.

- Experts should be pressed to provide their evidence base for theories and statistics.

- It is unwise to encourage experts too strongly to give definitive answers.

Judges weighing up the expert evidence fairly

Judges do not have to accept expert evidence, even if it is from a single joint expert, or from an 'illustrious source'. The function of expert evidence is to assist the judge, not to usurp the judge's role. Most expert evidence is not based upon direct observation of events by the expert at the material time, but is indirect evidence, which is technically hearsay. Experts offer opinions based upon factual evidence or versions of events. Experts should not give their opinion on the 'ultimate issue', whether this is finding facts or concluding that there has been negligence.

The weight that a judge will attach to expert evidence will depend upon a number of factors:

1. The 'factual evidence' adduced on the same issue and its likely accuracy and credibility.

2. The complexity and 'technical' content of the case.

3. The knowledge and experience demonstrated by the expert in the relevant field.

4. The thoroughness of the expert's instructions, investigations and report.

5. The judge's impression of the expert's objectivity and credibility, including in comparison with an opposing expert, especially if the expert gives oral evidence.

Sometimes, the judge's impression will be partly influenced by the expert's demeanour, confidence, voice, etc., particularly if the other expert, by contrast, appears timid or hesitant. This is a good reason for encouraging new experts to familiarise themselves with the courtroom and cross-examination (see above).

Judges rejecting expert evidence

If a judge rejects expert evidence, he must give detailed reasons – especially if that evidence is consistent with that of other experts.

The following are examples of judges rejecting expert evidence (for other examples where the judge concluded that the expert lacked independence (see Chapter 2).

1. **Where the Court of Appeal upheld the judge's rejection of the evidence.**

   In *BCCI SA v Ali (No 3)* [1999] 4 AER 83, ex-employees of the BCCI bank sued the then-collapsed bank for compensation for the alleged 'stigma' on their future job prospects of having worked for directors who had traded fraudulently. The employees relied upon a report from an expert, which relied heavily on interviews with a number of the ex-employees and which dealt generally with conditions in the labour market and hiring practices of employers. The judge rejected this evidence as he concluded that the interviews were partial and superficial, and the statistics too general to assist in deciding the 'stigma' issue. He preferred the factual evidence of the agency employed by BCCI to help the ex-employees find new jobs, as this demonstrated how actual employers had viewed the ex-employees' history.

Alexander v Midland Bank plc ([1999] 1 RLR 723) was a personal injury case about so-called Work-Related Upper Limb Disorder (WRULD). A rheumatology expert for the claimants concluded that there was a high probability that the claimants' condition was work-related but he admitted the condition was not well understood. A surgeon for the defendants said that the condition was psychosomatic. The judge rejected the surgeon's evidence, as he did not have the right qualifications and experience to express that view. The defendant's appeal was dismissed.

Royal Brompton NHS Trust v Hammond (No 7) ([2001] CILL 1714) was a case in which Judge Seymour QC rejected the claimant's architect's evidence in its entirety, because he had not mastered the relevant documents and because he had made assumptions, the accuracy of which were central to the questions which were to be addressed, and because he did not have knowledge of the practice in the profession contemporary to the events in the case.

Michael Hyde Associates v JD Williams ([2001] PNLR 233) was a professional negligence claim against an architect. The Court of Appeal was critical of the trial judge for accepting evidence from two architect expert witnesses, who had approached the issue from the perspective of what they would have done in the circumstances, not whether the architect's actions fell within the range of actions that a responsible body of architects would have done.

2. **Where the Court of Appeal overturned the judge's rejection of expert evidence.**

Lougheed v Safeway Stores plc ([2001] EWCA Civ 176) was a personal injury case in which liability was admitted. At issue at trial was whether the claimant's chronic pain was attributable to the accident. Experts for both parties agreed that she *was* suffering pain, and only differed on the cause. However, the judge decided that the claimant had not been honest with the doctors about the pain and that the accident did not cause her disability. The Court of Appeal ordered a retrial, as there was no evidence before the court questioning the claimant's veracity, and the judge had no basis, therefore, for rejecting the experts' evidence.

Judges attaching too little weight to expert evidence

Chappell v Imperial Design Ltd (31st October 2000, New Law 2002229701) was a personal injury claim for a 13-year old who gained access to flammable liquid left outside the defendant's factory. The expert for the claimant opined that few adults, let alone children, would have appreciated the risk of an explosion when air and chemical vapour mix, but the defendants should have been aware of this. The trial judge found the claimant 50% contributorily negligent, but the Court of Appeal said he had attached too little weight to the expert's report and adjusted the liability split to 50:50.

Judges comparing the evidence of opposing experts

Judges need to be careful when comparing the evidence of experts.

1. **Sometimes the Court of Appeal consider that the judge was right.**

   Coker v Barkland Cleaning Co, 6th December 1999 (unrep). (For the facts of this personal injury case, see Chapter 1.) Both parties adduced medical evidence on whether the claimant's back problems were caused by a pre-existing condition, or by the accident. The judge preferred the defendant's expert's opinion that it was the pre-existing condition, but concluded that the accident had accelerated the condition by two years, when the defendant's expert had said one year at most. The defendant's appeal was dismissed – the Court of Appeal said the judge was entitled to interpolate from the expert evidence.

   In *Bennett v Smith* [2003] EWHC 1006, the issue was whether a road traffic accident had caused the claimant's fibromyalgia. The judge preferred the evidence of the claimant's rheumatologist to that of the defendants' experts, because his reasoning was more consistent with that of all the other experts in their joint statement.

2. **Sometimes they conclude that he was wrong.**

Roadrunner Properties Ltd v Dean ([2003] EWCA Civ 1816) is an example of this. The defendant damaged the claimant's property when carrying out work on the house next door. The claimant's expert said the drill was the most likely cause of the damage to the house, but the defendant's expert said that it was purely coincidence that the damage had apparently occurred at the same time as the building work was being carried out next door and put the damage down to climatic change (although no evidence to support this hypotheses was adduced). On appeal, it was held that coincidence was a proper factor to take into account when drawing inferences from causation "if there is material from ... which a causal link can properly be established, I think a court, in those circumstances, should be slow to discard common sense in favour of expert hypothesis".

In *X v Brown* [2003] EWCA Civ 181, the claimant was kicked in the face in a karate class, suffering some physical injuries. After the accident she also developed some mental problems. Most of the medical evidence was agreed; the unresolved issue was the claimant's possibly fragile personality but neither psychologist expert considered the claimant to be malingering. The trial judge preferred the evidence of the defendant's psychiatrist – that the claimant would have developed a disabling psychogenic illness within one year in any event, regardless of the accident – to that of the claimant's expert. The Court of Appeal said that the reasoning the judge had applied to his analysis of the expert evidence did not support his conclusions. It was likely but by no means certain that the claimant would have developed mental problems but for the accident. The damages award was significantly increased.

3. **Sometimes the judge may be both wrong and right.**

Morris v Blackpool Victoria Hospital NHS Trust ([2004] EWCA Civ 1294) was a clinical negligence case, arising out of the birth of the claimant with cerebral palsy, in which the claimant alleged the pre-birth treatment of the mother was negligent. Three experts gave evidence on liability – two said the claimant suffered from intra-uterine growth retardation, the third said he did not (which was relevant to whether the Trust should have delivered the child sooner). The judge concluded that he did not, which the Court of Appeal said was an error, but not one that was so fundamental or one that so infected or undermined the rest of his conclusions (that the Trust had not been negligent) to justify a retrial.

4. **Judges need to be especially careful when neither expert is in court to give oral evidence.**

   Yousif v Jordan [2003] EWCA Civ 1852 was a dispute about whether the claimant had been warned about the risk that a rhinoplasty, to improve the appearance of his nose, could lead to a nasal obstruction and cause difficulty in breathing. The parties had an expert each. Neither gave oral evidence at trial. Relying mainly on the joint statement of the experts following an experts' discussion, the trial judge dismissed the action on the basis of there being no case to answer. However, the Court of Appeal held that the trial judge was wrong to conclude that there was no evidence linking the nasal obstruction to the operation. He had failed to keep in mind the contents of the claimant's expert's report on causation. A retrial was ordered.

Judges weighing the evidence of witnesses of fact against that of an expert

1. When the only expert evidence is given by a single joint expert, judges should be slow to prefer the evidence of a witness of fact on a point that is really a matter of opinion rather than observation. Three examples follow:

   In *Takenaka (UK) Limited v Frankl* (*The Independent*, 11th December 2000), the case arose out of the admitted publication of defamatory e-mails. The only issue was whether the defendant was the author. The single joint expert analysed the contents of the defendant's computer and concluded that traces of e-mail activity matched the dates and times of the malicious e-mails, so it was "most probable" that the defendant's computer was the source. The expert said he was confident that the proof required "on the balance of probabilities" had been reached. The judge commented that:

   "A judge tries the case upon the evidence and in this case the expert evidence is of the highest quality in an arcane field in which the judge must be guided by that expert evidence."

245

Miller v C&G Coach Services ([2003] EWCA Civ 442) was a claim arising from a road traffic accident, in which the issue was the likely speed of the coach which hit the pedestrian claimant. The expert concluded from where the claimant had landed after the impact that the coach was travelling at between 14 and 15 miles per hour. The claimant contended it was between 23 and 29 miles per hour. The judge preferred the expert's evidence and dismissed the claim. The Court of Appeal dismissed the claimant's appeal.

Coopers Payen Ltd v Southampton Container Ltd [2003] AER D 220 is discussed in more detail in Chapter 9. The issue was the likely speed of a tug; whereby the Court of Appeal said that the trial judge should have accepted the evidence of the single joint expert, as there was no other explanation for the accident other than that the tug was travelling too fast.

However, in *Armstrong and Connor v First York* [2005] EWCA CW 277 (also discussed in Chapter 9), the Court of Appeal upheld the first instance decision in which the trial judge believed that the claimants in an RTA had suffered the injuries for which they were claiming damages, although an expert engineer argued that the impact was too low for injuries to be sustained and the judge did not criticise the expert's evidence.

2. Occasionally witnesses of fact may have greater knowledge than an expert, causing a judge reasonably to prefer their evidence.

Two examples of this follow, both concerning disputed wills:

In *Wilkes v Wilkes* (8th June 2000) (unreported), the issue was the testamentary capacity of the testatrix. The claimant, who was disputing the will, called expert evidence from a physician who specialised in care of the elderly, who had access to the testatrix' medical records but had not met her. He concluded that she was unlikely to have had capacity as she had suffered brain damage, had Parkinson's disease and was very aged. The judge concluded that although he placed great weight on the evidence of the expert witness, which he found to be measured and objective, he could not ignore the evidence of three witnesses who were in frequent contact with the testatrix over substantial periods before her death, whose evidence was that she had capacity. The claim failed. There was no appeal.

In *Fuller v Strum* (*The Times*, 14th February 2001), the claimant, the testator's son, alleged that the will leaving half the estate to someone else was a forgery. Each party's handwriting expert came up with a different answer. The court ordered a further report from an eminent single joint expert, who concluded from detailed analysis that the signature on the will was a forgery. The expert did not give oral evidence to save costs, which the judge regretted. He went on to balance the other evidence, and decided that although the signature was different than the testator's usual one, on the balance of probabilities it was genuine. Again there was no appeal.

This case, and *Yousif v Jordan* (see above), is a warning to parties to balance the need to save costs against the effective presentation of expert evidence.

Judges failing to review literature relied upon by a party's expert

Experts should append to their reports, or make readily available well before trial, any literature on which they rely. This was not done in *Breeze v Ahmad* [2005] EWCA CW 223. The claimant was able to show that the literature relied upon by the defendant was unwittingly portrayed inaccurately and/or incompletely, which led the judge to place more reliance upon it than he should have done, as the judge had not seen the literature in question. A retrial was ordered.

Judges not treating witnesses of fact and expert witnesses equally

In *DN v Greenwich London Borough* [2004] EWCA Civ 1659, a professional negligence claim (discussed in detail in Chapter 1), the Court of Appeal were critical of the trial judge for adopting a "rigid rule" not to allow any examination in chief of a witness of fact while encouraging expert witnesses to expand at length in their evidence in chief – in one case well beyond the contents of his written report. This had disadvantaged the defendant's allegedly negligent main witness of fact, especially as the defendants had decided not to call any independent expert evidence on liability.

Judges should give reasons for their decisions on expert evidence

If a judge fails to give reasons for preferring one expert's opinion to another's, the appeal court might order a retrial. However, the judge should be invited to amplify the judgment before a decision is taken on the necessity of an appeal. See *English v Emery Reinbold* [2002] EWCA 605.

An example follows of when retrial was ordered:

In *Dyson v Leeds City Council* ([2000] CP Rep 42), the claimant was the executor of a plumber who died of asbestosis, allegedly contracted when he repaired the defendant's boilers in the 1960s. The judge preferred the evidence of the defendant's expert to that of the claimant's expert on when the defendant should have been aware of the risks posed to employees working with asbestos. He dismissed the claim. However, he gave no reasons for his preference, and the Court of Appeal sent the case back for a retrial.

ASSESSOR PREPARING A REPORT FOR THE COURT (CPR 35.15(3)A))

The role of assessors in assisting the judge at trial was discussed in Chapter 2. Assessors are rarely used, except in admiralty and patents cases and costs disputes. However, trial judges have to be very careful to ensure all parties have an opportunity to comment upon the assessor's brief and advice before the judge decides the case.

In *Owners of the Ship Bow Spring v Owners of the Ship Manzanillo II* [2004] EWCA Civ 1007, a dispute arising from a nautical collision, the Court of Appeal, *obiter*, said that the judge was correct to invite counsel to comment upon the questions that he intended to put to the nautical assessors, but that he should have done likewise with the assessors' answers before deciding whether to accept the assessors' advice. In *Global Mariner v Atlantic Crusader* [2005] EWHC Admiralty 380, the judge expanded upon these comments and recommended the following procedure:

● The range of topics on which advice might be sought from the assessors should be canvassed with counsel, at the latest, by the stage of final submissions.

● Questions put by the judge, and the assessor's answers, should be disclosed to counsel before the draft judgment is handed down.

● Generally, any further answers from the assessors, and the judge's decision, with reasons, in relation to that advice, will be recorded in the judgment without a further round of disclosure, on the grounds of proportionality.

AFTER THE TRIAL OR SETTLEMENT

The aftermath of a trial or settlement is often an anti-climax, even for the successful party. The solicitor's effort is concentrated, quite rightly, on explaining the outcome to the client, ensuring judgment and the order are entered correctly, carrying out the terms of the order and dealing with the costs.

The work of the expert witnesses is then completed. If you and the client are satisfied with their report and/or their performance at court, and you intend to instruct them again, do not neglect to:

1. Advise the experts of the outcome.

2. Thank them for their assistance.

3. Pay any outstanding fees as soon as possible.

You might also consider providing some feedback on the expert's work, as many expert witnesses have said to the author that frequently they hear nothing at all from the solicitor after they have sent their report (see also Chapter 14).

CONCLUSIONS

Preparing carefully for trial is essential. It may be hard, anxious work for the lawyers, as settlement is often being attempted while trial preparation goes ahead, and an ordeal for the client, but do not overlook the expert witnesses. It pays to develop a good rapport with the experts while respecting their independence. An expert who understands how his evidence fits into the case being advanced, and who has been kept up-to-date and fully briefed (without being coached), is likely to feel committed to doing his best to help to achieve a fair outcome at trial.

Nonetheless, experts do owe their first duty to the court; they may change their mind or waiver under cross-examination, or otherwise fail to impress the judge. Judges have to consider and weigh all the evidence; they are never bound to accept expert evidence but it will often be very persuasive on specialist issues, especially from a single joint expert. On occasions, however, judges do misunderstand technical matters, or fail to compare the expert evidence fairly (or to compare it fairly with the witness evidence), or fail to give sufficient reasons for preferring one expert to another. As the latter part of this chapter shows, sometimes appeals on a judge's failure to deal with the expert evidence well do succeed.

Chapter 13

PROBLEMS WITH EXPERT WITNESSES AND SOME SOLUTIONS

Expert evidence is often a vital ingredient in proving or defending a case. If producing that evidence goes wrong in any serious way, it can have a significant impact on the outcome of the case or on the client's liability for costs. This chapter summarises the problems that may occur and the possible, but limited, remedies.

PROBLEMS YOU MIGHT ENCOUNTER WITH EXPERT WITNESSES

The main problems solicitors and their clients might encounter with experts and their evidence concern experts who:

a) accept instructions outside their expertise;

b) accept instructions when they have a conflict of interest or are not independent;

c) fail to produce a report on time or at all;

d) produce deficient advice or a report which:

    i) does not comply with the CPR requirements or court directions;

    ii) does not comply with the instructions;

    iii) is inadequately researched;

    iv) is inaccurate in material respects;

    v) covers matters outside the expert's expertise;

    vi) is inconsistent or illogical; or

    vii) relies upon untested theories;

e) overcharge, e.g. by increasing the report fee, hourly rate, attendance at court fee or cancellation fee without discussion or justification, or by charging for disbursements or expenses which were not authorised;

f) fail to be objective or display bias in a report, or when giving oral evidence;

g) act inefficiently or unco-operatively with regard to follow-up work to the report – written questions, experts' discussion, etc.;

h) do not co-operate about availability for trial when oral evidence is necessary, or who ignore a witness summons to attend trial;

i) change their mind after the report has been disclosed, without informing the solicitor;

j) are less than honest about their qualifications or experience, or about their true opinion in a report or when giving oral evidence;

k) perform inadequately or inappropriately when giving oral evidence, e.g. by being over-dogmatic, or by 'playing advocate'.

Many of the above problems can be avoided by careful selection and instruction of an expert (see Chapters 4 and 5), and by keeping in regular contact with the expert as the case progresses.

If the problem occurs at an early stage before any report from the expert has been disclosed or before proceedings have been issued, it will usually be possible to instruct another expert, as a party cannot be required to disclose an expert's report at that stage, unless the party intends to rely on that report (see Chapter 7). The only consequence may be that the client or solicitor will have to bear the cost of the report, as it will not be recoverable from the other party even if the case succeeds.

If the problem occurs or becomes apparent after proceedings have been issued, and after the court has given permission for reliance upon expert evidence and possibly even for a named expert, the court might be persuaded that the loss of confidence in the expert justifies instruction of another one, but the penalty might be disclosure of the report from the first expert (see Chapter 10) and, again, non-recovery of the costs.

If one party instructs the expert only, deficiencies in the report might not cause long-term problems, if the expert is willing and able to amend the draft before disclosure. Similarly, with late reports or late answers to written questions, it will often be possible to persuade the other party or the court to slightly amend the timetable for disclosure, provided that the trial date will not be affected (see Chapters 8 and 11).

If a single joint expert's report is deficient, even after putting written questions to the expert, the only possibilities are to persuade the court that a second expert should be instructed, or that the first expert should give oral evidence (see Chapter 9).

However, problems that only occur or become apparent close to or at trial, may not have any attractive solutions. They may adversely affect the outcome of the case by leading to a settlement on less than favourable terms, or a less favourable decision at trial or, at best, additional costs may be incurred and may not be recovered.

THE LIMITED REMEDIES

If a problem with an expert or his evidence has significantly affected the outcome, there are limited options in terms of 'redress' against the expert. In fact, the client is more likely to begin a negligence claim against the solicitor for recommending the selection and instruction of an inappropriate or inadequate expert.

The only options may be:

a) not instructing the expert again;

b) not paying the expert;

c) complaining to the professional body or database/directory in which the expert was listed;

d) inviting or encouraging the judge to criticise the expert or make a complaint about him;

e) asking the court to invite the Attorney General to authorise prosecution for contempt of court or for perjury;

f) in very limited circumstances, making a claim in negligence against the expert;

g) making an application to the court for a costs order against the expert.

NOT INSTRUCTING THE EXPERT AGAIN

This is the easiest option and the only one solicitors and clients are likely to pursue if an expert gives a poor, but not very poor, service. The firm may wish to consider removing the expert's name from the firm's database. However, great care must be taken about making adverse comments about the expert to other lawyers, or other clients, to avoid the risk of a defamation action.

NOT PAYING THE EXPERT

The options here include:

1. Not paying any of the fee, e.g. for failure to produce a report at all or producing it so late that you had to instruct another expert (provided that the expert knew the importance of the deadline well in advance).

2. Paying part of the fees, e.g. for poor service or a poor report.

3. Declining to pay additional fees charged by the expert for further work, e.g. for amending the report when the work could have been carried out properly from the first instructions.

Before adopting any of these courses of action, it is important to check the expert's terms of business, the letter of instruction and any reply from the expert carefully, as they form the contract. If you did not query or object to specific terms at the outset, e.g. entitlement to first class travel, you may be bound. It is prudent to explain the reasons for any proposed reduction in fees in writing and give the expert an opportunity to respond. An expert disgruntled about payment of fees may complain to the senior partner of your firm or to the Law Society, or may even sue the firm for breach of contract in the County Court.

COMPLAINING ABOUT THE EXPERT

Complaining to another organisation about an expert is only justified if the failings were serious. This might include failing to declare a conflict of interest, or other breach of the expert's duty to the court, or very incompetent work. Again, it is courteous to put the complaint to the expert first.

Who should the complaint be put to?

1. The expert's employer or firm, if their expert witness work is carried out as part of that business.

2. The recommendation or source of the expert – this might include an expert's agency (mainly for medico-legal work), a directory or a database (particularly if some vetting is carried out prior to entry).

3. Their professional body or trade association, possibly after checking whether that organisation has a separate expert witness division and how the disciplinary or regulatory procedures work.

4. An expert witness organisation if they belong to one – the EWI and the Academy of Experts both have Codes of Practice for their members, which cover matters such as not accepting work outside the expert's expertise or where there is a conflict of interest. The EWI code also requires their members to comply with the codes or declaration required by their professional body.

5. The Council for the Registration of Forensic Practitioners (CRFP) if the expert has been accredited by them (see Chapter 1).

INVITING OR ENCOURAGING THE TRIAL JUDGE TO MAKE THE COMPLAINT

Judges have made such complaints in at least two reported cases.

Pearce v Ove Arup [2002] 25(2) IPD 25011 centred on an allegation that a leading international architect had dishonestly copied the claimant architects' design for a building. At the trial, these allegations were completely and utterly dismissed by the Honourable Mr Justice Jacob (now Jacob LJ). During the course of the trial, the claimant relied on an architect expert, Mr Wilkey.

Jacob J said:

"In my judgment, Mr Wilkey's 'expert' evidence fell far short of the standards of objectivity required of an expert witness. He claimed to have appreciated the seriousness of what he was saying but made blunder after blunder ... So biased and irrational do I find his 'expert' evidence that I conclude he failed his duty to the court."

Jacob J was particularly critical that the expert came to argue the claimant's case. He decided that Mr Wilkey should be reported to his professional body. He gave Mr Wilkey an opportunity to come to court and show why he should not be reported. He did not do so; hence the judge registered the complaint.

The Professional Conduct Committee of the Architects Registration Board heard the complaint, investigated several alleged breaches of duty by the architect and in every instance found him not guilty of serious professional misconduct, and that the quality of his instructions and the limitations of public funding had been very relevant factors in the way he carried out his work on the case.

Hussein v William Hill Group ([2004] EWHC 208 QB) was a personal injury claim arising from an alleged assault on the claimant at a bookmakers. The claimant acted in person. Two doctors, a GP and a consultant psychiatrist, who were friendly with the claimant, and who had allegedly treated him for his injuries, gave evidence for him. The judge, Hallett J, found that the claimant had greatly exaggerated his injuries and awarded him only £50 in damages. She did not believe most of the evidence from either doctor. The GP had virtually no records of the 'consultation and treatment', hence the judge concluded that he was prepared to say whatever he believed would help the claimant. The psychiatrist, she concluded, had been brought into the case later purely to support it, and she found it "incredible that a Fellow of the Royal College of Psychiatrists could allow himself to give evidence in these circumstances". The judge asked for her judgment and the papers to be referred to the General Medical Council.

Regardless of whether a professional body administers any sanction on an expert witness, trenchant criticism in a judgment given in public and a referral by a judge would be likely to have an impact on the expert's future conduct, and on his career as an expert witness.

CONTEMPT OF COURT (CPR 32.14)

Every expert witness report must include a statement of truth as follows:

"I confirm that insofar as the facts stated in my report are within my own knowledge I have made clear which they are and I believe them to be true, and that the opinions I have expressed represent my true and complete professional opinion". (CPR Part 35 Practice Direction paragraph 2.4.)

If an expert witness makes a false statement in a report, or other document verified by a statement of truth, without an honest belief in its truth, proceedings for contempt may be brought against him (CPR 32.14). False statements might include untruths about qualifications or experience, or about the findings of the expert's investigations in the case, or a dishonest statement of his opinion. The court dealing with the case has the power to act on the contempt if this is in accordance with the overriding objective, or may refer the matter to the Attorney General, with a request that he considers whether to bring proceedings for contempt. He will only do so if this is 'proportionate'. On a finding of contempt, the courts may imprison the contemner for a maximum of two years, impose a fine or 'take security for good behaviour'. The author is unaware of any reported cases of contempt proceedings against expert witnesses. (However, in *Dattel Europe Ltd (in liquidation) v Makki and Others*, the court allowed contempt proceedings to go ahead against a party who knowingly signed a false statement of truth.)

PROSECUTION FOR PERJURY

An expert witness' oral evidence is also given on oath or affirmation, hence false oral evidence at court could amount to perjury under the Perjury Act 1911. The prosecution would have to prove that:

- The statement was false.
- The expert made the statement wilfully, i.e. deliberately and not by mistake.

- The expert knew the statement was false or did not believe it to be true.

- The statement was material to the judicial proceeding.

It would be very difficult to prove to the criminal standard of proof (beyond reasonable doubt) that an expert witness deliberately misrepresented their opinion. The author is unaware of any case where an expert witness has been prosecuted for perjury.

NEGLIGENCE OR BREACH OF CONTRACT ACTIONS AGAINST EXPERTS

Witness immunity

The basic rule, which originates from the 1870s (*Dawkins v Lord Rokeby* [1873] 8 QB 25), is that witnesses, including experts, cannot be sued for what they say in court proceedings. This is a significant exception to the principle that a wrong should not be without a remedy, as well as to the rule established in *Hedley Byrne and Co Ltd v Heller and Partners Ltd* ([1964] AC 465) that, irrespective of contract, if someone possessed of a special skill undertakes to apply that skill for the assistance of another person who relies upon such a skill, a duty of care will arise. If the advice given in exercising that duty is such that no reasonable professional competent in the field and acting reasonably should give, then there may be a claim in negligence as the skilled person clearly owes a duty of care to the client (as well as to the court).

The courts have explained the public policy arguments for the immunity exception as follows:

1. It is in the interests of the administration of justice (not specifically the interests of the witnesses), that witnesses feel able to express themselves freely, and are not inhibited from giving frank evidence by the fear that they might be sued.

2. It is in the public interest to keep to a minimum the circumstances when court decisions can be challenged in collateral proceedings – in an action against a witness, the value of their evidence would be tested a second time and, if the action was successful, there could be grounds for appealing the original court decision.

3. In addition, with regard to expert witnesses, their overriding duty is to the court (now in CPR 35.3), to assist the court in the resolution of issues and to come to a just conclusion.

The leading recent case on experts' immunity from suit is *Stanton v Callaghan* [2000] 1 QB 75. The plaintiff consulted a surveyor, Mr Callaghan, about subsidence damage to his home, for a claim against his insurers. The surveyor reported that the house needed total underpinning. The surveyor later attended a meeting with the insurer's expert, at which it was agreed that there was an alternative, cheaper solution – the insurers refused to pay for total underpinning as they considered that this would amount to 'betterment'. The insurers paid the lower sum into court, which the plaintiff accepted. The plaintiff sold the house and sued his solicitor and the surveyor for the difference between the sale price and the value of the house if it had been underpinned, as the surveyor had originally proposed. At first instance, the deputy High Court judge declined to strike out the statement of claim against the surveyor, on the ground that the immunity might not extend to negligence that consisted of taking into account "extraneous matters", i.e. the insurer's position.

The Court of Appeal struck out the claim, concluding that the surveyor was immune because:

a) he was doing what he was instructed to do, so the main allegations could not amount to a breach of contract or negligence;

b) his report and attendance at the experts' meeting attracted immunity because it was in the interests of the administration of justice that expert witnesses should meet; and

c) experts should be free to make proper concessions and "to resile fearlessly and with dignity", so that trials should take no longer than is necessary to achieve justice in the particular case.

In very detailed judgments, the Court of Appeal considered the development of the law on witness immunity. With regard to experts, they concluded that:

1. The immunity extends to:

a) anything that the expert says in evidence at trial; and

b) the contents of the report, which he adopts as, or incorporates into, his oral evidence.

2. The immunity does not extend to protect an expert who has been retained to *advise* as to the merits of a party's claim in litigation, "notwithstanding that it (the litigation) was in contemplation at the time when the advice was given and that the expert would be a witness at the trial if that litigation were to proceed".

Otton LJ said:

"Immunity for pre-trial work is not indiscriminate. Not all work done prior to a hearing will be covered. It is a tailored immunity and whether or not immunity exists in respect of pre-hearing conduct rests on an assessment of whether the work in question is so intimately connected with the conduct of the case in court that it can fairly be said to be a preliminary decision affecting the way the cause is to be conducted when it comes to a hearing."

Simon Tuckey QC (as he then was), sitting as a deputy High Court judge, drew the lines similarly in the earlier case of *Palmer v Durnford Ford* [1992] 1 QB 483 (referred to with approval by the Court of Appeal in Stanton). The expert was an engineer who was retained by a firm of haulage contractors to prepare a report on the cause of the breakdown of a new lorry following an attempted repair. The engineer assured the plaintiff's solicitors that he had the necessary qualifications and experience. The engineer advised bringing actions against both the vendors and the repairers of the lorry. The plaintiff followed the advice. The engineer changed his mind about the claim against the vendors, after disclosure of their expert's report. Eventually, the entire claim was abandoned at trial, after the engineer had given evidence and, by consent, judgment was given for the two defendants, with costs. The plaintiffs sued their solicitors and the engineer for breaches of their contractual duties of care. The engineer claimed immunity. Tuckey allowed the claims in negligence in respect of the engineer's assurances to the client about his expertise, and his pre-action advice to proceed. Tuckey said that the principal purpose for which the work was done was the key to whether the immunity was engaged:

"The immunity would only extend to what could fairly be said to be preliminary to his giving evidence in court judged perhaps by the principal purpose for which the work was done. So the production or approval of a report for the purposes of disclosure to the other side would be immune but work done for the principal purpose of advising the client would not. Each case would depend upon its own facts with the court concerned to protect the expert from liability for the evidence which he gave in court and the work principally and proximately leading thereto."

Landall v Dennis Faulkner and Alsop [1994] 5 Med LR 268 concerned allegedly negligent advice by a consultant orthopaedic surgeon given in a medico-legal report for a personal injury claim. The surgeon advised that the plaintiff's back problems would be alleviated by a spinal fusion operation. The plaintiff had the operation. It was not successful. He sued the solicitor and the consultant. He argued that the consultant had a dual role – as an expert witness for the purposes of the litigation but also as a medical adviser. Mr Justice Holland rejected that submission and struck out the claim, as the report in which the advice was given was:

"... pre-trial work so intimately connected with the conduct of the case in court that it could fairly be said to be a preliminary decision affecting the way that the case was to be conducted when it came to a hearing."

However, in *Hughes v Lloyds Bank*, CA (3rd November 1997) (unreported except on Lawtel), it was held that immunity did not attach to letters from the plaintiff's GP which said that her injuries arising from an RTA would settle down with time. No proceedings were issued. The claim was settled for £600 (against the solicitor's advice). The injuries turned out to be much more serious and the plaintiff sued the GP, arguing that the early settlement was occasioned by his letters. The GP claimed immunity. At first instance, the claim was struck out. However, the Court of Appeal disagreed; as the GP's letters were preliminary advice, it was very unlikely that the plaintiff would have relied upon the GP if proceedings had been issued. The issue of her reliance on the letters merited testing at trial.

There has been one only reported case concerned with immunity of experts since the implementation of the CPR. In *Raiss v Paimano* [2001] PNLR 540, the claimant brought an action against a surveyor,

Mr Paimano, for wasted costs and losses allegedly caused by the surveyor's negligent advice when acting as an expert witness in proceedings against a firm of surveyors. Mr Paimano told the claimant that he was on the Panel of Arbitrators to the Royal Institute of Chartered Surveyors and that he had considerable knowledge and experience of open market property transactions in the Covent Garden area. He also advised that the claimant had a good claim against the surveyors. The surveyor's claims about his expertise were repeated in his report for the court; under cross-examination it became apparent that neither statement was true.

At first instance in the subsequent proceedings against the surveyor, the High Court Master drew a distinction between the statements about the surveyor's experience, and the deceit that he was on the RICS Panel, striking out the first from the particulars of claim but allowing the second to stand. However, on appeal, Eady J struck out both heads of claim as he considered that the immunity applied even to dishonest evidence, based on the authorities including *Stanton*.

Advocates' immunity

Until a few years ago, advocates were also immune from suit for similar public policy reasons to witnesses (to encourage freedom of speech in court and to avoid relitigation). Nonetheless, in *Arthur J S Hall & Co (a firm) v Simons* [2002] 1 AC 615 HL, advocates lost their immunity from actions in negligence in respect of their conduct and management of a case in court, and the pre-trial work immediately connected with it. The House of Lords concluded that the two century-old immunity no longer offered sufficient public benefit, particularly when other professionals, whose work posed equally stressful and ethical dilemmas, have no such immunity, and neither do advocates in many other jurisdictions. They also said that public confidence in the legal system is not enhanced by the existence of the immunity.

The future of expert witness immunity

At some stage, will the courts similarly decide that the public policy arguments in favour of expert witness immunity for their court-related work are outweighed by arguments against it? Certainly, it is arguable whether experts' immunity is consistent with Article 6 of the European Convention on Human Rights (right to a fair trial – see Chapter 2) particularly in a circumstance when there was no other redress for a client seriously disadvantaged by the actions or inactions of an expert. Commentators have also suggested that the jurisprudential basis for expert witness immunity has been substantially undermined by the decision in the *Hall* case.

Even if the courts were persuaded to remove or restrict the immunity, it could still be very difficult to prove that a party's losses were attributable to an expert witness' actions when there had been a trial, because while expert evidence informs and assists a judge, he/she has to make up their own mind based on *all* the evidence.

For the present, therefore, courts attach immunity to an expert witness' oral evidence and report for the proceedings, or to other work 'principally and proximately', leading to the giving of evidence in court. This is likely to include the expert answering written questions on their report under CPR 35.6, and work for, at and following an experts' discussion under CPR 35.12. Excluded from the immunity are advice pre-proceedings, and possibly advisory work during the litigation by 'shadow experts' (see Chapter 3) who are not preparing reports for disclosure and who will not give evidence at trial.

Yet grey areas remain; for instance, advice or a report from an expert pre-action, possibly when the parties are following a pre-action protocol procedure, when the same expert was retained subsequently for the proceedings; or advisory work by an expert who was initially instructed as a shadow expert, but who was then retained with the permission of the court, to prepare a report for disclosure and, if necessary, for trial.

COSTS ORDERS AGAINST EXPERT WITNESSES (CPR 48.2 & 48.7)

Section 51 of the Supreme Court Act 1981, as amended by section 4 of the Courts and Legal Services Act 1990, gives the court the power to make a costs order against (or in favour of) a person who is not a party to the proceedings. CPR 48.2 sets out the procedure for making such an application. In *Symphony Group plc v Hodgson* [1994] QB 179, the Court of Appeal said such orders should be exceptional, only when the non-party is guilty of wholly unjustifiable conduct, especially where the non-party could have been made a party to the action, or there was a cause of action against him. A second important criterion is the extent to which the conduct of the non-party caused loss to the applicant in the sense of occasioning or increasing costs. Orders tend only to be made when the non-party has been maintaining an action that failed, or played a substantial part in running or guiding such an action for their own interests.

The courts also have power, under CPR 48.7, to make "wasted costs" orders against solicitors and advocates whose seriously improper, unreasonable, or negligent conduct, "akin to an abuse of process", caused the applicant to incur unnecessary costs.

The procedure for a non-party costs order under CPR 48.2 is to apply to the court for permission to add the person as a party to the proceedings for the purposes of costs only, and for the person to be given a reasonable opportunity to attend the hearing when the court considers the matter further. Similarly, an application for a wasted costs order is heard after the conclusion of the proceedings, and the respondent must be told clearly what it is alleged they have done wrong, and be given an opportunity to "show cause why an order should not be made" (CPR 48.9(2)).

There are no reported examples of costs orders being made against expert witnesses, and only one against a witness of fact.

In *Locabail (UK) Ltd v Bayfield Properties Ltd and Others (No 3)*, (*The Times*, 29th February 2000), the issue was whether P.T., who was a witness of fact and the unsuccessful third defendant's husband, should be joined as a party for the purpose of a claim in costs. Lawrence Collins QC (as he then was), sitting as a deputy High Court Judge, concluded that the case was sufficiently exceptional to so order because:

a) P.T. had funded his wife's defence, knowing she could not pay the costs if she lost;

b) P.T. had identified "intensely" with her position and showed indifference to the legal and factual position; and

c) the trial judge had rejected "the factual basis" of P.T's evidence.

In a recent case, *Phillips & Others v Symes & Others (Costs No 2)* [2004] EWHC 2330 Ch, at a preliminary hearing to decide whether Mr Symes, a bankrupt, had the mental capacity to conduct the litigation, an expert witness (a consultant psychiatrist) concluded that he had not had capacity to manage his affairs for the previous 20 years, following a stroke. The judge, Smith J, seriously criticised the psychiatrist for not investigating the issue of capacity adequately (he saw Mr Symes for a total of one hour and only reviewed some of the other evidence), for persevering with his opinion for much too long in the face of that other evidence, and for "assuming the role of advocate" for Mr Symes.

The claimants sought a decision in principle that the psychiatrist could be joined as a respondent for costs purposes, particularly as Mr Symes had no assets. After a review of the authorities on experts' immunity and non-parties' liability for costs, the judge concluded that a claim for costs could be pursued against the expert because:

1. The courts have the power to order an expert witness to pay costs and that this would not operate as a deterrent to their giving evidence.

2. "In the administration of justice ... it would be quite wrong of the court to remove from itself the power to make a costs order in appropriate circumstances against an expert who, by his evidence, causes significant expense to be incurred and does so in flagrant disregard of his duties to the court".

3. The other available sanctions, e.g. reference to the expert's professional body, were nothing more than "blunt instruments".

4. No specific warning of the intention to make the application needed to be given to the expert, as the CPR and the expert's signed declaration on his report were sufficient.

However, the judge made it clear that a high level of proof would be required to establish gross dereliction of duty or recklessness by an expert. The claimants would have to prove that the psychiatrist was "in serious breach of his duties to the court by acting recklessly, irresponsibly and wholly outside the bounds of how any reasonable psychiatrist preparing an opinion for the court would properly have acted".

If this decision stands, and particularly if the application is pursued and a costs order is eventually made against this expert, for the first time a tangible means of redress will have become available against irresponsible and incompetent expert witnesses. Yet the test proposed is a higher one than to establish negligence, and it is not clear from the judgment whether any eventual order might be that the expert witness should pay the costs of the losing party (as in a non-party order) or pay the costs specifically incurred and wasted by his actions (as in a wasted costs order).

EXPERT WITNESSES AND INDEMNITY INSURANCE

Before embarking upon any claim against an expert witness, either in negligence or for a costs order, a check should be made on whether the expert is insured or has sufficient assets to satisfy any judgment or order.

The majority of professionals who provide expert witness services will have professional indemnity insurance cover arranged through their professional body. Those who work in professional partnerships, e.g. accountants, architects and surveyors, will usually have unlimited liability unless their terms of business for expert witness work, or the specific letter of engagement, states otherwise. The expert witness organisations recommend that their members maintain professional indemnity cover. The Expert Witness Institute says it should be "appropriate cover in respect of the full liability of the expert service". The Academy recommends "not less than £500,000" of cover.

CONCLUSIONS

If an expert witness performs poorly, particularly after proceedings have been issued and permission given to rely upon that evidence, frequently the only solution will be to settle the claim on the most favourable terms possible, and perhaps to reduce any fees yet to be paid to the expert. Making a complaint about the expert might benefit his future clients but will provide no redress for your client.

It will only be possible generally to pursue a claim in contract or negligence against an expert for deficient preliminary advice pre-proceedings, although several commentators have questioned the validity of the judgment in the *Stanton* case, given that an expert adviser and an expert witness are often doing the same job as far as the client is concerned, particularly now that advocates are no longer immune. Costs orders against expert witnesses might be possible following the *Phillips v Symes* case, but only if the expert has acted very irresponsibly or recklessly.

In short, with the limited remedies available for errors made by experts, it pays to take particular care when selecting and instructing an expert, and in developing an effective working relationship with them for the life of the case.

Chapter 14

THE EXPERT'S PERSPECTIVE

Many lawyers and experts have good working relationships, but most lawyers would benefit from viewing civil disputes from the expert's perspective from time to time. Why not invite experts with whom you work regularly to provide feedback? Alternatively, visit the websites of the main expert witness organisations or attend their conferences. Some of the organisations carry out regular surveys of their members and place newsletters and members' queries on their websites.

THE BOND SOLON ANNUAL SURVEY

Each autumn, before their annual conference, Bond Solon, the training company, conducts a survey of expert witnesses on their database. The results in 2004 in relation to experts' fees were discussed in Chapter 6.

Other interesting results from the 2004 survey are listed below.

The **number of instructions** received in the last year:

- 36% said they had increased.
- 40% said they had stayed the same.
- 21% said they had gone down.

Time spent working as an expert witness:

- 44% said 0-25% of their time.
- 19% said 16-50% of their time.
- 31% said 51-75% of their time.
- 6% said 76-100% of their time.

On **experts' discussions**:

- 28% found them very useful.
- 36% found them useful.
- 27% found them of some use.
- 4% found them not useful.
- 29% thought solicitors should draft the agenda, 43% thought the experts should, 15% said both should.
- 67% thought lawyers should not be present, 28% thought they should attend.

On **single joint experts**:

- 64% thought they were effective.
- 18% did not think they were effective.

On **training**:

- 97% said experts need training.
- 54% said training should be mandatory.

On **accreditation**:

- 48% were in favour.
- 46% were considering applying.
- 84% thought professional bodies should be able to prevent members from being expert witnesses if they fell below standard.

On **working with firms of solicitors**:

- 63% said there were firms with whom they would never work again!

On expert witness **work for the future**:

- 12% were very optimistic.
- 47% were optimistic.
- 7% were pessimistic.

THE AUTHOR'S EXPERIENCE

The author has spent a significant amount of time with expert witnesses in the last six years, at conferences, seminars, training days and on committees. She has often invited the experts to comment upon what solicitors might do better. The following inadequacies of solicitors have tended to top the lists (not listed in the order of frequency of mention):

1. Failing to tell the expert the names of the parties, solicitors and experts involved, to enable the expert to check for conflicts of interest.

2. Failing to sign the expert's terms of business or otherwise confirm the contract.

3. Sending instructions late and thereby setting a very tight timetable for the report (confirmed in the Bond Solon survey when 22% of experts said they were instructed late, 34% just in time and 43% in good time).

4. Sending vague instructions, e.g. "Please do your usual report" (in the Bond Solon survey, solicitors did rather better – only 11% said their instructions were poor, 39% adequate and 49% excellent).

5. Sending seemingly random documents with the instructions that have not been organised or paginated.

6. When they instruct a single joint expert, sending 'very economical' instructions and materials.

7. Forgetting to keep the expert 'in the loop' with additional documents and reports.

8. Failing to acknowledge receipt of the report after a period of frequent contact when the report was in preparation.

9. Expecting the experts to change parts of the report which are germane to the opinion (in the Bond Solon survey, only 51% said that the lawyers encouraged real independence, 44% said they did not).

10. Failing to advise the expert when their report has been disclosed, so that the receipt of questions comes as a surprise.

11. Raising long repetitive lists of questions on reports which go beyond clarification.

12. Expecting questions to be answered and experts' discussions arranged, at very short notice.

13. Failing to provide an agenda for an experts' discussion.

14. Failing to check availability for trial sufficiently early or, alternatively, expecting the expert to keep two weeks blocked out in their diary for months or longer.

15. When they have a single joint expert who is attending court, failing to 'look after' them.

16. Failing to write to the expert at all when the case settles.

17. Not providing feedback on reports or performance at court.

18. Failing to pay fees promptly (in the Bond Solon survey, only 17% said they were paid promptly, 65% said they were paid late and 16% said they were paid very late).

With regard to number 17 in the list, Dame Elizabeth Butler Sloss, writing in the *Journal of the Royal Society of Medicine* in September 2002 ("Expert Witness, Courts and the Law"), said for many expert witnesses "participation in court proceedings can be intimidating, time-consuming, confrontational, complex and unpleasant". She recommended in particular that there should be feedback to expert witnesses at the end of the case, not just to let them know the outcome but to help them improve their performance. She cited one High Court judge who arranges for his judgments to be provided to the experts who gave evidence and who recommends a debriefing letter from the solicitor who instructed the expert.

CONCLUSION

There is clearly room for improvement in the way in which solicitors treat experts.

Chapter 15
CONCLUSIONS

THE IMPACT OF THE CPR

The implementation of the CPR has undoubtedly influenced the use parties make of expert evidence in civil disputes.

However, very limited empirical research into the impact of the reforms has been carried out. The only substantive piece of work is the Law Society and Civil Justice Council study into pre-action behaviour and the protocols. There has also been some research into small claims, court annexed ADR schemes, judges' attitudes to case management, and pre-action costs in low value RTA personal injury cases. Some *ad hoc* but very useful surveys of solicitors have been carried out by the Law Society, and of experts by Bond Solon, the Expert Witness Institute and others. The Lord Chancellor's Department has also published two general evaluation reports largely based on anecdotal evidence, plus some analysis of trends using Judicial Statistics. However, the opportunity has now been lost to carry out comprehensive 'before and after' studies, which might isolate the impact of the CPR from the other changes which have taken place in the last few years, particularly to the funding of many disputes.

Generally it seems to be agreed that the CPR has:

- Made the civil system less complicated for all who use it by the introduction of the same new rules in the High and County Courts.

- Led to a significant fall in the number of new claims issued in all courts – the pre-action protocols and offers to settle have been major factors here.

- Greatly improved the pre-trial settlement rate – offers to settle and encouragement of ADR have influenced this.

- Reduced the time between issue and trial, particularly for cases allocated to the fast track – through judicial case management and the application of tighter timetables which are judicially 'policed'.

- Encouraged a less adversarial, more co-operative culture – as 'conduct' can result in adverse costs orders.

However, Lord Woolf's other aim of reducing costs may not have been achieved. The work on cases is now more 'frontloaded' through the impact of the protocols (research carried out for the Civil Justice Council suggested that in low value personal injury claims, pre-issue costs had increased by a significant percentage post-1999) and in responses to Law Society surveys, solicitors have said that completion of the case management questionnaires, and case management conferences, have increased the work on individual cases and, therefore, costs have increased, particularly in cases that do not settle early. The implementation of predictable costs for low value personal injury claims from October 2003 may reverse the trend for cases that fall within the scheme. Other schemes, or more widespread use of budgeting and cost capping, may follow.

With regard to expert evidence, it is difficult for this author to do more than suggest from her experience the main ways in which the CPR might have changed the use of expert evidence.

- The emphasis in Part 35 on the experts' duty to the court, and the several decisions of the appellate courts concerning experts' conflicts of interest and independence, has encouraged a more professional approach by the vast majority of experts. Examples of very partisan behaviour are now relatively rare, and practitioners and judges say that the worst offenders from the past no longer appear as expert witnesses.

- The strengthening of court control has led to a more disciplined approach by lawyers and clients to the instruction of experts; the knowledge that the case management judge might not permit expert evidence at all or might restrict it to a single joint expert, or limit the fees payable or recoverable, has reduced the use of expert evidence to 'bolster' cases, and has possibly controlled expenditure on experts, at least in some cases.

- Judicial case management, the earlier disclosure of experts' reports and the introduction of written questions on reports and experts' discussions, mean that experts less frequently need to give oral evidence at trial – always the most difficult part of their work.

Experts at fast track trials are very rare and single joint experts also hardly ever give oral evidence. Furthermore, when expert evidence at trial is necessary, the issues and any areas of disagreement between experts for the parties are usually clear, reducing the time the expert has to spend at court. This should have reduced costs.

• Written questions to experts and experts' discussions probably have another advantage – encouraging experts to write clearer, properly researched and well-argued reports, and not to include theories or opinions that do not flow from the evidence. No expert likes to have to admit to inaccuracy or poor reasoning when challenged by their peers.

It may also be significant that:

• Part 35 and its Practice Direction have only been amended three times (see Chapter 2), whereas many other rules have been subject to frequent change (there have been 39 sets of amendments to the CPR up to May 2005).

• The implementation of the Human Rights Act 1998 in October 2000 has produced very few challenges to Part 35 and these have not succeeded (see Chapter 2).

• Experts make very little use of the power in CPR 35.14 to apply to the court for directions (see Chapter 10). There are no reported cases and the author has only seen two applications. While this could be because many experts do not realise that they have the facility to write to a judge, it is also likely that lawyers and experts can usually resolve most difficulties by discussion without troubling the court.

OTHER INFLUENCES FOR CHANGE

The professionalisation of expert witnesses

In the long term the civil justice reforms may not be as significant an influence for change in the use of experts as the concern about the miscarriages of justice in the criminal system, arising from the discredited forensic expert evidence in certain notorious cases in the 1980s and 1990s, and from the sudden infant death and child abuse cases more recently (see Chapter 12). It seems likely that judges in all courts (criminal, family and civil) will be increasingly wary in future of allowing expert evidence alone to determine crucial disputes as to fact and causation.

The professionalisation of expert witnesses is generally to be welcomed, whatever the reasons. Some of the professional bodies have played a major role here, setting up specialist divisions and producing guidance for expert witnesses (the RICS and Institute of Chartered Accountants in particular – see Chapter 2). The expert witness organisations (the Academy of Experts, the Expert Witness Institute and the Society of Experts) provide an excellent service to their members in the form of specimen terms of business, model report formats, newsletters, seminars and training events. In addition, in-depth training and guidance for experts is also provided by Bond Solon, Cardiff University, the Inns of Court School of Law and others. The author has been impressed with the knowledge and commitment portrayed by the many expert witnesses she has met at events organised by all these bodies over the last seven years.

However, more formal and official accreditation and regulation of expert witnesses is not universally supported. The arguments for and against accreditation are discussed in Chapter 1. The arguments against it are that there is insufficient evidence that there exists a problem to be remedied, the costs of the administration of a universal scheme would be significant, the quality of the assessment would be only as good as that of the assessors, accreditation could not be made a requirement for giving evidence as this would exclude the occasional but really 'expert in his field' expert, and that the potentially dangerous eminent specialist prepared to use the courtroom to advance his own theories, would almost certainly not be screened out by an accreditation system. These are powerful arguments but not dissimilar to those used in the past against the accreditation and regulation of professionals generally, and it was long ago decided that machinery to discipline lawyers and doctors, etc. was essential in modern society.

The arguments for a *form* of accreditation are that clients, lawyers, and judges would have some assurance that the expert in question understood his role within the legal system, and was likely to be able to fulfil it reasonably, most typically by producing a useful written report that complied with the rules, court directions and instructions.

Accreditation could also save lawyers some time in checking experts' professional qualifications and references, and could provide some disciplinary machinery if a complaint against the expert became necessary.

In the author's view it would be beneficial if the government and judiciary encouraged professional bodies and regulators, such as the RICS and the GMC, to produce standards and guidance for their members who act as expert witnesses against which performance would be measured in case of a complaint, and if the expert witness organisations, either of their own accord or through the Council for the Regulation of Forensic Practitioners, developed voluntary accreditation schemes for other civil expert witnesses who are not members of professional bodies.

Experience from the family and criminal jurisdictions

Procedures in the civil family and criminal jurisdictions have been growing closer together in recent years. Single joint experts have a longer tradition in family cases than civil, as court welfare officers, and most of the recent guidance issued on instructing single joint experts in the family courts (see Chapter 9) is equally applicable in civil cases. Likewise, the 2004 report of the Royal Colleges of Pathologists and Paediatrics and Child Heath on investigation and evidence in sudden infant death cases (see Chapter 12), although aimed at cases decided in the criminal and family courts, is clearly relevant to doctors and pathologists giving evidence in civil cases. Judges, senior government officials and lawyers have opportunities to cross-fertilise ideas and should continue to make use of them.

PART 35 – WHAT NEXT?

There are, of course, critics of the CPR and of Part 35 in particular. The criticism seems to be focused on the following aspects of the Rules.

- Both Part 35 and its Practice Direction are very short and provide little practical guidance even upon the operation of the new elements of the rules, e.g. how parties might select and instruct a single joint expert, and how an experts' discussions should be organised.

- The preference for single joint experts can prevent parties from preparing and presenting their evidence as they(rather than a judge who knows little about the case) see fit. Furthermore, SJEs inevitably in practice 'decide' the more technical aspects of cases which the lawyers and even the judge cannot challenge without a second opinion.

- The wide scope of case management judges' discretion means that it is very difficult to predict whether a judge will permit expert evidence to be adduced in a particular case and, if so, whether by party expert or SJE, and to appeal any surprising decisions.

- Case management judges can set impracticable timetables for expert witness work, especially for experts answering written questions and holding discussions in the run-up to trial, and show little understanding of the practical problems involved in securing an expert's availability for trial.

The Protocol for the Instruction of Experts

The intention of the heads of civil justice in the late 1990s was that there should be a code of guidance for expert evidence to assist clients, lawyers and experts in applying the rules (see Chapter 2). It was clearly very unfortunate that two codes were published, each with its supporters and which were different in detail. However, the welding together of the codes has at last been achieved and it is sincerely to be hoped that *The Protocol for the Instruction of Experts* (see Appendix 2) will help with the first point of difficulty listed above.

Practitioners working more closely with judges

In the author's view the remedy for many of the other practitioner criticisms, including those listed above, lies in better preparation and 'written advocacy' by practitioners. In many cases, especially fast track and lower value multi-track cases in the County Court, case management decisions on expert evidence are taken on paper based upon the completed allocation questionnaires and pre-trial checklists. In the author's experience these are often poorly completed. They are treated as a box-ticking exercise with no supporting argument given if, for instance, a party wants to instruct their own expert in a fast track case. Questionnaires are not always exchanged with the other party (as they should be), and either no draft directions are provided or, less than usual, are provided but lacking in any explanation. A recent trend seems to be for parties to submit 'consent directions' for a case management conference arranged by the court, which do not deal with the problems identified by the judge, or which do so in an unsatisfactory way, and then to fax or telephone an apology for 'non-attendance' on the day of the conference.

Courts have demonstrated considerable flexibility about expert evidence, including over the identity of a proposed SJE, whether a second expert to an SJE might be justified, whether an SJE might give oral evidence at trial (see Chapter 9), on when a party might change his expert or in allowing late expert evidence (see Chapter 10). Nonetheless, judges need to understand *why* a departure from the norm is being sought and must be persuaded that it is justified. Attaching a letter or note to the particular questionnaire, application or directions and attending case management conferences is time well spent.

Privilege and experts

An area that has caused difficulty is in relation to privilege and experts, discussed in Chapter 5. Recent decisions of the Court of Appeal have clarified that instructions and attached material will remain privileged unless the expert's summary of his instructions is clearly inaccurate and incomplete, and that draft reports are also privileged. *The Protocol for the Instruction of Experts* suggests that advice that the parties do not intend to adduce in litigation is also likely to be privileged. However, uncertainties remain, especially when an expert is instructed to advise in the early stages of a dispute and is then retained for the litigation, and in relation to privileged material not disclosed to the other party but relied upon by the expert.

Experts' fees

Lawyers' fees in litigation are subject to control and assessment through fixed advocacy costs or fast track trials, fixed success fees in personal injury conditional fee cases, predictable costs in some low value personal injury claims, guideline rates for summary assessment, scrutiny of estimates and, in a few cases, judges setting budgets or costs caps and proportionality checks on detailed assessment. By contrast, experts' fees are very lightly controlled, largely through the contractual negotiations with the instructing parties. Judges only infrequently limit recoverable fees or rates, and reduction of experts' fees on assessment rarely affects the contract – leaving the solicitor to pay for the shortfall between the expert's charges and the assessed fee, or to negotiate with the expert. It is difficult for judges to set reasonable rates or fee limits when there is limited information available about what experts charge and why (see Chapter 6).

However, this too may soon be subject to change. The Civil Justice Council has started to look at setting experts' fees in predictable costs personal injury cases. In the author's view, some official guideline rates for the mainstream experts would be useful for all concerned.

Experts' immunity

Witnesses, including experts, are largely immune from negligence actions for their work for the court. While there may have been policy reasons for this originally, once barristers lost their immunity the case for experts retaining theirs was not strong (see Chapter 13). The principle seems to have survived because the Court of Appeal has not had an opportunity to review the law since the CPR were implemented. Judges' attempts to hold expert witnesses to account for very poor performance – by the trial judge sending a complaint to the professional body – is clearly a blunt instrument. Costs orders against expert witnesses who do not comply with their CPR 35.3 duty to the court may now provide a remedy in some cases but a review of *Stanton v Callaghan* is now long overdue.

New ways of using and testing expert evidence

The English civil courts have been cautious, post the implementation of the CPR, about introducing new ways of using and assessing expert evidence.

The potential role of assessors, who sit with the judge, has been underused outside Admiralty cases (see Chapter 2). Now that there has been some procedural guidance to safeguard the ECHR Article 6 concerns (see Chapter 12), maybe the courts will extend the use of assessors to other cases as Lord Woolf recommended.

In the larger High Court cases, the American Daubert deposition hearing, when experts are cross-examined at pre-trial hearings, has its attraction (see Chapter 1), as does the Australian 'hot-tubbing', when the judge questions both experts together during the trial (see Chapter 12).

Whatever further changes in the use of expert evidence are made in the next few years, it seems highly likely that the subject will remain on the agenda for the next Civil Justice Review.

Appendix 1
CIVIL PROCEDURE RULES – PART 35 AND PRACTICE DIRECTION

Duty to restrict expert evidence

35.1   Expert evidence shall be restricted to that which is reasonably required to resolve the proceedings.

Interpretation

35.2   A reference to an 'expert' in this Part is a reference to an expert who has been instructed to give or prepare evidence for the purpose of court proceedings.

Experts – overriding duty to the court

35.3   (1) It is the duty of an expert to help the court on the matters within his expertise.

(2) This duty overrides any obligation to the person from whom he has received instructions or by whom he is paid.

Court's power to restrict expert evidence

35.4   (1) No party may call an expert or put in evidence an expert's report without the court's permission.

(2) When a party applies for permission under this rule he must identify –

(a) the field in which he wishes to rely on expert evidence; and

(b) where practicable the expert in that field on whose evidence he wishes to rely.

(3) If permission is granted under this rule it shall be in relation only to the expert named or the field identified under paragraph (2).

(4) The court may limit the amount of the expert's fees and expenses that the party who wishes to rely on the expert may recover from any other party.

General requirement for expert evidence to be given in a written report

35.5 (1) Expert evidence is to be given in a written report unless the court directs otherwise.

(2) If a claim is on the fast track, the court will not direct an expert to attend a hearing unless it is necessary to do so in the interests of justice.

Written questions to experts

35.6 (1) A party may put to –

(a) an expert instructed by another party; or

(b) a single joint expert appointed under rule 35.7,

written questions about his report.

(2) Written questions under paragraph (1) –

(a) may be put once only;

(b) must be put within 28 days of service of the expert's report; and

(c) must be for the purpose only of clarification of the report,

unless in any case –

(i) the court gives permission; or

(ii) the other party agrees.

(3) An expert's answers to questions put in accordance with paragraph (1) shall be treated as part of the expert's report.

(4) Where –

(a) a party has put a written question to an expert instructed by another party in accordance with this rule; and

(b) the expert does not answer that question,

the court may make one or both of the following orders in relation to the party who instructed the expert –

(i) that the party may not rely on the evidence of that expert; or

(ii) that the party may not recover the fees and expenses of that expert from any other party.

Court's power to direct that evidence is to be given by a single joint expert

35.7 (1) Where two or more parties wish to submit expert evidence on a particular issue, the court may direct that the evidence on that issue is to given by one expert only.

(2) The parties wishing to submit the expert evidence are called 'the instructing parties'.

(3) Where the instructing parties cannot agree who should be the expert, the court may –

(a) select the expert from a list prepared or identified by the instructing parties; or

(b) direct that the expert be selected in such other manner as the court may direct.

Instructions to a single joint expert

35.8 (1) Where the court gives a direction under rule 35.7 for a single joint expert to be used, each instructing party may give instructions to the expert.

(2) When an instructing party gives instructions to the expert he must, at the same time, send a copy of the instructions to the other instructing parties.

(3) The court may give directions about –

(a) the payment of the expert's fees and expenses; and

(b) any inspection, examination or experiments which the expert wishes to carry out.

(4) The court may, before an expert is instructed –

    (a) limit the amount that can be paid by way of fees and expenses to the expert; and

    (b) direct that the instructing parties pay that amount into court.

(5) Unless the court otherwise directs, the instructing parties are jointly and severally liable (GL) for the payment of the expert's fees and expenses.

Power of court to direct a party to provide information

35.9   Where a party has access to information which is not reasonably available to the other party, the court may direct the party who has access to the information to –

    (a) prepare and file a document recording the information; and

    (b) serve a copy of that document on the other party.

Contents of report

35.10 (1) An expert's report must comply with the requirements set out in the relevant practice direction.

    (2) At the end of an expert's report there must be a statement that –

        (a) the expert understands his duty to the court; and

        (b) he has complied with that duty.

    (3) The expert's report must state the substance of all material instructions, whether written or oral, on the basis of which the report was written.

    (4) The instructions referred to in paragraph (3) shall not be privileged (GL) against disclosure but the court will not, in relation to those instructions –

        (a) order disclosure of any specific document; or

        (b) permit any questioning in court, other than by the party who instructed the expert,

    unless it is satisfied that there are reasonable grounds to

consider the statement of instructions given under paragraph (3) to be inaccurate or incomplete.

Use by one party of expert's report disclosed by another

35.11 Where a party has disclosed an expert's report, any party may use that expert's report as evidence at the trial.

Discussions between experts

35.12 (1) The court may, at any stage, direct a discussion between experts for the purpose of requiring the experts to –

(a) identify and discuss the expert issues in the proceedings; and

(b) where possible, reach an agreed opinion on those issues.

(2) The court may specify the issues which the experts must discuss.

(3) The court may direct that following a discussion between the experts they must prepare a statement for the court showing –

(a) those issues on which they agree; and

(b) those issues on which they disagree and a summary of their reasons for disagreeing.

(4) The content of the discussion between the experts shall not be referred to at the trial unless the parties agree.

(5) Where experts reach agreement on an issue during their discussions, the agreement shall not bind the parties unless the parties expressly agree to be bound by the agreement.

Consequence of failure to disclose expert's report

35.13 A party who fails to disclose an expert's report may not use the report at the trial or call the expert to give evidence orally unless the court gives permission.

Expert's right to ask court for directions

35.14 (1) An expert may file a written request for directions to assist him in carrying out his function as an expert.

(2) An expert must, unless the court orders otherwise, provide a copy of any proposed request for directions under paragraph (1) –

(a) to the party instructing him, at least 7 days before he files the request; and

(b) to all other parties, at least 4 days before he files it.

(3) The court, when it gives directions, may also direct that a party be served with a copy of the directions.

Assessors

35.15 (1) This rule applies where the court appoints one or more persons (an 'assessor') under section 70 of the Supreme Court Act 1981 or section 63 of the County Courts Act 1984.

(2) The assessor shall assist the court in dealing with a matter in which the assessor has skill and experience.

(3) An assessor shall take such part in the proceedings as the court may direct and in particular the court may –

(a) direct the assessor to prepare a report for the court on any matter at issue in the proceedings; and

(b) direct the assessor to attend the whole or any part of the trial to advise the court on any such matter.

(4) If the assessor prepares a report for the court before the trial has begun –

(a) the court will send a copy to each of the parties; and

(b) the parties may use it at trial.

(5) The remuneration to be paid to the assessor for his services shall be determined by the court and shall form part of the costs of the proceedings.

(6) The court may order any party to deposit in the court office a specified sum in respect of the assessor's fees and, where it does so, the assessor will not be asked to act until the sum has been deposited.

(7) Paragraphs (5) and (6) do not apply where the remuneration of the assessor is to be paid out of money provided by Parliament.

PRACTICE DIRECTION – EXPERTS AND ASSESSORS, PART 35

Part 35 is intended to limit the use of oral expert evidence to that which is reasonably required. In addition, where possible, matters requiring expert evidence should be dealt with by a single expert. Permission of the court is always required either to call an expert or to put an expert's report in evidence.

Expert evidence – general requirements

1.1 It is the duty of an expert to help the court on matters within his own expertise: rule 35.3(1). This duty is paramount and overrides any obligation to the person from whom the expert has received instructions or by whom he is paid: rule 35.3(2).

1.2 Expert evidence should be the independent product of the expert uninfluenced by the pressures of litigation.

1.3 An expert should assist the court by providing objective, unbiased opinion on matters within his expertise, and should not assume the role of an advocate.

1.4 An expert should consider all material facts, including those which might detract from his opinion.

1.5 An expert should make it clear:

(a) when a question or issue falls outside his expertise; and

(b) when he is not able to reach a definite opinion, for example because he has insufficient information.

1.6 If, after producing a report, an expert changes his view on any material matter, such change of view should be communicated to all the parties without delay, and when appropriate to the court.

Form and content of experts' reports

2.1 An expert's report should be addressed to the court and not to the party from whom the expert has received his instructions.

2.2   An expert's report must:

(1) give details of the expert's qualifications;

(2) give details of any literature or other material which the expert has relied on in making the report;

(3) contain a statement setting out the substance of all facts and instructions given to the expert which are material to the opinions expressed in the report or upon which those opinions are based;

(4) make clear which of the facts stated in the report are within the expert's own knowledge;

(5) say who carried out any examination, measurement, test or experiment which the expert has used for the report, give the qualifications of that person, and say whether or not the test or experiment has been carried out under the expert's supervision;

(6) where there is a range of opinion on the matters dealt with in the report –

(a) summarise the range of opinion, and

(b) give reasons for his own opinion;

(7) contain a summary of the conclusions reached;

(8) if the expert is not able to give his opinion without qualification, state the qualification; and

(9) contain a statement that the expert understands his duty to the court, and has complied and will continue to comply with that duty.

2.3   An expert's report must be verified by a statement of truth as well as containing the statements required in paragraph 2.2(8) and (9) above.

2.4   The form of the statement of truth is as follows:

"I confirm that insofar as the facts stated in my report are within my own knowledge I have made clear which they are and I believe them to be true, and that the opinions I have expressed represent my true and complete professional opinion."

2.5   Attention is drawn to rule 32.14 which sets out the consequences of verifying a document containing a false statement without an honest belief in its truth.

(For information about statements of truth see Part 22 and the practice direction which supplements it.)

Information

3   Under Rule 35.9 the court may direct a party with access to information which is not reasonably available to another party to serve on that other party a document which records the information. The document served must include sufficient details of all the facts, tests, experiments and assumptions which underlie any part of the information to enable the party on whom it is served to make, or to obtain, a proper interpretation of the information and an assessment of its significance.

Instructions

4   The instructions referred to in paragraph 2.2(3) will not be protected by privilege (see rule 35.10(4)). But cross-examination of the expert on the contents of his instructions will not be allowed unless the court permits it (or unless the party who gave the instructions consents to it). Before it gives permission the court must be satisfied that there are reasonable grounds to consider that the statement in the report of the substance of the instructions is inaccurate or incomplete. If the court is so satisfied, it will allow the cross-examination where it appears to be in the interests of justice to do so.

Questions to experts

5.1   Questions asked for the purpose of clarifying the expert's report (see rule 35.6) should be put, in writing, to the expert not later than 28 days after receipt of the expert's report (see paragraphs 1.2 to 1.5 above as to verification).

5.2   Where a party sends a written question or questions direct to an expert, a copy of the questions should, at the same time, be sent to the other party or parties.

5.3   The party or parties instructing the expert must pay any fees charged by that expert for answering questions put under rule

35.6. This does not affect any decision of the court as to the party who is ultimately to bear the expert's costs.

Single expert

6   Where the court has directed that the evidence on a particular issue is to be given by one expert only (rule 35.7) but there are a number of disciplines relevant to that issue, a leading expert in the dominant discipline should be identified as the single expert. He should prepare the general part of the report and be responsible for annexing or incorporating the contents of any reports from experts in other disciplines.

Orders

6A   Where an order requires an act to be done by an expert, or otherwise affects an expert, the party instructing that expert must serve a copy of the order on the expert instructed by him. In the case of a jointly instructed expert, the claimant must serve the order.

Assessors

7.1   An assessor may be appointed to assist the court under rule 35.15. Not less than 21 days before making any such appointment, the court will notify each party in writing of the name of the proposed assessor, of the matter in respect of which the assistance of the assessor will be sought and of the qualifications of the assessor to give that assistance.

7.2   Where any person has been proposed for appointment as an assessor, objection to him, either personally or in respect of his qualification, may be taken by any party.

7.3   Any such objection must be made in writing and filed with the court within 7 days of receipt of the notification referred to in paragraph 6.1 and will be taken into account by the court in deciding whether or not to make the appointment (section 63(5) of the County Courts Act 1984).

7.4   Copies of any report prepared by the assessor will be sent to each of the parties but the assessor will not give oral evidence or be open to cross-examination or questioning.

Appendix 2
PROTOCOL FOR THE INSTRUCTION OF EXPERTS TO GIVE EVIDENCE IN CIVIL CLAIMS

1. Introduction

Expert witnesses perform a vital role in civil litigation. It is essential that both those who instruct experts and experts themselves are given clear guidance as to what they are expected to do in civil proceedings. The purpose of this Protocol is to provide such guidance. It has been drafted by the Civil Justice Council and reflects the rules and practice directions current [in June 2005], replacing the Code of Guidance on Expert Evidence. The authors of the Protocol wish to acknowledge the valuable assistance they obtained by drawing on earlier documents produced by the Academy of Experts and the Expert Witness Institute, as well as suggestions made by the Clinical Dispute Forum. The Protocol has been approved by the Master of the Rolls.

2. Aims of Protocol

2.1   This Protocol offers guidance to experts and to those instructing them in the interpretation of and compliance with Part 35 of the Civil Procedure Rules (CPR 35) and its associated Practice Direction (PD 35) and to further the objectives of the Civil Procedure Rules in general. It is intended to assist in the interpretation of those provisions in the interests of good practice but it does not replace them. It sets out standards for the use of experts and the conduct of experts and those who instruct them. The existence of this Protocol does not remove the need for experts and those who instruct them to be familiar with CPR35 and PD35.

2.2   Experts and those who instruct them should also bear in mind para 1.4 of the Practice Direction on Protocols which contains the following objectives, namely to:

(a)   encourage the exchange of early and full information about the expert issues involved in a prospective legal claim;

(b)   enable the parties to avoid or reduce the scope of litigation by agreeing the whole or part of an expert issue before commencement of proceedings; and

(c)   support the efficient management of proceedings where litigation cannot be avoided.

3. Application

3.1   This Protocol applies to any steps taken for the purpose of civil proceedings by experts or those who instruct them on or after 5th September 2005.

3.2   It applies to all experts who are, or who may be, governed by CPR Part 35 and to those who instruct them. Experts are governed by Part 35 if they are or have been instructed to give or prepare evidence for the purpose of civil proceedings in a court in England and Wales (CPR 35.2).

3.3   Experts, and those instructing them, should be aware that some cases may be "specialist proceedings" (CPR 49) where there are modifications to the Civil Procedure Rules. Proceedings may also be governed by other Protocols. Further, some courts have published their own Guides which supplement the Civil Procedure Rules for proceedings in those courts. They contain provisions affecting expert evidence. Expert witnesses and those instructing them should be familiar with them when they are relevant.

3.4   Courts may take into account any failure to comply with this Protocol when making orders in relation to costs, interest, time limits, the stay of proceedings and whether to order a party to pay a sum of money into court.

Limitation

3.5   If, as a result of complying with any part of this Protocol, claims would or might be time barred under any provision in the Limitation Act 1980, or any other legislation that imposes a time limit for the bringing an action, claimants may commence proceedings without complying with this Protocol. In such circumstances, claimants who commence proceedings without complying with all, or any part, of this Protocol must apply, giving notice to all other parties, to the court for directions as to the timetable and form of procedure to be adopted, at the same time as they request the court to issue proceedings. The court may consider whether to order a stay of the whole or part of the proceedings pending compliance with this Protocol and may make orders in relation to costs.

4. Duties of experts

4.1 Experts always owe a duty to exercise reasonable skill and care to those instructing them, and to comply with any relevant professional code of ethics. However when they are instructed to give or prepare evidence for the purpose of civil proceedings in England and Wales they have an overriding duty to help the court on matters within their expertise (CPR 35.3). This duty overrides any obligation to the person instructing or paying them. Experts must not serve the exclusive interest of those who retain them.

4.2 Experts should be aware of the overriding objective that courts deal with cases justly. This includes dealing with cases proportionately, expeditiously and fairly (CPR 1.1). Experts are under an obligation to assist the court so as to enable them to deal with cases in accordance with the overriding objective. However the overriding objective does not impose on experts any duty to act as mediators between the parties or require them to trespass on the role of the court in deciding facts.

4.3 Experts should provide opinions which are independent, regardless of the pressures of litigation. In this context, a useful test of 'independence' is that the expert would express the same opinion if given the same instructions by an opposing party. Experts should not take it upon themselves to promote the point of view of the party instructing them or engage in the role of advocates.

4.4 Experts should confine their opinions to matters which are material to the disputes between the parties and provide opinions only in relation to matters which lie within their expertise. Experts should indicate without delay where particular questions or issues fall outside their expertise.

4.5 Experts should take into account all material facts before them at the time that they give their opinion. Their reports should set out those facts and any literature or any other material on which they have relied in forming their opinions. They should indicate if an opinion is provisional, or qualified, or where they consider that further information is required or if, for any other reason, they are not satisfied that an opinion can be expressed finally and without qualification.

4.6   Experts should inform those instructing them without delay of any change in their opinions on any material matter and the reason for it.

4.7   Experts should be aware that any failure by them to comply with the Civil Procedure Rules or court orders or any excessive delay for which they are responsible may result in the parties who instructed them being penalised in costs and even, in extreme cases, being debarred from placing the experts' evidence before the court. In[1] *Phillips v Symes* Peter Smith J held that courts may also make orders for costs (under section 51 of the Supreme Court Act 1981) directly against expert witnesses who by their evidence cause significant expense to be incurred, and do so in flagrant and reckless disregard of their duties to the Court

5.   Conduct of experts instructed only to advise

5.1   Part 35 only applies where experts are instructed to give opinions which are relied on for the purposes of court proceedings. Advice which the parties do not intend to adduce in litigation is likely to be confidential; the Protocol does not apply in these circumstances.[2, 3]

5.2   The same applies where, after the commencement of proceedings, experts are instructed only to advise (e.g. to comment upon a single joint expert's report) and not to give or prepare evidence for use in the proceedings.

5.3   However this Protocol does apply if experts who were formerly instructed only to advise are later instructed to give or prepare evidence for the purpose of civil proceedings.

6.   The need for experts

6.1   Those intending to instruct experts to give or prepare evidence for the purpose of civil proceedings should consider whether expert

---

[1]   *Phillips v Symes* [2004] EWHC 2330 (Ch).
[2]   *Carlson v Townsend* [2001] 1 WLR 2415.
[3]   *Jackson v Marley Davenport* [2004] 1 WLR 2926.

evidence is appropriate, taking account of the principles set out in CPR Parts 1 and 35, and in particular whether

(a)   it is relevant to a matter which is in dispute between the parties;

(b)   it is reasonably required to resolve the proceedings (CPR 35.1);

(c)   the expert has expertise relevant to the issue on which an opinion is sought;

(d)   the expert has the experience, expertise and training appropriate to the value, complexity and importance of the case; and whether

(e)   these objects can be achieved by the appointment of a single joint expert (see section 17 below).

6.2   Although the court's permission is not generally required to instruct an expert, the court's permission is required before experts can be called to give evidence or their evidence can be put in (CPR 35.4).

7.   The appointment of experts

7.1   Before experts are formally instructed or the court's permission to appoint named experts is sought, the following should be established:

(a)   that they have the appropriate expertise and experience;

(b)   that they are familiar with the general duties of an expert;

(c)   that they can produce a report, deal with questions and have discussions with other experts within a reasonable time and at a cost proportionate to the matters in issue;

(d)   a description of the work required;

(e)   whether they are available to attend the trial, if attendance is required; and

(f)   there is no potential conflict of interest.

7.2   Terms of appointment should be agreed at the outset and should normally include:

(a)   the capacity in which the expert is to be appointed (e.g. party appointed expert, single joint expert or expert advisor);

(b)   the services required of the expert (e.g. provision of expert's report, answering questions in writing, attendance at meetings and attendance at court);

(c)   time for delivery of the report;

(d)   the basis of the expert's charges (either daily or hourly rates and an estimate of the time likely to be required, or a total fee for the services);

(e)   travelling expenses and disbursements;

(f)   cancellation charges;

(g)   any fees for attending court;

(h)   time for making the payment; and

(i)   whether fees are to be paid by a third party;

(j)   if a party is publicly funded, whether or not the expert's charges will be subject to assessment by a costs officer.

7.3   As to the appointment of single joint experts, see section 17 below.

7.4   When necessary, arrangements should be made for dealing with questions to experts and discussions between experts, including any directions given by the court, and provision should be made for the cost of this work.

7.5   Experts should be informed regularly about deadlines for all matters concerning them. Those instructing experts should promptly send them copies of all court orders and directions which may affect the preparation of their reports or any other matters concerning their obligations.

Conditional and contingency fees

7.6   Payments contingent upon the nature of the expert evidence given in legal proceedings, or upon the outcome of a case, must not be offered or accepted. To do so would contravene experts' overriding duty to the court and compromise their duty of independence.

7.7   Agreement to delay payment of experts' fees until after the conclusion of cases is permissible as long as the amount of the fee does not depend on the outcome of the case.

8. Instructions

8.1 Those instructing experts should ensure that they give clear instructions, including the following:

(a) basic information, such as names, addresses, telephone numbers, dates of birth and dates of incidents;

(b) the nature and extent of the expertise which is called for;

(c) the purpose of requesting the advice or report, a description of the matter(s) to be investigated, the principal known issues and the identity of all parties;

(d) the statement(s) of case (if any), those documents which form part of standard disclosure and witness statements which are relevant to the advice or report;

(e) where proceedings have not been started, whether proceedings are being contemplated and, if so, whether the expert is asked only for advice;

(f) an outline programme, consistent with good case management and the expert's availability, for the completion and delivery of each stage of the expert's work; and

(g) where proceedings have been started, the dates of any hearings (including any Case Management Conferences and/ or Pre-Trial Reviews), the name of the court, the claim number and the track to which the claim has been allocated.

8.2 Experts who do not receive clear instructions should request clarification and may indicate that they are not prepared to act unless and until such clear instructions are received.

8.3 As to the instruction of single joint experts, see section 17 below.

9. Experts' acceptance of instructions

9.1 Experts should confirm without delay whether or not they accept instructions. They should also inform those instructing them (whether on initial instruction or at any later stage) without delay if:

(a) instructions are not acceptable because, for example, they require work that falls outside their expertise, impose unrealistic deadlines, or are insufficiently clear;

(b)   they consider that instructions are or have become insufficient to complete the work;

(c)   they become aware that they may not be able to fulfil any of the terms of appointment;

(d)   the instructions and/or work have, for any reason, placed them in conflict with their duties as an expert; or

(e)   they are not satisfied that they can comply with any orders that have been made.

9.2   Experts must neither express an opinion outside the scope of their field of expertise, nor accept any instructions to do so.

10. Withdrawal

10.1   Where experts' instructions remain incompatible with their duties, whether through incompleteness, a conflict between their duty to the court and their instructions, or for any other substantial and significant reason, they may consider withdrawing from the case. However, experts should not withdraw without first discussing the position fully with those who instruct them and considering carefully whether it would be more appropriate to make a written request for directions from the court. If experts do withdraw, they must give formal written notice to those instructing them.

11. Experts' right to ask court for directions

11.1   Experts may request directions from the court to assist them in carrying out their functions as experts. Experts should normally discuss such matters with those who instruct them before making any such request. Unless the court otherwise orders, any proposed request for directions should be copied to the party instructing the expert at least seven days before filing any request to the court, and to all other parties at least four days before filing it. (CPR 35.14).

11.2   Requests to the court for directions should be made by letter, containing.

(a)   the title of the claim;

(b)   the claim number of the case;

(c)   the name of the expert;

(d)   full details of why directions are sought; and

(e)   copies of any relevant documentation.

12. Power of the court to direct a party to provide information

12.1   If experts consider that those instructing them have not provided information which they require, they may, after discussion with those instructing them and giving notice, write to the court to seek directions (CPR 35.14).

12.2   Experts and those who instruct them should also be aware of CPR 35.9. This provides that where one party has access to information which is not readily available to the other party, the court may direct the party who has access to the information to prepare, file and copy to the other party a document recording the information. If experts require such information which has not been disclosed, they should discuss the position with those instructing them without delay, so that a request for the information can be made, and, if not forthcoming, an application can be made to the court. Unless a document appears to be essential, experts should assess the cost and time involved in the production of a document and whether its provision would be proportionate in the context of the case.

13. Contents of experts' reports

13.1   The content and extent of experts' reports should be governed by the scope of their instructions and general obligations, the contents of CPR 35 and PD35 and their overriding duty to the court.

13.2   In preparing reports, experts should maintain professional objectivity and impartiality at all times.

13.3   PD 35, para 2 provides that experts' reports should be addressed to the court and gives detailed directions about the form and content of such reports. All experts and those who instruct them should ensure that they are familiar with these requirements.

13.4   Model forms of Experts' Reports are available from bodies such as the Academy of Experts or the Expert Witness Institute.

13.5   Experts' reports must contain statements that they understand their duty to the court and have complied and will continue to comply with that duty (PD35 para 2.2(9)). They must also be verified by a statement of truth. The form of the statement of truth is as follows:

"I confirm that insofar as the facts stated in my report are within my own knowledge I have made clear which they are and I believe them to be true, and that the opinions I have expressed represent my true and complete professional opinion."

This wording is mandatory and must not be modified.

Qualifications

13.6   The details of experts' qualifications to be given in reports should be commensurate with the nature and complexity of the case. It may be sufficient merely to state academic and professional qualifications. However, where highly specialised expertise is called for, experts should include the detail of particular training and/or experience that qualifies them to provide that highly specialised evidence.

Tests

13.7   Where tests of a scientific or technical nature have been carried out, experts should state:

(a)   the methodology used; and

(b)   by whom the tests were undertaken and under whose supervision, summarising their respective qualifications and experience.

Reliance on the work of others

13.8   Where experts rely in their reports on literature or other material and cite the opinions of others without having verified them, they must give details of those opinions relied on. It is likely to assist the court if the qualifications of the originator(s) are also stated.

Facts

13.9   When addressing questions of fact and opinion, experts should keep the two separate and discrete.

13.10 Experts must state those facts (whether assumed or otherwise) upon which their opinions are based. They must distinguish clearly between those facts which experts know to be true and those facts which they assume.

13.11 Where there are material facts in dispute experts should express separate opinions on each hypothesis put forward. They should not express a view in favour of one or other disputed version of the facts unless, as a result of particular expertise and experience, they consider one set of facts as being improbable or less probable, in which case they may express that view, and should give reasons for holding it.

Range of opinion

13.12 If the mandatory summary of the range of opinion is based on published sources, experts should explain those sources and, where appropriate, state the qualifications of the originator(s) of the opinions from which they differ, particularly if such opinions represent a well-established school of thought.

13.13 Where there is no available source for the range of opinion, experts may need to express opinions on what they believe to be the range which other experts would arrive at if asked. In those circumstances, experts should make it clear that the range that they summarise is based on their own judgement and explain the basis of that judgement.

Conclusions

13.14 A summary of conclusions is mandatory. The summary should be at the end of the report after all the reasoning. There may be cases, however, where the benefit to the court is heightened by placing a short summary at the beginning of the report whilst giving the full conclusions at the end. For example, it can assist with the comprehension of the analysis and with the absorption of the detailed facts if the court is told at the outset of the direction in which the report's logic will flow in cases involving highly complex matters which fall outside the general knowledge of the court.

Basis of report: material instructions

13.15 The mandatory statement of the substance of all material instructions should not be incomplete or otherwise tend to mislead. The imperative is transparency. The term "instructions" includes all material which solicitors place in front of experts in order to gain advice. The omission from the statement of 'off-the-record' oral instructions is not permitted. Courts may allow cross-examination about the instructions if there are reasonable grounds to consider that the statement may be inaccurate or incomplete.

14. After receipt of experts' reports

14.1   Following the receipt of experts' reports, those instructing them should advise the experts as soon as reasonably practicable whether, and if so when, the report will be disclosed to other parties; and, if so disclosed, the date of actual disclosure.

14.2   If experts' reports are to be relied upon, and if experts are to give oral evidence, those instructing them should give the experts the opportunity to consider and comment upon other reports within their area of expertise and which deal with relevant issues at the earliest opportunity.

14.3   Those instructing experts should keep experts informed of the progress of cases, including amendments to statements of case relevant to experts' opinion.

14.4   If those instructing experts become aware of material changes in circumstances or that relevant information within their control was not previously provided to experts, they should without delay instruct experts to review, and if necessary, update the contents of their reports.

15. Amendment of reports

15.1   It may become necessary for experts to amend their reports:

(a)   as a result of an exchange of questions and answers;

(b)   following agreements reached at meetings between experts; or

(c)   where further evidence or documentation is disclosed.

15.2   Experts should not be asked to, and should not, amend, expand or alter any parts of reports in a manner which distorts their true opinion, but may be invited to amend or expand reports to ensure accuracy, internal consistency, completeness and relevance to the issues and clarity. Although experts should generally follow the recommendations of solicitors with regard to the form of reports, they should form their own independent views as to the opinions and contents expressed in their reports and exclude any suggestions which do not accord with their views.

15.3   Where experts change their opinion following a meeting of experts, a simple signed and dated addendum or memorandum to that effect is generally sufficient. In some cases, however, the benefit to the court of having an amended report may justify the cost of making the amendment.

15.4   Where experts significantly alter their opinion, as a result of new evidence or because evidence on which they relied has become unreliable, or for any other reason, they should amend their reports to reflect that fact. Amended reports should include reasons for amendments. In such circumstances those instructing experts should inform other parties as soon as possible of any change of opinion.

15.5   When experts intend to amend their reports, they should inform those instructing them without delay and give reasons. They should provide the amended version (or an addendum or memorandum) clearly marked as such as quickly as possible.

16. Written questions to experts

16.1   The procedure for putting written questions to experts (CPR 35.6) is intended to facilitate the clarification of opinions and issues after experts' reports have been served. Experts have a duty to provide answers to questions properly put. Where they fail to do so, the court may impose sanctions against the party instructing the expert, and, if, there is continued non-compliance, debar a party from relying on the report. Experts should copy their answers to those instructing them.

16.2   Experts' answers to questions automatically become part of their reports. They are covered by the statement of truth and form part of the expert evidence.

16.3   Where experts believe that questions put are not properly directed to the clarification of the report, or are disproportionate, or have been asked out of time, they should discuss the questions with those instructing them and, if appropriate, those asking the questions. Attempts should be made to resolve such problems without the need for an application to the court for directions.

Written requests for directions in relation to questions

16.4   If those instructing experts do not apply to the court in respect of questions, but experts still believe that questions are improper or out of time, experts may file written requests with the court for directions to assist in carrying out their functions as experts (CPR 35.14). See Section 11 above.

17. Single joint experts

17.1   CPR 35 and PD35 deal extensively with the instruction and use of joint experts by the parties and the powers of the court to order their use (see CPR 35.7 and 35.8, PD35, para 5).

17.2   The Civil Procedure Rules encourage the use of joint experts. Wherever possible a joint report should be obtained. Consideration should therefore be given by all parties to the appointment of single joint experts in all cases where a court might direct such an appointment. Single joint experts are the norm in cases allocated to the small claims track and the fast track.

17.3   Where, in the early stages of a dispute, examinations, investigations, tests, site inspections, experiments, preparation of photographs, plans or other similar preliminary expert tasks are necessary, consideration should be given to the instruction of a single joint expert, especially where such matters are not, at that stage, expected to be contentious as between the parties. The objective of such an appointment should be to agree or to narrow issues.

[No paragraph 17.4 appears in the Protocol as published.]

17.5   Experts who have previously advised a party (whether in the same case or otherwise) should only be proposed as single joint experts if other parties are given all relevant information about the previous involvement.

17.6   The appointment of a single joint expert does not prevent parties from instructing their own experts to advise (but the costs of such expert advisers may not be recoverable in the case).

Joint instructions

17.7   The parties should try to agree joint instructions to single joint experts, but, in default of agreement, each party may give instructions. In particular, all parties should try to agree what documents should be included with instructions and what assumptions single joint experts should make.

17.8   Where the parties fail to agree joint instructions, they should try to agree where the areas of disagreement lie and their instructions should make this clear. If separate instructions are given, they should be copied at the same time to the other instructing parties.

17.9   Where experts are instructed by two or more parties, the terms of appointment should, unless the court has directed otherwise, or the parties have agreed otherwise, include:

(a)   a statement that all the instructing parties are jointly and severally liable to pay the experts' fees and, accordingly, that experts' invoices should be sent simultaneously to all instructing parties or their solicitors (as appropriate); and

(b)   a statement as to whether any order has been made limiting the amount of experts' fees and expenses (CPR 35.8(4)(a)).

17.10 Where instructions have not been received by the expert from one or more of the instructing parties the expert should give notice (normally at least 7 days) of a deadline to all instructing parties for the receipt by the expert of such instructions. Unless the instructions are received within the deadline the expert may begin work. In the event that instructions are received after the deadline but before the signing off of the report the expert should consider whether it is practicable to comply with those instructions without adversely affecting the timetable set for delivery of the report and in such a manner as to comply with the proportionality principle. An expert who decides to issue a report without taking into account instructions received after the deadline should inform the parties who may apply to the court for directions. In either event the report must show clearly that the expert did not receive instructions within the deadline, or, as the case may be, at all.

Conduct of the single joint expert

17.11 Single joint experts should keep all instructing parties informed of any material steps that they may be taking by, for example, copying all correspondence to those instructing them.

17.12 Single joint experts are Part 35 experts and so have an overriding duty to the court. They are the parties' appointed experts and therefore owe an equal duty to all parties. They should maintain independence, impartiality and transparency at all times.

17.13 Single joint experts should not attend any meeting or conference which is not a joint one, unless all the parties have agreed in writing or the court has directed that such a meeting may be held[4] and who is to pay the experts' fees for the meeting.

17.14 Single joint experts may request directions from the court - see Section 11 above.

17.15 Single joint experts should serve their reports simultaneously on all instructing parties. They should provide a single report even though they may have received instructions which contain areas of conflicting fact or allegation. If conflicting instructions lead to different opinions (for example, because the instructions require experts to make different assumptions of fact), reports may need to contain more than one set of opinions on any issue. It is for the court to determine the facts.

Cross-examination

17.16 Single joint experts do not normally give oral evidence at trial but if they do, all parties may cross-examine them. In general written questions (CPR 35.6) should be put to single joint experts before requests are made for them to attend court for the purpose of cross-examination.[5]

18. Discussions between experts

18.1 The court has powers to direct discussions between experts for the purposes set out in the Rules (CPR 35.12). Parties may also agree that discussions take place between their experts.

18.2 Where single joint experts have been instructed but parties have, with the permission of the court, instructed their own additional Part 35 experts, there may, if the court so orders or the parties agree, be discussions between the single joint experts and the additional Part 35 experts. Such discussions should be confined to those matters within the remit of the additional Part 35 experts or as ordered by the court.

---

[4] *Peet v Mid Kent Area Healthcare NHS Trust* [2002] 1 WLR 210.
[5] *Daniels v Walker* [2000] 1 WLR 1382.

18.3   The purpose of discussions between experts should be, wherever possible, to:

(a)   identify and discuss the expert issues in the proceedings;

(b)   reach agreed opinions on those issues, and, if that is not possible, to narrow the issues in the case;

(c)   identify those issues on which they agree and disagree and summarise their reasons for disagreement on any issue; and

(d)   identify what action, if any, may be taken to resolve any of the outstanding issues between the parties.

Arrangements for discussions between experts

18.4   Arrangements for discussions between experts should be proportionate to the value of cases. In small claims and fast-track cases there should not normally be meetings between experts. Where discussion is justified in such cases, telephone discussion or an exchange of letters should, in the interests of proportionality, usually suffice. In multi-track cases, discussion may be face to face, but the practicalities or the proportionality principle may require discussions to be by telephone or video conference.

18.5   The parties, their lawyers and experts should co-operate to produce the agenda for any discussion between experts, although primary responsibility for preparation of the agenda should normally lie with the parties' solicitors.

18.6   The agenda should indicate what matters have been agreed and summarise concisely those which are in issue. It is often helpful for it to include questions to be answered by the experts. If agreement cannot be reached promptly or a party is unrepresented, the court may give directions for the drawing up of the agenda. The agenda should be circulated to experts and those instructing them to allow sufficient time for the experts to prepare for the discussion.

18.7   Those instructing experts must not instruct experts to avoid reaching agreement (or to defer doing so) on any matter within the experts' competence. Experts are not permitted to accept such instructions.

18.8   The parties' lawyers may only be present at discussions between experts if all the parties agree or the court so orders. If lawyers do attend, they should not normally intervene except to answer questions put to them by the experts or to advise about the law.[6]

18.9 The content of discussions between experts should not be referred to at trial unless the parties agree (CPR 35.12(4)). It is good practice for any such agreement to be in writing.

18.10 At the conclusion of any discussion between experts, a statement should be prepared setting out:

(a)   a list of issues that have been agreed, including, in each instance, the basis of agreement;

(b)   a list of issues that have not been agreed, including, in each instance, the basis of disagreement;

(c)   a list of any further issues that have arisen that were not included in the original agenda for discussion;

(d)   a record of further action, if any, to be taken or recommended, including as appropriate the holding of further discussions between experts.

18.11 The statement should be agreed and signed by all the parties to the discussion as soon as may be practicable.

18.12 Agreements between experts during discussions do not bind the parties unless the parties expressly agree to be bound by the agreement (CPR 35.12(5)). However, in view of the overriding objective, parties should give careful consideration before refusing to be bound by such an agreement and be able to explain their refusal should it become relevant to the issue of costs.

19. Attendance of experts at court

19.1   Experts instructed in cases have an obligation to attend court if called upon to do so and accordingly should ensure that those instructing them are always aware of their dates to be avoided and take all reasonable steps to be available.

19.2   Those instructing experts should:

(a)   ascertain the availability of experts before trial dates are fixed;

---

6   *Hubbard v Lambeth, Southwark and Lewisham HA* [2001] EWCA 1455.

(b)   keep experts updated with timetables (including the dates and times experts are to attend) and the location of the court;

(c)   give consideration, where appropriate, to experts giving evidence via a video-link.

(d)   inform experts immediately if trial dates are vacated.

19.3   Experts should normally attend court without the need for the service of witness summonses, but on occasion they may be served to require attendance (CPR 34). The use of witness summonses does not affect the contractual or other obligations of the parties to pay experts' fees.

Appendix 3

LETTER OF INSTRUCTION TO AN EXPERT

Parties and solicitors

We are instructed by (*client's full name, address and telephone number(s)*) in connection with a dispute (*claim*) concerning (*explain type of case*). At this stage the other party is (*their name and address*). They are represented by (*the other party's solicitors name and address*).

Type of instruction

We would like you to act as an expert (*witness*) in this case to advise (*or to prepare a report and whether the latter is for court proceedings*) on (*liability or quantum*). (*The other experts instructed so far are for our client ..... and for the other party ..... names and addresses*).

Single joint expert

The parties have agreed (*or the court has ordered*) that you are to be instructed as a single joint expert and that each party will be responsible for (*half or give %s*) of your fees. All correspondence and your report must be copied to both parties and no steps in your investigation taken without both parties' consent.

Specific instructions

The main facts of the case in summary are..... and our instructions to you are ..... (*Set out instructions in detail including any issues on which the expert's opinion is specifically requested*). (*If a single joint expert explain whether this is a joint letter of instruction or whether the other party will be ending a separate letter and if so by what date*).

Materials

Enclosed are the following materials to assist you (*or annex the list to the letter if there are many materials. The materials might include background reports and documents, correspondence between the parties, statements of case, and disclosed witness statements and other experts' reports. Tell the expert if any of the materials have not been disclosed and/or are privileged and that these are being sent to him for background only and are not to be referred to in the report. Also tell the expert if any of the materials should be kept confidential and used only for the purpose of the case).*

Expert to confirm instructions

Please let me know if these instructions are not clear, or if you consider you require any other materials. Please also confirm that your particular expertise is appropriate for this case, and that, as far as you know, you will have no conflict of interest.

Timing of advice/report and court directions

We require your advice (report) by (*the date*). I would be grateful if you could confirm that you are able to do this. (*Or please let me know how soon you can provide the report*). (*If proceedings have been issued provide the expert with the name of the action, the court reference number and court address. If directions have been given annex these to the letter and highlight in the letter any direction of particular relevance to the expert, including whether the permission given to rely on an expert's report names him specifically, or any restriction on his fees. Also tell the expert if a trial date or window has been fixed and ask him to confirm his availability*).

Fees

We will need to agree your fee before you begin work. Please send me your terms of engagement, or telephone me on receipt of this letter. I suggest you provide an estimate for preparing the advice (*report*) and an hourly rate for any subsequent work (such as answering written questions on your report, attending an experts' discussion or a conference with counsel.) It would also be helpful if you could explain your charges for attending court to give oral evidence, should that become necessary, including cancellation fees. We (*or the client or shared with the other party if a single joint expert*) will be responsible for paying your reasonable fees but please note that (*our or the client's and/or the other party's*) prior authority will be needed if your estimate is likely to be exceeded. (*If the solicitor wants the expert to wait for his fees until the end of the case this should be made clear in the letter*).

311

At this stage we estimate the approximate value of our client's case as (*give a bracket*). We would ask you to bear in mind that the courts expect the costs of proceedings, including expert evidence, to be proportionate to what is in dispute. Do telephone me if you would like to discuss this.

For new experts

For experts with whom you have not worked before or who are new to expert witness work, consider requesting a CV, references or examples of their work. Also consider whether to attach to the letter Part 35 and the Practice Direction, or your firm's own guidance to experts, and whether to refer the expert to the Protocol for the Instruction of Experts (see Chapter 2 and Annex 2).

End of the case

At the end of the case we will expect the papers to be returned to us (*or please confirm that you will keep the papers for at least six years after the case is concluded*).

We hope that you will be able to accept these instructions and look forward to hearing from you.

Notes

Parts of the letter in italics are optional.

See Chapter 5 for more detailed guidance on drafting specific instructions.

In many cases the solicitor will have had a telephone discussion with the expert before the letter of instruction is sent and will have received the expert's terms of engagement - in which case the fees paragraph can be much simpler.

If there has not been a prior telephone discussion, be wary of sending all the papers with the first letter, especially privileged or very confidential ones, in case the experts turns out to have a conflict of interest.

Appendix 4

STANDARD DIRECTIONS ON EXPERT EVIDENCE

No expert evidence necessary

No expert evidence being necessary no party has permission to rely upon any expert evidence.

Single joint experts

Permission is given to the parties to rely upon the written evidence of a single joint expert on the issue of ..... in the field of ..... *(state the discipline and name if agreed / approved).*

If the parties cannot agree by ..... who that expert is to be, either party may apply to the court for further directions *(providing CVs, availability and the estimated fee of the expert they propose and reasoned objections to any other expert proposed).*

Instructions are to be provided to the expert by ..... 2005, and the report is to be prepared and served by ..... 2005.

Unless the parties agree in writing or the court orders otherwise, the expert's fees and expenses shall be paid by the parties equally (or *as to ..... % by claimant & ..... % by defendant*) (*and/or shall be limited to £ .....).*

Separate experts

Permission is given to the parties to rely upon the written evidence of an expert in the field(s) of ..... . *(state the discipline(s) and name(s) if agreed / approved).*

Parties shall simultaneously exchange experts' reports by ..... 2005, (*or there shall be sequential disclosure of experts' reports, the claimant's to be served by ..... 2005, and the defendant's by ..... 2005).*

No party shall recover from another party more than £ ..... for the fees and expenses of the expert in (name discipline and expert).

The written reports of the experts shall be agreed if possible and if not agreed *(see below for directions on written questions and discussions)*.

The evidence of any expert who has not complied with his duty to the court or with court directions may not be admitted at trial without the consent of the court.

Small claims

Permission is given to the parties to rely upon the written report of a single joint expert in the field of ..... (state the discipline and name if agreed /approved).

The parties are reminded that the maximum fee the court may order a party to pay towards the cost of expert evidence is £200.

Personal injury

The claimant has permission to rely on the written expert evidence of (name the expert) annexed to the particulars of claim and any supplementary updating report from that expert shall be served by ..... 2005.

The defendant may put written questions to the claimant's expert(s) by ..... 2005.

The expert shall reply to the defendant's questions by ..... 2005.

Literature relied upon by the expert

If an expert proposes to rely upon any textbook, article or other publication, he shall serve copies with his report, *(or he shall file and serve the literature by at least (one month) before trial)*. No reliance may be placed on literature not served in accordance with this direction without permission of the trial judge.

Separate trials on liability and quantum

Parties shall not incur any further expenditure on expert evidence in relation to quantum until after the trial on liability.

Premature application for expert evidence

The claimant's application to adduce evidence from an expert in (name the discipline) is refused. The application may be renewed following disclosure of (e.g. other specified experts' reports).

Written question on reports

Written questions may be put to the experts on their reports by ..... 2005.

The experts are to respond in writing to the questions by ..... 2005 (usually 14-28 days later).

Subject to any order for costs made in due course, the expert's fee for replying to the written questions shall be borne by ..... (name the party).

Expert's discussions

If the experts' reports are not agreed, the experts (in like disciplines) shall discuss the case on a without prejudice basis by ..... 2005 and shall serve and file a joint statement of areas of agreement and disagreement by ..... 2005.

The parties' solicitors shall agree an agenda for the experts' discussion by ..... In default of agreement either party may apply to the court for further directions .

The parties' solicitors are (are not) permitted to attend the meeting of experts.

Permission to rely upon oral evidence at trial *(usually given at Pre-trial Checklist stage)*

The parties have permission to rely at trial upon the oral evidence of the following expert witnesses ..... .

The parties shall agree the days on which the experts will be required to attend to give oral evidence.

Notes

The more common type of directions are in regular type. Italics are used for options and for the less common types of directions.

315

Appendix 5

CODE OF PRACTICE FOR EXPERTS

Preamble

This Code of Practice shows minimum standards of practice that should be maintained by all Experts.

It is recognised that there are different systems of law and many jurisdictions in Europe, any of which may impose additional duties and responsibilities which must be complied with by the Expert.

There are in addition to the Code of Practice, General Professional Principles with which an Expert should comply.

These include the Expert:

● Being a "fit and proper" person.

● Having and maintaining a high standard of technical knowledge and practical experience in their professional field.

● Keeping their knowledge up to date both in their expertise and as Experts and undertaking appropriate continuing professional developments and training.

The Code

1. Experts shall not do anything in the course of practising as an Expert, in any manner which compromises or impairs or is likely to compromise or impair any of the following:

   a) the Expert's independence, impartiality, objectivity and integrity,

   b) the Expert's duty to the Court or Tribunal,

   c) the good repute of the Expert or of Experts generally,

   d) the Expert's proper standard of work,

   e) the Expert's duty to maintain confidentiality.

2. An Expert who is retained or employed in any contentious proceeding shall not enter into any arrangement which could

compromise his impartiality nor make his fee dependent on the outcome of the case nor should he accept any benefits other than his fee and expenses.

3. An Expert should not accept instructions in any matter where there is an actual or potential conflict of interests. Notwithstanding this rule, if full disclosure is made to the judge or to those appointing him, the Expert may in appropriate cases accept instructions when those concerned specifically acknowledge the disclosure. Should an actual or potential conflict occur after instructions have been accepted, the Expert shall immediately notify all concerned and in appropriate cases resign his appointment.

4. An Expert shall for the protection of his client maintain with a reputable insurer proper insurance for an adequate indemnity.

5. Experts shall not publicise their practices in any manner which may reasonably be regarded as being in bad taste. Publicity must not be inaccurate or misleading in any way.

6. An Expert shall comply with all appropriate Codes of Practice and Guidelines.

REFERENCES

Books

Bond C., Solon M., Harper P., and Burn, S., *The Expert Witness in Court – A Practical Guide*, Shaw & Sons, 1999.

Brooke L.J. and others (eds.), *Civil Procedure* (the 'White Book'), Sweet and Maxwell, 2005.

Clements R., Davis N., Palmer R., Patel R., *Medical Evidence*, RSM Press, 2001.

Day J. and Le Gat L., *Expert Evidence under the CPR*, Sweet and Maxwell, 2001.

Department of Constitutional Affairs, *Civil Procedure Rules 1998*.

Family Division Ancillary Relief Advisory Group, *Best Practice for Instructing a Single Joint Expert*, Family Division, 2002.

Freckleton I. and Selby H., *Expert Evidence*, Lawbook Co, 2002.

Goriely T., Moorhead R. and Abrams P., *More Civil Justice? The impact of the Woolf Reforms on pre-action behaviour*, Research Study No 43, Civil Justice Council and Law Society, 2002.

Graham Hall J. and Smith G., *The Expert Witness*, Barry Rose Law Publications, 2001.

Holburn C., Bond C., Solon M., Burn S., *Healthcare Professionals as Witnesses to the Court*, GMM, 2000.

Jacob J., *Civil Evidence for Practitioners*, EMIS Publishing, 2003.

James C., *Expert Witnesses*, Clarendon Press, 1994.

Kendall J., *Expert Determination*, Sweet and Maxwell, 2001.

Law Society, *The Guide to the Professional Conduct of Solicitors*, Law Society Publishing, 1999.

Peysner J. and Burn S., *Civil Litigation Handbook*, Law Society, 2001.

Reynolds M., *Construction Litigation Practice*, CLT Professional Publishing, 2000.

Sime S., *Civil Procedure*, OUP, 2002.

Sweet and Maxwell, *The Expert Witness Directory*, Sweet and Maxwell, 2005.

Townley L. and Ede R., *Forensic Practice in Criminal Cases*, Law Society, 2004.

Wall Mr Justice, *A Handbook for Expert Witnesses in Children Act Cases*, Family Law, 2000.

Woolf Lord, *Access to Justice*, Interim Report 1994 and Final Report 1996, HMSO.

Zuckerman A., *Civil Procedure*, LexisNexis Butterworths, 2003.

Journals and newsletters

Expert Witness Institute – see websites below.

Journal of Personal Injury Law, Sweet and Maxwell.

Law Society Gazette – especially the twice yearly Expert Witness Supplement.

New Law Journal – especially the twice yearly Expert Witness Supplement.

Solicitors' Journal – especially the twice yearly Expert Witness Supplement.

Websites

Academy of Experts: www.academyofexperts.org

Bond Solon: www.bondsolon.com

Civil Justice Council: www.civiljusticecouncil.gov.uk

Clinical Disputes Forum: www.clinical-disputes-forum.org.uk

Council for the Regulation of Forensic Practitioners: www.crfp.org.uk

Department of Constitutional Affairs: www.dca.gov.uk

Expert Witness Institute: www.ewi.org.uk

General Medical Council: www.gmc-uk.org

Institute of Chartered Accountants: www.icaew.co.uk

Law Society: www.lawsociety.org.uk

Lawtel – subscription only: www.lawtel.com

Legal Services Commission: www.legalservices.gov.uk

Royal Institute of Chartered Surveyors: www.rics.org

Society of Expert Witnesses: www.sew.org.uk

UK Register of Expert Witnesses: www.jspubs.com

INDEX